2795

A Woman's Ministry

A volume in American Civilization,
a series edited by Allen F. Davis

Temple University Press

PHILADELPHIA

A Woman's Ministry

Mary Collson's Search for Reform
as a Unitarian Minister, a
Hull House Social Worker, and a
Christian Science Practitioner

Cynthia Grant Tucker

Temple University Press, Philadelphia 19122
© 1984 by Temple University. All rights reserved
Published 1984
Printed in the United States of America

Library of Congress Cataloging in Publication Data

Tucker, Cynthia Grant.
  A woman's ministry.

  (American civilization)
  Bibliography: p.
  Includes index.
    1. Collson, Mary Edith, 1870–1953. 2. Social
reformers—United States—Biography. 3. Social workers—
Illinois—Chicago—Biography. 4. Feminists—United
States—Biography. 5. Women clergy—United States—
Biography. I. Title. II. Series.
HQ1413.C64T83   1984   305.4'2'0924 [B]   83-18191
ISBN 0-87722-338-6

Frontispiece: Mary Collson (*top right*) with members of Iowa
Zeta Chapter, Pi Beta Phi Sorority at State University of Iowa,
1897. Photo from *Hawkeye* yearbook (1897). Courtesy University
of Iowa Archives.

$5k, 27.95/14.00/8/3/84$

This book is for many friends
who have kept the Collson spirit alive.

Contents

Preface

No reader is likely to recognize the subject of this book, for her name slipped into obscurity when she died thirty years ago. Yet in her lifetime, which began shortly after the Civil War, Mary Collson was rarely overlooked or forgotten. Growing up among Unitarians in frontier Iowa, she became, by dint of a quick intellect and precocious interest in churchwork, the darling of the liberal community. The town's unusual leadership, a prodigious group of feminist ministers known as the Iowa Sisterhood, recognized the youngster's promise, groomed her to join their ranks, and helped send their "designated daughter" to college and seminary.

Even after her schooldays, Collson's critical mind, love of books, and unorthodox goals brought her notice, if not applause. As a pastor newly settled in a conservative farming community, she discovered that some congregations had little taste for learned sermons, and disliked them all the more when a female delivered them. Unprepared for rejection and no longer certain about her proper place in the world, she suffered the first of a series of nervous breakdowns, and found relief only when she redirected her energies from pulpit to parish service.

Mary Collson found welfare work so rewarding that after a few years she left her Iowa pastorates for a job as a juvenile court probation officer at Jane Addams' Hull House in Chicago. There, as the 19th ward's only full-time court caseworker at the turn of the century, Collson did the real work of the settlement, spending long days and many nights in the homes of the district's most troubled families. To be sure, she was invisible in the circles dominated by such "worthies" as Jane Addams, Florence Kelley, and Julia Lathrop, but at the grass roots she was one of the best known and most respected of all the Hull House women.

Collson gained visibility at the upper eschelons, too, when after another nervous breakdown early in the new century, she joined Mary Baker Eddy's Christian Science organization and embarked on a new career as a mind-cure practitioner. Well spoken, sympathetic, and able to instill confidence, she attracted a large and loyal clientele, and her following boosted her into positions of leadership in the local church. However, her demands for a rational, uplifting, and egalitarian religion put her at odds with the Eddyites' chain of command, which, as Collson tells it, promoted a white, middle-class, male elitism and a metaphysics that generated enormous, irrational fears. The turbulence of her relationships with associates and church authorities was felt at the highest administrative levels, and by the time the maverick withdrew from the membership rolls after thirty years, her name was as well known in Christian Science boardrooms as it had been in Chicago's 19th ward and the Iowa parishes.

Yet in old age, the threads that hold human lives together weaken and fray, and the patterns that have been woven into the fabric over the years disappear. "Blessed" by longevity, Mary Collson outlived almost all the old friends and family who had connected her to her rich past. She became, as the elderly so often do, a marginal figure in society. She had neither a bank account nor a steady address; it sometimes took months for her mail to catch up with her. To her great distress, most of her few belongings and all of her personal papers were lost a full six years before her death, when she was hospitalized and her things were "picked and shifted around and scattered about by other people" who did not expect her to recover. It is terrible but not surprising, then, that even before the end came, the circumstances of old age had so despoiled Mary Collson's history that practically no one knew anything about it. There were no memorials or even obituaries when she died on August 29, 1953; and the remnant of her identity was effaced officially by her death certificate, which described her as a female who had spent "most of her working life" not in the ministry, social work, or mental therapeutics, but in doing "housework at home."

The record can now be set straight only because Mary Collson believed that others would profit from her experiences and took steps to see that they might. Soon after leaving Christian Science at the age of sixty-one, she wrote an account of her search for a means of "shaping the Age of Gold," of finding a cure for all the world's social and spiritual ills. Focussing on the period of "jostling faith, doubts, questionings, and repressions" after she entered Christian Science, she analyzed her adopted religion's conflict with her liberal heritage and explained why she remained in the Eddy movement so long. Unfortunately, in her concern that her exposé avoid anything libelous, Collson deliberately left out dates and most names of people and places, and in doing so produced an opaque style that was sometimes maddening in its elusiveness. Moreover, without a defined social context in which to stage her personal drama, the script seemed to some who read it more eccentric than significant. For these and other reasons, the memoir was never published. However, it did survive, and when discovered provided the clues that led slowly to the full recovery of Collson's life.

On a personal level, this story is an intensely committed woman's search for fulfillment, a search periodically derailed by nervous collapse, by conflicts with a power structure often represented by men, and by struggles with her own aspirations and conscience. It is the record of how a nineteenth-century "hysterical woman" tried to overcome her excessive sympathies and the problems of being an ambitious woman in a man's world. But as its self-proclaimed "heroine" knew even then, the story concerns more than this.

Collson's struggle is that of an entire generation of liberal reformers who tried to combat the world's sickness, corruption, and poverty. Beneficiaries of an earlier individualistic tradition, Collson's contemporaries remained attached to their fore-fathers' faith in unrestrained human potential, self-sufficiency, and laissez faire; at the same time, however, they embraced nineteenth-century positivism, which rejected much of this Romantic legacy. The positivists attacked self-absorption, so-cial isolation, and nonconformity, and sought to establish the individual's moral and creative worth within a scientifically organized, balanced society. The old liberalism expected that automatic social progress would follow from the improvement of individuals; the new liberalism believed that the problem lay in flawed social structures. When the new programs failed to deliver satisfactory results, however, it was natural for the reformers to reconsider the Romantic solutions they had aban-doned earlier, and which they now tried to adapt to the world of modern science.

In this respect, Collson's search was paradigmatic of Amer-ican liberalism for over a century. Collson constantly wavered between trying to save the world by improving its laws and institutions, and trying to save the world by making its people better individually. In college, signalling what was to follow, she vacillated between majors in economics and philosophy. Later, her ministries of parish calls, teaching, one-on-one case-work, and personalized religio-therapy alternated with political forays into the labor struggle, woman's suffrage campaigns, and socialism. The woman's entire reform career, from appren-ticeship to retirement, was marked by this fundamental uncer-tainty about how to get at the root of society's problems, and by repeated strategical disappointments.

Collson's quest was also typical in its profound and enduring respect for science. As a liberal clergywoman, she was more concerned with sickness than sin, with achieving good living conditions than eternal salvation. To keep her parish work up to date, she attended discussions of scientific topics at confer-ences and read all she could about the latest empirical findings

of modern research. She moved on to the juvenile court program in Chicago because it was endorsed by sociologists and
psychologists as the best way of tackling urban problems
through rational, scientific management. When Collson's
efforts through these avenues of social science proved futile,
she returned to scientistic religion, this time in the guise of
Eddyism, which claimed all the distinctions of a systematic and
provable science and promised instantaneous results. By the
same token, she renounced Christian Science three decades
later because it had failed to be the rational and scientific
reform movement she had expected.

On another level, Collson's story is that of a woman whose
early relationships to family and mentors implanted the lifelong
"habit of thought" which she summed up as "Ladies First!"
Like many nineteenth-century girls who grew up to champion
women's rights—such as Lucy Stone, Charlotte Perkins,
Louisa May Alcott, and Amelia Jenks—Mary Collson had a
father who failed to give his family adequate emotional and
material support. For the daughter, this failure undercut any
popular Romantic notions of men as dependable providers and
protectors; it also left her with an indelible image of depriva-
tions suffered by women and their children. Mary's mother, on
the other hand, was a devoted parent whose caring had the
effect Nancy Chodorow describes as "reproducing motherhood" in the daughter. That is, it heightened the daughter's
capacity for, and inclination toward, caretaking roles. It was no
coincidence that as an adult Collson time and again took up
work that allowed her to vent mothering energies. As the minister tending to the needs of her fold, as the surrogate parent of
delinquent boys, and as the mother-confessor and healer in
Christian Science, she was able to gather her children under
her wings "as a hen does her brood at night," to borrow the
phrase she used to describe the impulse.

Though it was untraditional, the Iowa Sisterhood's model of
productive womanhood unattached to a husband or home did
not conflict with their protégée's nurturant interests. Their

generation of career women presented professional work as an extension of woman's work at home, and therefore within the bounds of True Womanhood. As society's housekeepers, they sought to ply the principles of social science to make the public sector, as well as private life, healthier and more harmonious.

Collson's motto, "Ladies First," became the working principle of her life. She looked first to women when casting about for counselors and comrades in arms, and whatever her crusade, she plotted its destination with an eye to her sisters' special needs. Her pastoral energies went into establishing welfare centers for mothers and speaking out for woman's right to vote. During her social settlement days, she became an active socialist and worked with labor organizers to improve the lot of working women. Collson also expected that Eddyism, with its female founder and largely female following, its visible organizational roles for women, both on the local level and in the matronly healing ranks, would give her the opportunity to advance woman's cause. In fact, her feminist hopes were so strong that it took years before she fully admitted that the church's enticing vision of liberated womanhood had never given her the slightest evidence of promoting its female members' advancement as a group, of encouraging their ethical growth, or of nourishing personal friendships among them.

In light of Collson's intense identification with women's concerns and the value she placed on relationships with other females, it is startling to discover that she actually spent much of her life alone. Sometimes Collson's "humble origins" created the barriers. As a social worker, for instance, she felt closer in many ways to the immigrant women in the Hull House neighborhood than to "the Lady Janes," whose personal comforts, composure, and administrative absorptions prevented them, Collson suspected, from truly understanding the slum dwellers' deprivation. Yet when Collson joined the socialists, her comrades were not immigrants but middle-class intellectuals and political radicals with cultural backgrounds much like her own. As Mari Jo Buhle points out in *Women and Socialism*, the native-born middle-class feminists that Collson invited as speakers for her Socialist Woman's Club wanted the socialist program to secure women's right to outside employment; most immigrant women, however, looked to reform that would free them to stay at home and were therefore hostile to radical feminists.

For many years, of course, it was Collson's religious affiliation, even more than class values or political sympathies, that separated her from other women. Within Christian Science itself, where doctrine discouraged involvement in outside organizations and devalued personal attachments, a rigid vertical network undermined lateral bonding. The lower ranks were expected to be loyal to their superiors, and those nearer the top were given authority over those below. At the higher levels, the healers and teachers Collson knew were "more competitive than co-operative," and their rivalries tended to seep down and create fissures among their constituencies. Outside her own clientele, Collson encountered very little real affection among Eddyites and had "no friend to whom to say good bye" when she left after thirty years.

While a pervasive "sameness" and a "total lack of variety" kept Collson from finding satisfying relationships within the Eddy community, her views on religion made her "different" and suspect to non-Eddyites whose goals for reform she shared. In this way, her conversion first severed connections with friends and mentors in the liberal church, settlement work, and labor circles, and later "stood in the way" when she tried to approach the radical Marxists.

The difficulties Collson encountered in trying to achieve reform and live out her ideal of sisterhood give us new insight into the complex ways gender interacts with factors of public and private life in the formation of feminist alliances. Indeed, because she comes to us today as a forgotten figure, unpreceded by mystique or reputation, she appears with particular clarity as the representative figure she was: a committed liberal who faced the social and cultural problems of her age with all the perceptual and analytical tools available, and who shared fully in her generation's disappointments, flounderings, ill health—and resilience.

Acknowledgments

This book could not have been written without the assistance of numerous libraries, archives, and historical organizations. My special gratitude goes to the Iowa State Department of History and Archives, particularly to Lida L. Greene, who first helped me connect Mary Collson to the town of Humboldt and to Mary Safford's "strange household of women"; Carl Seaburg, at the Unitarian Universalist Association; Cate Hitchings, of the Universalist Historical Society, who introduced me to the "Iowa Sisterhood"; and to Meadville Theological School's librarian, Neil W. Gerdes, whose generosity never failed me. I am also indebted to the Andover-Harvard Theological School Library; the Cherokee (Iowa) Public Library; the Chicago Historical Society; the Des Moines Unitarian Society; the Evansville Williard Library; the Illinois State Historical Library; the Mississippi Valley Collection at Memphis State University; the New York Public Library; the Schlesinger Library at Radcliffe College; the State Historical Society of Iowa City; the Swarthmore College Peace Collection; the Unitarian Universalist Society of Iowa City; the University of Illinois at Chicago Circle Library; and the University of Iowa Library.

Peter Clark and Mary Lynn McCree of the Jane Addams Papers Project at Hull House were always hospitable. Kim Ashby of the Zeta Chapter of Pi Beta Phi led me back to the early years of Collson's college sorority. For historical information about First Church of Christ, Scientist, in Evansville, Indiana, I am grateful to Jane Steber, church clerk. I would also like to acknowledge Steve Howard and Robert Peel of the archives and library of the First Church of Christ, Scientist, at the Christian Science Center in Boston, where the vigilant staff restricted my access to holdings but was always courteous.

Donald R. Gordon graciously lent me papers and photographs left by his aunt, Reverend Eleanor Gordon. Glenda Riley shared information about Reverend Gordon and Mary Collson's other Iowa mentors. For helping me reach other distant sources of information, I am grateful to Deborah Brackstone, director of Memphis State's interlibrary loan, whose energy and expertise worked miracles for me.

A research grant from Memphis State University gave me several quiet months in the summer of 1978 to devote to research and writing, and an additional stipend from the university helped defray some of the cost of securing a professional typist. I especially appreciate the support of my department chairman, Joseph K. Davis, and Jerry N. Boone, vice president for academic affairs.

While I alone am responsible for the weaknesses in my work, the comments and suggestions of Allen Davis, Elizabeth Drewry, Phillip Grant, and Barbara Welter had much to do with this book's strengths. My friends' and colleagues' willingness to listen patiently was also a great help to me.

Most of all, my thanks go to my husband, David M. Tucker, who first found the memoir that sparked my interest in writing a book about Collson's life, and never in the many years since allowed me to doubt I would someday complete it and actually see it in print.

A Woman's Ministry

CHAPTER I

The Feminist Forge

From the clear memory of childhood, Mary Collson saw her mother and father make a fresh start on the frontier after the Civil War, "building a new home in a new land" in an atmosphere of "high hope and adventure."[1] Yet her family's inability ever to achieve prosperity left her with deep impressions of poverty and spoiled relationships. As a girl, she resolved to become "somebody" and do something worthwhile in life. Throughout her quest for distinction she tried to grasp the significance of her parents' failure, but she never determined whether the blame lay in some flaw of her father's character or in the ruthless capitalistic society which had defeated him.

Members of a vast migration which pushed America's frontier out to the Great Plains, Andrew and Martha Davenport Collson arrived in northwest Iowa with two little girls a few years before Mary Edith, their third child, was born in September 1870. Collson, a struggling carpenter idled by the postwar depression, had followed traditional wisdom in moving his family from upstate New York to the mythical "Garden" of the West, where all were said to prosper.[2] The Collsons settled not in a sod house on the land, but on the edge of the prairie in an upstart town called Humboldt.

Colonized by Unitarians, a westering eddy of Transcendentalism and liberal reform, the fledgling community had been planted in the interest of "freedom and unity in religion," "human helpfulness," and "equal rights for all, both black and white, male and female."[3] The founding fathers, scouting the area, had recognized in the untamed beauty of a white-water river and rich timberland the makings of a saw and grist mill, "and in connection with such improvement . . . the blacksmith, the dry goods store, the cabinet shop, the grocery, the school and [the] church."[4] Their vision had been so compelling that within a year Humboldt actually stood as the site of a mill, and soon a network of roads intersected the settlement, weaving scattered homes and structures into a modest commercial center. The railroad connected the colony with the outside world, and Humboldt began to behave like a typical booster town: it put up a hotel, established a college to draw in more easterners, and started a paper to advertise vast opportunities for new wealth.

Yet the promised prosperity always eluded the Collsons, as it did most Americans who went west in search of a better life without sufficient capital.[5] The myth of a western paradise collapsed in the face of declining grain prices, which so depressed the agriculture of the 1870s that commercial centers simply stopped growing. When the boom came to a halt, the best Mary's father could do for his family, which grew to include eight altogether, was to scrape out a living by tending shop for a grocer and doing odd jobs on the side. Overworked, bitter, and prematurely aged, the man had neither time nor energy to leave his mark on Humboldt's civic life. The town's watchful chroniclers barely caught sight of him.[6]

But more important, Andrew Collson was equally peripheral in the mental landscape his daughter later painted of her childhood. In all her autobiographical writings and existing correspondence, in which she mentions relatives often and her mother with particular affection, she says almost nothing about her father except that he was a religious sceptic who scoffed at her liberal church loyalties, and that she "heeded [her] mother more."[7] Plainly, Andrew Collson did not inspire in his daughter a high opinion of men as either protectors or strong authority figures.

But Mary was devoted to her mother, whose stable parental virtues expanded in the vacuum left by her husband's emotional distance and ineptitude. While Andrew was chronically absent in Mary's recollections of family crises, Martha was "always to be found where she was needed most."[8] She seemed to Mary "the most unselfish person" she had ever known, someone "who abandoned all thought of self in a constant habit of care for others."[9] Mary herself was an appealing, if rather plain child, with a little pug nose, a high broad forehead, and the clear blue eyes and brown hair of her English ancestors. Digestive problems and poor vision made her skinny and inclined to squint. Yet whatever she lacked in robust good looks was compensated by a quick wit, contagious enthusiasm, and a generous, affectionate nature.

As the family member most often ailing or convalescing, Mary enjoyed an abundance of her mother's loving attention, and through this intimacy developed a great desire to nurture others. She took "for granted that all human beings were tenderly cared for" when they were injured or ill, and being "very sensitive to the evidence of pain and suffering," she was "eager to effect immediate relief." When not helping to care for her younger siblings or the neighbors' babies, she ministered to. the town's injured birds, hungry dogs, stray cats, and lame horses. One of her greatest loves was a pet hen which she had rescued as a chick. "This little thing's leg was broken," she later explained, "and I took [her] and bound up her broken member and proceeded to raise her by hand. She grew from a little starch-box nest to a cigar box and finally to a nail-keg which my mother allowed me to have for her roost at night."[10]

Mary remembered her mother often reassuring the children that the family's "privation would never last," though the problems persisted and grew.[11] The unrelieved strains of poverty led to frequent domestic quarrels. Illnesses and accidents left one of the two boys paralyzed, and Mary—who, as a curious toddler, swallowed some lye—with a chronic digestive impairment. In time, Mary's bright impressions of childhood were darkened by the harsh contours of the family's life. "My mother," she told Jane Addams years later, "found life so hard that she always said it was easier to die than to live" and "always observed, when she heard of a death, 'Well, that one is out of her trouble.' "[12]

Perhaps it was inevitable that the Unitarian fellowship came to displace the troubled home as the center of Mary's life. Church suppers, festivals, lectures, and study groups made the girl feel a part of a stimulating extended family whose members included not only her hometown neighbors, but the brightest minds in New England and the modern scientific world. "We were decidedly reared to be 'liberals,'" she later wrote of her upbringing. "Always our faces were turned to Boston, our Mecca, and before we reached the age of twelve, we were reading and 'discussing' Emerson."[13] At home, her father, a follower of Robert Ingersoll, ridiculed Bible stories, telling them to the children "as jokes," but in the Unitarian Sunday School, Mary learned the stories as myths; there, she recalled, "we read our Bible in the light of 'the Higher Criticism.'"[14] "I never heard the old theology presented by anyone who believed in it until I was 16 years old."[15] "Reared to love freedom," she "never felt compelled to do anything" because she had been threatened with the devil.[16]

The 1884 calendar of Humboldt's Unity Club suggests the typical syllabus of Mary Collson's early religious training. There were lectures and discussions on early Unitarians, including William Ellery Channing, Margaret Fuller, Amos Bronson Alcott, Theodore Parker, and Ralph Waldo Emerson.[17] Club members reviewed the origins of Unitarianism as a revolt against the Calvinist formulations of predestination and innate human depravity. They discussed how the new religion's apostles had challenged the widespread belief in miracles as a necessary support of Christian revelation, and how its more radical communicants, finding their liberalized theology too cold and materialistic, had turned to the Romantic ideas of the Transcendentalists.

It was Emerson who had the greatest appeal for the Collson girl. Temperamentally drawn to his warm and affirmative idealism, she savored his celebrations of Nature, which nourished her own incipient faith in the power of cosmic good to overcome evil. Similarly, his doctrine of "man's moral nature" shaped her belief in divinity's presence within every human being. Mary was also drawn to Emerson as a person who suffered disillusionment and grew less confident of what he preached. Her elders explained that the blight of slavery had forced the Concord sage to question his early individualistic faith in the wise and righteous men who would make the State unnecessary. She learned that the Darwinian perspective had further diminished Emerson's estimate of human influence, so that by middle age he was no longer sure that the individual's will to reform himself would be enough to reform the world at large.

Emerson, Parker, Alcott, and their followers in distant Humboldt still evoked Transcendentalism in the name of positivist reform, and still reserved a place in their beliefs for the mystical experience of the divine, but their focus was shifting. For they "had read and studied enough," as one Humboldt school teacher put it, "to know a new word had been spoken, that the universe had changed front, so to speak."[18] If liberals like Humboldt's modified Comte's epistomology to make a place for their deepset intuitive theism, they were prodded out of any lingering social detachment by Comte's definition of God as Collective Humanity, and they committed themselves to improving society by applying scientific solutions.[19] "In the first faint flush of this great inspiration," one of the church members later wrote, "we [forgot] that we were practically exiled in the snow drifts with only one train each way a day, that we were 100 miles from Des Moines, 400 from Chicago and practically across the continent from New York and Boston." If they did remember at all, it was to wonder "if people who lived so far away were thinking and studying with as much interest" as they were.[20]

Mary Collson belonged to the first generation to hear this

liberal religion preached by women ministers. Educated middle-class women, in small but significant numbers, had been
infiltrating the formerly all-male ranks of the Liberal ministry
ever since the war had extended their "proper place" beyond
the Sunday schools and church kitchens. Unwilling to return
to the narrower spheres of work, Liberal women now insisted
that the inherent freedoms of faith and thought espoused by
their church included the freedom to serve that church in
whatever ways they chose, even if this meant occupying the
pulpit. Denominational flexibility in such matters enabled a
few, like Caroline Dall, to become Unitarian preachers in the
late 1860s without formal training or ordination. These women
worked to "reconcile congregations" to their presence in the
pulpit "by giving them a service likely to make them forget"
which sex had delivered it.[21] By 1873 there were enough female
ministers to answer those who thought it "preposterous that
women could do anything constructive through organization."[22] They assembled at a "Woman's Preachers' Convention"
convened by Julia Ward Howe, and thereafter caucussed frequently at local, regional, and national levels, working out
successfull strategies for gaining a stronger hand in church
business and bringing more women into the field.

The distaff's invasion of traditionally male territory was
never warmly received by Liberals in the East. There the view
persisted that ladies were "unfit" for high church positions,
which demanded "much business capacity," and that if they
were allowed to serve, they would just "displace capable
men."[23] However, in the West, where men were in critically
short supply, liberal denominations were "fairly committed" to
ordaining women and saw no reason to "keep so dark about it."
With "work enough in the Lord's vineyard for every laborer,"
surely "no little minister need fear" being "crowded out by
women."[24] One of Mary Collson's first heroes was the feminist
Reverend Jenkin Lloyd Jones, who became missionary secretary of the West in 1875, and soon after started editing *Unity*,
the Western Conference's weekly. In his advocacy of women's

rights, "Uncle Jenk" collaborated with his wife in her efforts as president of the Women's Unitarian Conference. In contrast to their colleagues back east, Jones and a number of his associates saluted those women who made bold to leave conventional work to take a place behind pulpits. They were, Jones said, "the rising factor of hopefulness" in the West's Liberal cause.[25]

Two such women were Mary Safford and Eleanor Gordon of Hamilton, Illinois, who in 1880 took over the Liberal leadership in Mary Collson's community. Schoolteachers in their late twenties, they had been best friends since their girlhood and had made a pledge to carry out their life's work as a team. They took the first step in the late 1870s, starting a Unitarian congregation in their hometown, with Safford as minister and Gordon as her assistant. The church grew beyond expectations, produced several satellites in the country, and drew loud applause from the missionary office. The women were encouraged by their success, and when they heard of Humbolt's need for a minister and a public school principal, they offered their services jointly. "We had decided four years before to work together," Gordon later explained, "and now the opportunity had come for establishing our home."[26]

Safford and Gordon shifted their base of operations to an upstairs apartment of five rooms in a large, rustic house near Humboldt's Unity Church. There were, of course, none of the modern conveniences, and the women had to carry all their water and fuel upstairs and all garbage and ashes down. But there were many hands to help with the chores, for the newcomers arrived not as a party of two, but as a "family" of six. With the new minister and school principal were four teenage girls, who attended the normal school and were pressed into service as teachers' aids and pastoral assistants. In a female world that had long been bound by support networks among women, the arrangement was more conspicuous than anomalous. Through intimate mother-daughter relationships, the young had always been systematically, almost ritualistically trained by mothers and other older women in the domestic arts they would need in their adult roles.[27] Now that real alternatives to housewifery and motherhood were presenting themselves, Safford and Gordon saw the need for apprenticeships under surrogate mothers that prepared the young for useful occupations outside the home.

Mission headquarters hoped that Humboldt's enterprising leadership would spur "other earnest, intelligent young women . . . who might be willing to come out of their obscurity in public school houses or elsewhere and help do this missionary work."[28] These hopes were not disappointed. Within a few years, the Collsons' town stood as the hub of a prodigious network of Unitarian female ministers known throughout the region as the "Iowa Sisterhood." In Humboldt, Marian Murdock, the first woman to receive a B.D. from a Unitarian theological school, took up the pastorate in 1885, freeing Mary Safford to carry the liberal cause elsewhere. Murdock's younger sister Amelia accompanied her as a parish assistant.[29] The Sisterhood also established Reverend Ida B. Hultin, an experienced preacher and an active suffragist, in nearby Algona. Indeed, before their power diminished early in the next century, scarcely a liberal pulpit in Iowa or along the boundaries of neighboring states was not at one time or another occupied by a woman; and the regiment's influence extended well beyond. Boasting more than a dozen capable workers, the organization recruited and trained its own probationary members and conferred ordination by its own authority. Working in concert, the Sisters filled each other's pulpits when they were emptied by illness, transfers, vacations, or conferences. Occasionally they shared the pastoral duties of a single church, not because it took two women to make one man, they emphasized, but because it sometimes took "two persons to make one good pastor.[3] The Sisterhood soon dominated state and regional church offices, had editorial control of *Old and New*, the Iowa liberals' monthly, and eventually capped its triumphs by seating its guiding spirit, Mary Safford, as national director of the American Unitarian Association.

II

No one was happier to see the Sisterhood's new household settle in Humboldt than nine-year-old Mary Collson, whose hard-pressed family had no social life or recreation beyond what the church provided. Under the newcomers' leadership, the liberal community took on new life, and Mary quickly became one of the church's most ardent lay workers. "While using but a single digit to tell my age," she later testified, "I was a very busy worker in our Band of Mercy . . . seeking to increase the membership . . . and to distribute its literature."[31] Recognizing the girl's potential, Safford and Gordon took the irrepressible youngster under wing, as they had the four girls in their household, and from that moment, as she expressed it many years later, Mary Collson was "destined" to become a Unitarian minister and a lifelong feminist. For she had entered the tutelege not simply of religious liberals, but of a band of "strongminded" women she grew accustomed to seeing daily in positions of leadership, women who earned the respect of prominent men and beckoned her to follow in their footsteps.

Eleanor Gordon proved to be a popular and efficient principal with remarkable business acumen. She surpervised "some thirty-five scholars" enrolled in the ten-level public school, and as "preceptress of the upper room" taught the eighth, ninth, and tenth grades herself.[32] Like other feminist educators, she deplored the cultivation of woman's affectional nature to the neglect of her intellect. In an age when everything from social questions to theology was thought to be governed by fixed laws and principles, reformers insisted that women's minds must be made capable of approaching whatever was studied "in the true scientific spirit; the aim being, not merely to imbibe the thoughts of others, but to obtain a clear perception of truth by . . . observation and reasoning."[33] To this end, despite the objections of the school board's Congregationalists, Gordon taught evolution, which her critics took to be "synonymous with teaching Unitarianism." She also made sure that all her students received "a very rationalistic training" that led the responsive ones, like the Collson girl, to expect "a full and logical explanation" for everything.[34] The novels of George Eliot, a Comtean humanist beloved by feminists for her "genial altruism" and "scientific knowledge," dominated Gordon's reading lists, while mathematics, logic, and the scientific method were prominent features of her school curriculum.[35]

The educational climate stimulated what Mary Collson later called a "mathematical intelligence"; throughout adulthood she attempted to "formulate and reduce life to algebraic equations" in a quest for "scientific" solutions to personal and social problems.[36] This tendency was revealed in embryo by an incident that occurred in Gordon's algebra class. The girl had been working problems and proving her answers simply "for the pleasure of the proof," when she found what appeared to be a mistake in the textbook. Gordon was skeptical, since the book was a standard text she had used for several years, during which time many students' computations had brought the authorized result. But Mary was not satisfied with this defense. "I pointed out that I could prove my answer, while the answer in the text could not be proven," she later explained. Before she would take her seat and be quiet, as Safford requested, she stated for the record that she "did not consider an answer correct just because it was given in a book." After a few days of wrangling, Gordon agreed to send the girl's work to the editors, and this concession "greatly comforted" the youngster because she "had such perfect confidence in the proof." Much to her delight, a letter of thanks from the publishers arrived a week or so later acknowledging that the book had indeed been in error all along.[37]

While Eleanor Gordon modernized the school curriculum, Mary Stafford and Marian Murdock arranged activities in the church that would "build character" and encourage what they called "soul growth." "No matter how deep the drifts or how low the mercury," church members met for "mental culture," to hear papers on anything from the New Science to recent poetry and fiction. "We were afraid of no subject," Gordon later recalled; "we were awake, were asking questions, seeking for light."[38] Nor was the life of the church "all reading poetry or studying modern science." The fellowship was, Safford boasted, as energetic "as any large city society with an environment of clammoring demands."[39] As activists who wanted to see their religion's ideals of beauty and truth take "practical form in everyday living," the Humboldt Sisters brought in scores of visitors, "men and women reformers from the outside world," who could give them advice and encouragement. One winter, Safford and Gordon had as their houseguest Mary Livermore, the prominent Universalist writer and advocate of temperance, suffrage, and sanitation reform. "We would sit down close to the hard coal base burner, for the weather was intensely cold, and listen to her wonderful experiences in her reform work," Gordon later recalled. They devoured every word as their guest told about her part in establishing women's aid societies and in founding *The Agitator*, which later merged into the *Woman's Journal*. For with the woman's engaging blend of humor and "earnestness," and her connections with well-known figures her hosts "admired at a distance," Livermore's conversation was "bread for the hungry."[40]

While "soul growth" and individual character were always of prime concern, Mary Collson's mentors aimed at the well-being of the whole person, body as much as soul. "The number of our burdens which are due to ignorance is appalling," Gordon declared from the forum of *Old and New*, which she helped to edit. "We bear the burden of ill health because we have not learned how to dress and eat and exercise properly."[41] To educate their parishioners in matters of preventive hygiene, sanitation, and physiology, the clergywomen closed ranks with "household scientists" and health societies. They called for better sanitation in grocery stores and meatmarkets and urged their congregations to boycott poorly kept shops. "The instinct for cleanliness," they pointed out, was "a true instinct, as the germ theory has proved, and where that instinct prompts a shopper to turn from a dirty store, she will do well to obey it without hesitation."[42]

Concerned that the young people's "injudicious use of food" was "planting the seeds of life-long misery," they supported the public cooking schools which, by teaching the principles of good nutrition, would "work a revolution in the [people's] physical life . . . and lay the foundation for a higher morality."[43] They encouraged physical fitness and regular use of the YMCA, the Turning Societies, and the Outing Clubs, and where there were no such facilities for their parishioners, they organized exercize programs in makeshift gymnasiums set up in schoolrooms or church social halls.

Some of the Sisterhood opened public kindergartens where the children might develop a spirit of give and take and a wholesome sense of community instead of the self-centeredness believed to be fostered by isolation. The feminist clergy also joined forces with social-science affiilates in teaching that criminals and prostitutes were not self-made, but created by social conditions that threatened everyone. They tried as educators, not as agitators, to harness their congregations' empathy to gain support for prison reform, the construction of asylums, and the operation of homes for alcoholics and prostitutes.[44] At their pastors' suggestion, the Humboldt congreation included among its philanthropies, the Women's Christian Temperance Union, a local "Humane Society," and the Benedict Home, a hospice for derelict women in Des Moines.[45]

Because Mary Collson's counselors viewed balance in all aspects of society as essential to collective and individual health, political equality for women was always "another burning question" for them.[46] Both Safford and Gordon served terms as president of the Iowa Woman's Suffrage Association, though as postwar feminists they had abandoned the old liberalism of conflict. They waged their campaigns in a spirit of cooperative and orderly reform, advocating the reconciliation, not the further division, of the sexes. Their mission, Gordon once said, was to lead people "to respect and love each other [even] when they think differently."[47] They liked to reach back to their New England forebears, who praised the "feminine principle," to reinforce the claim that females had special credentials for realizing this modern, positivist ideal: by using their "feminine nature" to offset society's crass, aggressive "masculine" traits, women would help to balance and harmonize the communal order.[48]

Mary's mentors were especially sensitive to the inequities which hampered females pursuing careers in the ministry. They knew from their own experiences that family and economic pressures made it more difficult for women than men to attend theological school. Insufficient funds had forced Gordon to drop out of Iowa's state university after just a year, and she had had to continue her education piecemeal by taking night courses. Safford's plans to enter seminary had been thwarted when her sister took ill and she was called home to care for her. Yet they also knew that even those women who did earn the credentials required to make application rarely received unbiased consideration from the seminaries.[49] The denomination's divinity school at Harvard had long been a notorious stronghold of male privilege and continued to stand firm in its rejection of female applicants.

It was understandable, then, that the Sisterhood focussed on discriminatory admission policies as a major target for reform. With the *Unity* men as their seconds, they persistently challenged Harvard's exclusion of women and howled when that institution proposed an exclusively female school for the training of parish assistants. They pounced on the implication that one sex was suited for the dominant office of minister, and the other fit only for a subordinate role. If anything, Safford argued, extraordinary encouragement should be given to females aspiring to be ministers because they had extraordinary obstacles to surmount.[50] Behind the scenes, Murdock prepared a series of pamphlets for women, in which she identified possible openings in theological schools and suggested strategies for gaining access to them.

From the Collson girl's vantage point, however, the Sisterhood's ambitions for her always seemed uncomplicated and within reach. As Gordon pointed out, if the issue of women pastors was hotly debated elsewhere, "there was not much opportunity for argument . . . in Humboldt."[51] Mary never doubted that she would someday become a minister with as thorough a training as Reverend Murdock herself. Murdock had not only been to college and seminary, but was planning to do additional study at Oxford and on the Continent. As this seemed "a proper preparation for a woman minister," the girl decided that she would retrace her pastor's steps.[52] She realized that getting this education would be a "herculean task," especially when her family was so poor, but she was sure that she could surmount any barrier with enough effort—and with the financial help her mentors promised her.

Nor did the girl ever doubt that she would be happy as a career woman. For one thing, the conventional option of married life had little appeal. Though like her sisters, she had been exposed to the popular lore about marriages "made in heaven" and "happy Newlyweds" who vacationed at Niagara Falls, she herself was "inclined to be of independent disposition" and resolved to visit the honeymoon spot without paying the price of a wedding.[53] Any notions of domestic bliss had been badly damaged by the reality of her parents' troubles at home, and dealt yet another blow by her oldest sister's marriage to a man Gordon wrote off as "undesirable."[54] Nor was the girl's view of marriage improved by her mentors' avoidance of it. Murdock, fiercely independent and averse to any kind of frilly "woman's work," was fully and happily committed to the single life.[55] Gordon found the outlook for ambitious women "dreary enough" and saw no reason to make matters worse by entering into wedlock. She had two hands and a brain of her own, she said, and she intended to use them without having someone else dictate to her "as to ways and means."[56] Though a few of the

Iowa Sisterhood did marry, most—including those Mary knew best—did not. Like their vintage of college women generally, they doubted that they could entertain both a marriage and a career, and decided a career was the more important.[57]

What made the Sisters' choice especially easy for the Collson girl, whose greatest pleasures came from caring for children and the nurturing aspects of homemaking, was that it remained squarely in the realm of domesticity. For if her mentors denied men's exclusive rights to the ministry, they thought of their own contributions to the field in distinctly female terms. Like the WCTU's Frances Willard, whom they quoted frequently, they seemed to want to "make the whole world HOMELIKE."[58] Though they chose not to marry, they saw themselves as homemakers-at-large, uniquely equipped by virtue of their sex to harmonize society by promoting the ideals of marriage and family. Safford, who liked being known as the "mother" of her congregations, enjoyed the fact that her work as a minister sometimes meant that she "preach and sweep," "pay bills and . . . wait on tables."[59] As Gordon explained to a male colleague, there was no conflict between their "home duties" and church work because both were facets of one life undivided in its service to the church family.[60]

Except when there were objections from "unruly" traditional bridegrooms who were seeking the hands of Unitarian girls, the women ministers counseled young couples about their conjugal obligations and then had them take their vows.[61] They arranged special services of "dedication" where parents pledged "to do all in their power" to make their children "good, true, loving, and useful citizens."[62] They also delivered sermons that stressed the domestic responsibilities of married people, reminding the husbands that they no longer "belonged" to themselves once they had families depending on them, and warning the wives against becoming "professional reformers."[63] They deplored the married woman who had too strong a sense of mission and was "so busy caring for the world that she [had] no time to care for her household"—leaving her own home "a foreign missionary field for someone else to cultivate."[64] On at least one occasion, the Iowa Sisters joined forces to dedicate a family's new house and took the opportunity to celebrate "The Ideal Home."[65] With this domestic emphasis, Mary Collson was able to set her sights on a church career like the Sisters', untroubled by fears that it would mean her exile from the sphere of family and home.

The highlight of the last summer Mary Collson spent in Humboldt was the town's 1886 Independence Day festival. The event provoked the playful *Unity* men to accuse "the efficient Sisterhood of preachers" of "having a sort of ministerial institute all by themselves," but for the girl, the gathering had a more sobering effect.[66] For the entire sweep of her past was represented in its service, its participants, and its setting. There, along with the town's founding fathers and her family and childhood companions, were Safford and Gordon leading an informal procession of adoring children, just as they had once played Pied Piper to her. Murdock and Hultin welcomed the church's newest members, taking them by the hand and evoking memories of a similar service when Mary's name was entered in the church registry. And finally, there were speeches in which the Sisters hitched their hopes for social reforms and women's unabbridged rights to patriotic ideals of a better America. Altogether, the celebration reenacted the laying on of hands by which feminists have long been consecrated.

CHAPTER II

No Cowled Churchman

I

Eleanor Gordon had known all along that her small, ten-grade
school would not prepare her protégée for college entrance
examinations, and had decided to send the girl to live with an
older sister in Fort Dodge, where the school curriculum was
more extensive. The move was made late in the summer of
1886, and after another three years of "much striving . . .
pecuniary juggling, pinching, and saving," Mary Collson received her high-school diploma at the age of eighteen and took a
job that Gordon had found for her in the country schools. Like
most single women in the later nineteenth century who wanted
employment outside the home, the new graduate thought first
of teaching, since it was the main road, if not to great wealth or
prestige, at least—as Catherine Beecher had said—"to honour-
able independence and extensive usefulness" well within "the
prescribed boundaries of feminine modesty."[1]

Collson's intention was to be a "schoolma'am" only for a year
or two, just long enough to save the money she needed to go to
college. To economize, she worked for her board and walked
several miles to school and back each day, but her hard-earned
financial advances were reversed by a string of "personal misfortunes," which involved some minor illnesses and a family
crisis back home. Though it is unclear whether Andrew Collson's final separation from his family was accomplished by
death or desertion, it is known that at some point while Mary

was teaching, Martha was left without a provider and had to move in with a daughter and son-in-law who were living in Fort Dodge. As the oldest wage-earning child in the family, the young teacher was expected to help with her mother's support, though her salary barely allowed it. As a result, she found herself four years after her high school graduation with only fifty dollars put aside. Convinced that she would never get to college unless she just "packed up and went," she took her meager savings "and fate in hand," asked Gordon to advance her tuition, and started for Iowa City, seat of the state university.[2]

The State University of Iowa, the first state school in the nation to admit both sexes on an equal footing, had always been a favorite of reform-minded women in the West. In the 1870's Safford and Gordon had both left their home state of Illinois to take advantage of Iowa's egalitarian policies. As mainstream feminists, they championed coeducation, rejecting claims that college life overtaxed the coeds' "weaker" minds and bodies and corrupted their feminine purity. Citing their own authorities, advocates of the open-door policy argued that women's health was in fact more likely to flourish than fail in a coeducational climate. They contended that active females who were becoming more balanced through further intellectual development were less susceptible to illnesses than those who secluded themselves in unnaturally one-sided settings. As for the students' moral well-being, educational reformers believed that open and daily encounters between men and women who studied side by side, more as brothers and sisters than as sexual *provocateurs*, were exposed to much less of the unhealthy excitement that led to undesirable behavior.[3]

Granted, Iowa's Board of Trustees had made some distinctions between the sexes. They had introduced programs of physical education to strengthen the women's bodies and keep them from being debilitated by their strenuous studies. Funds were also freed for constructing a tunnel between campus buildings to shield the female scholars from the assaults of the harsh prairie weather. However, no special adjustments were made when it came to curricular matters.[4]

Collson enrolled along with the men in the "Philosophical Course" leading to a B. Ph. degree. The program included classes in ancient and modern languages, logic, literature, mathematics, psychology, and ancient history, as well as electives in major and minor concentrations. An avid and rapid reader, the new student was able to carry a full 18 hour load each term and still find time for numerous extracurricular activities. She joined a literary society and was invited to take part in "a select Conversation Club" where students and faculty met to talk about current events, social problems, and the latest "scientific research."[5] She found a vent for her feminist concerns in a local Women's Political Equality Club, one of several women's rights groups to have sprung up in the area, and also renewed her commitment to animal and child welfare by resurrecting "a defunct Humane Society."[6] At church, she supervised a Sunday School of six classes, took care of the library, and helped to arrange monthly student teas and other sociables.[7] She even belonged to a social fraternity, thanks to the generosity of a well-to-do Humboldt woman who paid for the membership.[8]

Posing with her sisters of Pi Beta Phi for the 1897 yearbook, a thin young woman in spectacles, handsome in a fashionable, high-collared gown with mutton-leg sleeves, Collson looked pleased with her station in life. Indeed, her later recollection of these years might have furnished the caption: "I loved social life . . . I was never a grind. Everything connected with college . . . was of interest to me."[9] To meet expenses, Collson held several jobs. She earned petty cash by doing clerical work for the Unitarian minister, and she worked for her board in the home of an economics professor, where she assisted the husband with his research, and his wife with the care of the children. Remarkably, even with so many outside obligations,

Collson was able to finish her course of study, designed for four years, in just three.

It was less remarkable that with the new independence and broader experiences afforded by university life, the young woman began to have second thoughts about her plans for a church career. Collson had considered herself "very well acquainted with poverty," but had always thought of it more as a personal cross than a national crisis.[10] But in 1893, the year she started college, the nation's worst economic depression of the century struck. The economy's collapse saw the failure of five hundred banks and sixteen thousand businesses, with twenty percent of the nation's workers forced into unemployment. The crisis continued into the next year, accompanied by violent labor strikes and the first protest march on Washington, and the urban middle classes feared revolution. Now the talk among students and faculty, on campus, at church, and in the economist's home where Collson boarded, was of widespread unemployment, labor unrest, urban squalor, and the need for social reform. All this so excited the new student's interest in studying economics, that she was tempted more than once to change her major and "half-way decided to side-track" her ministerial career.

Her prior exposure to economic theory had been limited to classical laissez-faire and evolutionary doctrines. Eleanor Gordon, whose economics had always been more conservative than her religion, had made sure that her students were well versed in John Stuart Mill and Herbert Spencer, whose *Data of Ethics* she once reviewed for Humboldt's Unity Club.[11] But in Iowa City, Collson found more than Social Darwinism. She discovered a new economics rejecting Spencer's position that laborers should simply accept their lot uncomplainingly, since inequalities in the distribution of wealth resulted from the unequal distribution of talent and the survival of the fittest. Collson's first course, which used F. A. Walker's *Political Economy* as a major text, caused her to question whether the solution of current problems ought really to be entrusted to natural law when there was no evident correspondence between laissez faire in theory and practice. The actual failure of competition to operate well, Walker argued persuasively, worked unsufferable hardships on the laboring class, whose welfare could be protected only through legislative controls.

In other economics courses—"The Industrial Revolution and Modern Social Questions," "Recent Economic Theory," and "Applied Economics"—the students delved into such issues as "the relations of labor and capital, monopolies, and trusts . . . the problem of poverty, socialism, and the theory of surplus value."[12] Collson later recalled discussing *Das Kapital* and *Progress and Poverty* "along with Free Silver and similar subjects" in an intense, if rather "dilettante" sort of way among friends.[13]

Collson's interest in economics quite naturally tilted toward sociology, where such scholars as Lester Frank Ward aimed "at the organization of happiness" and sought to apply scientific knowledge in practical ways to heal and harmonize society.[14] With her penchant for orderly, nonpolitical remedies for social ills, social science was a more comfortable area for her, as for many reformist women, who looked upon it as the "feminine" counterpart of political economy and their sex's "peculiar field" of endeavor.[15] This orientation was particularly evident during Collson's last year. For then, even while violent strikes and workers' unrest were erupting throughout the country, she was busily writing a paper on the labor struggle, in which she minimized its disruptive features and expounded on the uplifting potential of "organization as a means of *educational*, as well as economic, progress for the working class."[16]

Even though Mary Collson never actually shifted her major, but took "all the philosophy and psychology" Iowa offered, she toyed with the idea of changing professional goals right through graduation. In fact, instead of going directly to seminary as planned, she remained at Iowa to work on an economics

thesis, which she hoped would earn her a scholarship to graduate school in New York. Her idea was to study under Franklin
H. Giddings, the Columbia University socio-economist, whose
connections with the growing social settlement movement
appealed to her penchant for child welfare work.

Needless to say, the Iowa Sisters were less than enthusiastic
about their protégée's shelving the plans they had carefully
drafted and paid for, and at the first opportunity, they moved to
regain their influence. This opportunity came in 1895, when
Gordon helped the Iowa City parish purchase a church and
then agreed to accept the congregation's pastorate. The errant
student, once again under the minister's watchful eye and close
counsel, "remembered" her indebtedness to those who had
helped her through college. Before the year was out, her old
enthusiasm for philosophy and religion "experienced a revival,"
and she could see once again that it would take "more than the
intellectual" to succeed in the world. The most persuasive
theories of philosophers and economists were of little use, she
told a November conference of Iowa Unitarians "when the
lessons of experience seem[ed] dimly written." The clarifica-
tion needed, she said, could come only from a higher faith that
would lift the soul above the world's vices and vanities. If she
neglected her "religious faculty," she would be only "half-
living" and would stumble along, trying to do on her own "the
things God meant to help [her] do."[17] Collson dropped her
advanced work in economics at the end of the winter term and
left for Meadville Theological School in northwestern Pennsylvania.

The seminary in Meadville, where religious liberals pre-
dominated, had for years welcomed women as warmly as men.[18]
When the Iowa Sisterhood's Marian Murdock, an alumna who
soon would become a trustee, gave the main address at the
institution's Semi-Centennial celebration in 1894, she congratulated the school for proving that women, accepted simply
"as students" and given full privileges, demonstrated "the same

capacity" as men. They were "as intensely eager to solve the insolvable problems of ethics and philosophy and quite as tenacious over disputed interpretations of Scripture." With "no traditions to hamper it, no powerful 'Establishment' to frown upon it, no General Assembly to dictate terms of its existence," and "no desire to play fast and loose with ecclesiasticism," Meadville promised to become "one of the noblest and most complete institutions" the country could offer for ministerial training.[19] Satisfied that their protégée would be in the best of hands, Collson's mentors sent her to Meadville with another loan for tuition and letters of introduction to their many faculty friends.

One of five women in a student body of twenty-eight, the new seminarian soon felt at home. She was happy to have a sabbatical from economics and social theory, and she settled into the quiet study of the New Testament, Old World geography, church history, Hebrew literature, and Judaism.[20] She had an enjoyable part-time job reading to the school's president, George L. Cary, an aging biblical scholar who was trying to conserve his eyesight, and for pocket money, she gave public readings of Keats and Browning and some of her other favorite poets. If the faculty teased her about being always "tiptoe with delight," it was, she later conceded, entirely justified. She was "an excellent illustration of Victorian optimism." When someone once asked her why she was always smiling, her reply was ready: "Why shouldn't everybody smile when things are moving *and* moving in the right direction?"[21]

It was only a matter of months, however, before the direction changed. Back in Iowa, Safford and Gordon were desperate for someone to serve a new church they had started in Ida Grove. The first minister they had placed resigned suddenly, leaving the congregation floundering and church business in chaos. The Sisters had unsuccessfully scouted the area for a replacement, and now, left with no other recourse, they summoned their protégée. Though surprised, Collson welcomed the call, for she had begun to weary of the student's life. She was anxious to earn a living and repay her debts, and above all, to put her education to use.

II

Mary Collson arrived in Ida Grove eager to present her opinions and the "rich harvest" of academic material she had been saving since high school. Her first lesson as a minister, however, was that congregations did not always share their preachers' enthusiasms. Ida Grove's Unitarians cared little for abstract religious debate, as one man told Collson quite bluntly when she asked what he liked to hear on Sunday mornings. The general feeling was, as he put it, that "everything savoring of theology as distinguished from religion" ought to assume "an entirely secondary and unimportant place." The "effort of the pulpit" should be "directed with strength, emphasis, and enthusiasm to the field of moral reform, the upbuilding of noble, ideal character, the development of the divine in the human." "Throw theology to the dogs," was the recommendation, and turn instead "to the burning necessities of the present day and generation . . . to that great mass of humanity that is now chiefly non-church going."[22]

The mood in Ida Grove followed the nationwide pattern of shifting concerns among liberal, progressive congregations. The finespun religious controversies of the past hardly seemed relevant at a time when enormous domestic crises threatened to destroy the ideal of a free and safe society. As one of Collson's sister ministers said of the climate in her parish, there was a "growing distaste for all the theological discussion which was so active" five years before. It was clear that unless the clergy could "prove" that they had something to offer, something that was "vital to human needs . . . something better than pointing out the errors of orthodoxy," the people would take no interest in their message.[23] "Sociological questions are the ones now up for discussion," she noted, "and the interest in psychic research has absorbed the old controversies on future punishment."[24]

Collson, of course, was equipped to take up social and economic questions and would gladly have given her major effort to sermonizing on current events. But she found that the congregation was no more willing to accept her sermons on economics than they were her sermons on religion. Better that a woman devote herself to the life of the parish.

The Ida Grove minister therefore adopted the policy of avoiding theology and social theory—where there was little concensus or interest, and even her own views were becoming "a little less certain." She concentrated on social service and left the real business of worship and individual reform to each parishioner's conscience. Instead of disputing His nature, she tried to help the church express the divine by doing good works in the parish. Using a vacant theater attached to a skating rink as her church, she organized an active Sunday School and a Unity Club. When the membership grew and became financially capable, she suggested they purchase their meeting place and convert it into a recreational facility for the town. As she saw it, Ida Grove's two thousand residents were already "blessed," if not "possessed," by seven sanctuaries, and they did not need another "inflicted" on them. By improving the theater and skating rink, the Unitarians would spare the town another church edifice, while providing a community center for "the better class of entertainments," where "both old and young could find amusements, literary culture . . . and good things to eat." The plan was approved, and when the new facility opened, the exultant minister "personally taught some of the more bashful townsfolk to dance."[25]

By the end of the year, Reverend Collson was able to report that her church had lost all sense "of being 'new'" and now felt "quite sedate and permanent." The congregation's history buffs were reading about the French Revolution; the Young People's Dramatic Club had recently presented a "parlor theatrical;" and a "vigorous and enthusaistic Ladies' Society" had been meeting weekly to study science, art, poetry, and short stories. Altogether, the minister was satisfied that her church was "growing not only in numbers," but also in the kind of activities that were "broadening, ennobling, and make for righteousness."[26] It was much more agreeable "being a leader than being a preacher," she found.[27]

Still, Collson was uneasy in her position. As the liberals' religious leader, she bore the brunt of the community's deep prejudice against her unorthodox faith. Even after the Unitarians were invited to take part in the town's yearly Thanksgiving program, from which they had formerly been excluded, there were those in attendance who simply would not accept their legitimacy. One "pious" woman, Collson remembered, came up to her after the service "to say she had felt . . . unable to bow her head when I offered the prayer."[28]

The discomfort of being rejected on religious grounds was compounded by the further disapproval of women who stepped outside their sphere and trespassed on what was considered male turf. The emerging New Woman had by no means replaced the housebound angel glorified by the mystique of True Womanhood.[29] The litany was that woman's greatest calling was to make a happy home, a noble work in which she could best display the "female attributes" of generosity, moral strength, spiritual purity, and understanding. During Mary Collson's girlhood, the Sisterhood's authority and Humboldt's progressive enclave had served as a buffer against the worst of that mythology's assault. They had provided her with sturdy armament for her "unwomanly" ambitions, allowing her to plot her future with a forgetfulness of gender that postponed any doubts that she could, or should, succeed in "a man's profession."

But most Americans in the nineteenth century had been brought up to believe that religiosity, the very essence of True Womanhood, had been given to woman by God to make her "man's auxilliary," not his leader, in the world's reform. Though religious service became a corridor through which many of the distaff found adventure outside the home, society encouraged churchwork precisely because it was thought to promote domesticity.[30] Unlike the Humbolt of Collson's girlhood, where a large contingent of maverick liberals supported its feminist leadership, Ida Grove's townsfolk expected women to confine their activities to those areas where their womanly nature would not be violated. They looked askance at the Unitarians' female minister, who not only served in the sanctuary, but involved herself in such "manly concerns" as property development and mortgages. Collson's broad community involvement maximized her exposure to criticism, and she was notified daily that "it was quite a novelty to see a Unitarian woman preacher" claiming "equality with respectably conservative reverend gentlemen."[31]

It is unlikely that Collson found many even among her own congregation who were entirely comfortable having a pastor in skirts. Unitarians as a body had never courted women preachers; they had only accepted them on the frontier in default of available men. With the growing idealization of womanhood, female ministries had become even less popular, and women no longer sought pastorates with their former vigor. Reluctant to throw off the True Woman's mantle, only a very few still forged apostolates of political feminism. Eager to end the battle of the sexes and bring men and women together in an orderly, conflict-free society, a new generation of feminists refrained from attacks on home and family life, and could not be counted on to support their sisters' professional pursuits.

Elizabeth Bogart, writing for the liberals' *Unity*, was typical in her retreat from the hard-line positions of the past. In an article on "The New Woman" (which regular subscribers like Collson would normally have read) Bogart congratulated her "modern" sisters for attaining high rank in the public realm. But she emphasized more the importance of those "womanly qualities" that equipped women "to join heart and hand with noble manhood." Since few could both be "eminent and make happy homes," she suggested that the New Woman should expect her professional life to last "but a season," until her "greatest reward," the "magnet of her heart," lifted her "into woman's noblest estate."[32]

None of this made Collson any easier in her pastoral role. She soon "had little relish for the title of Reverend"—which the townspeople used in addressing her even though she was not yet ordained—or the other clerical accessories which made her the object of criticism from many sides. Though she would not acknowledge it openly, her correspondence sometimes betrayed a longing to retreat from the grownup world and a ministry which had lost its glitter. A letter written to Jenkin Lloyd Jones about his visiting Ida Grove finds the twenty-eight-year-old woman assuming the persona of a "little girl from Humboldt" who was "still . . . in a humble way" trying to build up the cause.[33]

By the time the Sisterhood offered to ordain her at the end of her first year, Collson had grown "so averse to ecclesiasticism" that she declined, explaining she needed more time before taking the step. Confused by her reluctance, she reassured herself that "in this particular" she was merely following "the lead of Emerson," who had also felt shackled by denominational ties and had eventually left his pulpit for a freer ministry. However, no amount of historical sanction could really ease her misgivings, since they reflected a struggle for self-approval and personal identity. All her life she had enjoyed generous praise from family, friends, and employers, and habitually made a great effort to satisfy others' hopes for her. Many years later she understood how much this effort had cost her, and identified the "desire to please and be what somebody else wanted me to be" as her "greatest weakness."[34] But at the time, she was still "a glutton for admiration" and could not function well under criticism. She began to be troubled by bouts of nervousness, depression, tearfulness, and disabling fatigue—the classical "hysterical" symptoms commonly displayed by women faced by, and unable to cope with, unsatisfying life situations. The translation of psychological discomfort into physical illness gave

Collson a brief respite from the conflicts of her position. So long as she was unwell, she could relinquish the assertive, public role that produced the tension and rejection, and assume the private, dependent posture society sanctioned.[35]

By the end of her second year at Ida Grove, Collson's hysterical spells had become so frequent and severe that they forced her to take an extended leave of absence. *Unity* announced the unhappy turn of events with regret, recalling that "during a recent visit . . . it seemed to us as though here [was] a fine chance for what began in a protest against intolerable creeds to grow into an emphasis on neighborhood needs, village culture, and the religious life of the people," for here the work was "synthesis and not analysis." "The earnest young pastor of this vigorous movement" was now obliged "to retire temporarily, from overwork."[36] Safford prepared to step in until a replacement arrived, and her protégée "put on as brave a face" as she could and returned to Fort Dodge, where her mother and oldest sister were living.

The illness Mary Collson suffered after her years as a student followed a familiar pattern. Self-doubt and depression leading to physical collapse were so prevalent among Victorian intellectuals that the syndrome emerged as a major motif in the literature of the period. Hysteria was common among college women, who found, upon leaving their closely-knit campus communities, that the edited views of life they had received at college bore little correspondence to the world they discovered when they left. These middle-class graduates schooled in the liberal arts were traumatized when they found that they had been educated to fill positions that did not exist. But it was equally wrenching for trained ministers to be called to parishes only to hear that they ought not be there because they were women. Even with their close, supportive network, the Iowa Sisterhood showed the effects of this psychological displacement in a high incidence of "breakdowns," "exhaustion," "collapse," and "failing health."[37]

Mary Collson's case was diagnosed as "simple exhaustion,"

and the patient resisted any diagnostic amplification. She dismissed out of hand all attempts to apply to her ailment the current wisdom that the female's nervous system was more delicate than the male's and thus more likely to be overstimulated.[38] Years later she still insisted, "I did not break down because I was a woman, but because all my life I had worked harder than any young person should be allowed to work."[39] This explanation, of course, took no account of the fact that her health had held up all through her strenuous college and seminary days, when she was brimming with confidence about her abilities and the direction of her life. Whatever part overexertion played, and it doubtless played a part, Collson's illnesses must be seen in relation to her belated discovery, after years of preparation and enormous expense (by her standards), that the career she had worked so hard for was not, after all, what she wanted.

When Collson recovered her strength, she accepted new pulpits in Cherokee and Washta, two of Safford's young Iowa congregations. The Sisterhood was grateful to have her back, for it was hard to find workers with her dedication and willingness to sacrifice. Inquiries Eleanor Gordon received about open positions in Iowa pastorates convinced her that male ministers just emerging from Harvard and Meadville were thinking "of everything but . . . the task of saving souls." "They do not ask for a place where they may wrestle with superstition, ignorance, materialism, [and] godlessness," she complained to Boston headquarters, "but where there is a church built, where the work has been done, where all they have to do is write an essay once a week, and perhaps lead a Browning Club. —If only they might have some of the Browning spirit."[40] Mary Collson had that generous, idealistic spirit, and her counselors cherished her for it.

If Collson's illness in 1898 made her no more conscious of its causes, it did intensify her sympathy with the sick and depressed, and it persuaded her to give more of her time to her parishioners' physical and emotional needs. The idea of a ministry that linked Christian service, economics, and the social sciences was not new. Earlier in the century, Reverend Caroline Dall, one of the first women to occupy a Unitarian pulpit, had specifically recommended that women pastors concern themselves not with "pulpit graces," but with the "tender, reverent caretaking" of troubled people. Instead of getting caught up in the bureaucracy of the "narrow" church, which was "nowhere so narrow as in its human sympathies," the woman minister ought to be the head of a "religious household" and lead a "Committee of Comfort" that reached out to the parish's poor, friendless, and emotionally broken.[41] This kind of rehabilitative, nonsectarian ministry had attracted many progressive women by the end of the 1890s. So many, in fact, that the Unitarian yearbooks began to show "a perceptable dropping away" from the Sisterhood itself, as members left the field for broader careers in social service.[42]

Collson was also leaning in this direction. "Personally, I have no sectarian enthusiasm," she told Jones after returning to the Sisterhood, "but there are other ties that bind." In her new pastorates, she devoted herself to human relief activities that maximized the opportunities for nurturant ministering and minimized the troublesome churchly trappings. She began to organize nondenominational child welfare groups and social relief centers in small towns surrounding her parishes, and to advance this work she went to Chicago in May 1899 to attend the Conference of Settlements in the United States. At this conference she met Jane Addams for the first time.

Collson had been following Addams' settlement work for a decade, ever since *Unity*'s Jones had welcomed the social reformer to Chicago and started using his pulpit and press to commend her "academic work brought down to date." Sensing that the vague humanitarian force behind the settlement was akin to his own religious fervor, the liberal minister recommended "the sage of Hull House" as a worthy model for those intent upon recovering the spiritual ground the church had lost.[43] What most interested Collson when she heard Addams speak in Chicago, and again some months later at Tower Hill, Wisconsin, were the accounts of the settlement's programs for poor and neglected youths. Seeing an opportunity "to stimulate" her own modest efforts along the same lines, she arranged for Addams to lecture at her welfare stations in and near Cherokee.[44]

As it turned out, it was not the lecturer's expert advice so much as her presence and example that influenced the minister. For Addams, the secular servant of God, had perfected the very role Collson was groping for. Her pragmatic spirituality gave her the aura of a worldly priestess who was yet ensconced within the traditional boundaries of domesticity. She was eminently female and maternal in her calm ministry to the earth's downtrodden, yet as a scholar, activist, and executive, still "the best man in Chicago."[45] In short, Collson found Addams the ideal minister liberal churchmen envisioned when they now declared that "the saint must become a social reformer," must seek his or her ennobling vision of God "in the slums, not in the religious leisure of the monastery."[46] Addams thus became Collson's new model and inspirator.

The two women expected to meet again a year later when the Sisterhood's new Okoboji Summer School opened in August 1900. Both had been scheduled to give lectures. The reunion, however, was hastened by the sudden death in June of Alzina P. Stevens, the Hull House Juvenile Court parole officer. Collson was asked if she would step in and take over Stevens' work, and a few weeks later, the public learned of her response from *Unity*'s Jones, who ran this special notice:

Miss Mary Collson, whose work in connection with the Unitarian ministry of Iowa has been so favorably known, has laid down the pastorate at Cherokee and has come to Chicago and taken up residence at the Hull House. For the time being she is trying to keep going the work so well inaugurated by the late lamented Mrs. A. P. Stevens, among the friendless and criminal boys. Miss Collson comes to study the new applications of the old law of love in connection with the struggling and suffering portions of society. It

is another illustration of Emerson's lines and the experience back of
them:
   "I like a church, I like a cowl

   . . . .
   Yet not for all his faith could see
   Would I that cowled churchman be."

Collson's decision, Jones pointed out, was one more example of
"how many ministers in these days" were feeling "the irritation
of the 'vest' " even though they stood "in the freest of pulpits"
and had their hands "full of good work." Regrettably, the
church's self-image and sense of mission were "not yet adjusted to the lines which sociology" was "slowly surveying and
with which co-operative ethics and organized religion must
reckon." Though Collson had left the pulpit and denominational service, she had not left the ministry, Jones pointed out,
reminding his readers that "the old work and the new are one
work in the hands of the devoted."[47]

CHAPTER III

Hull House

I

When Mary Collson arrived at her new home in one of Chicago's worst slums, she counted twenty-two names on the Hull House directory, and discovered that scores of nonresidents also contributed in various ways to the settlement enterprise.[1] She later recalled that "each one's work was more or less independently carried on as a department of settlement programs," with the staff teaching classes in almost every conceivable subject and making "all kinds of interesting, amusing, and instructive efforts" to broaden "otherwise hedged-in lives." There were open forums and debates, and "continuous experiments" to find ways of assimilating the immigrant population. "Social affairs were given exclusively for the elderly, and a kindergarten and day nursery looked after the young children while mothers were at work." Eminent Americans and foreign dignitaries also visited frequently. "In short," Collson wrote, "Hull House as I knew it was a place where great and simple and commonplace people" created "a miniature ideal of a democracy," a "miracle of people."[2]

The newcomer found she had much in common with this sprawling family of reformers, whose members were largely young, unmarried, Protestant women of English or Scotch-Irish ancestry, highly educated, and brought up in a tradition of public service.[3] But she also quickly discovered an important difference. The other residents were either administrative staff

or students and professional people who spent their off-hours at
Hull House, where slum life might be momentarily transformed, while she was a full-time case worker, whose rounds in
the neighborhood placed her in ghetto conditions that bore little
semblance to the "miracle of people" back at the settlement.

After some shuffling of rooms among the other occupants of
the main house—young residents always scrambled for better
assignments when personnel changes were made—the new
social worker moved into a small third-floor bedroom. It was
comfortably furnished, but being directly under the roof was
terribly hot in the summers—and especially now, when a
blistering heat wave hovered over the city. Her unenclosed
office, little more than a desk and some chairs, was downstairs
on the ground floor, just to the side of a spacious hall where a
steady stream of traffic flowed through the house from dawn to
dark.

The summer was vacation time for most of the regular Hull
House staff, and many were away when Mary Collson moved
in. Jane Addams and Julia Lathrop were at the Paris Exposition,
Florence Kelley was in New York on business for the Consum-
ers' League, several residents were attending the Hull House
Summer School in Rockford, Illinois, and others had scattered
for visits to friends and family. Those who stayed behind or
came in to take up the slack discovered, however, that summer
was anything but a slow season at Hull House. There was
always plenty to do for neighborhood families in need of jobs,
food, clothing, rent, loans, even proper burials, and the summertime program sent several thousand children to fresh air
camps in the suburbs and arranged almost daily outings for
hundreds more.

The Hull House probation officer's work was actually
heaviest in the summertime, when school was out and the
number of domestic problems rose with the temperatures. Collson was anxious to get settled and see just how much she could
do. "I faced a very great vacancy when I arrived at Hull House,"
she remembered. "I heard of [Alzina Stevens'] wonderful sym-

pathy and devotion on every side and [I knew of her] great initiative and executive ability."[4] One of the state's most effective union organizers and a highly respected friend of women's groups, Stevens had used her influence to get a Juvenile Court bill written and passed in the 1899 state legislature.[5] In her first nine months as chief probation officer of the "Kindergarten Court," the first of its kind in the nation, Collson's predecessor had supervised almost two hundred children and visited each at least once. She had gathered reports from teachers and employers, located jobs and safe homes for some youngsters, and delivered needed medical and material aid for families of others.[6] Yet even with the help of a volunteer force from the women's clubs, the work had been so demanding that plans had been under way to bring Collson in as Stevens' assistant. That "assistant," now suddenly elevated to the director's position, wondered how she would ever be able to "fill the place" with so little preparation.

The idea behind the new court system was simple. Being young, children in trouble were still malleable enough to be rehabilitated and therefore should be treated differently from adult offenders and hardened criminals. To save as many as possible from a life of crime, the court would place its young delinquents under the supervision of sympathetic officers who would try to steer their charges back on the right course. Yet what seemed easy in its conception was made difficult in the early days by staff shortages and inadequate funding. When Collson stepped into her job, not quite a year after the program's inception, the Juvenile Court had just six full-time workers and youngsters enough to occupy thirty. Salaries, which came from private sources, were never enough for a living free from financial worries. As one of the court's early patrons observed, "The labors of [the] officers were heroic, but generally unsung. Even when they were paid, they received only $60.00 a month, $720.00 a year, a pitiful remuneration." It was not a job "for mere place hunters or political derelicts."[7]

The work week began early on Monday morning when Collson and the other court personnel gathered at the County Building to await the arrival of the latest group of children—anywhere from ten to twenty boys, and on a rare occasion, a girl or two—who were brought by horse-drawn police wagon from the juvenile detention home. As the youngsters arrived, they were ushered into Judge Richard S. Tuthill's courtroom and seated up front to the left of the bench. The room, as one observer reported, "was always crowded; the air was heavy; there was almost no ventilation. Women of many nationalities filled the place, accompanied by solid looking husbands, and many times they held the women's babies in their arms."[8]

The probation officers, all women, took their places at the judge's right and prepared to represent the children's interest in the proceedings. It was their job to assist the judge as requested and help put the youngsters at ease. Tuthill, soft-spoken and amiable, called the boys to his desk one by one for questioning. He spoke to the children informally "in a kind, fatherly manner," warning them "against the wrong," and urging them "to make a start in the right direction."[9] "I have always felt, and endeavored," he said of his handling of the court, "to act in each case, as I would were it my own son who was before me in the library at home, charged with some misconduct."[10] Those whom he judged capable of reform were placed under the charge of a general district probation supervisor, like Miss Collson, who knew upon leaving the courtroom that her work was just beginning.

As the head officer in the settlement's district, Collson was responsible for looking after the welfare of nearly two hundred children who, through delinquency or dependency, had become court wards. "Some of these boys and girls," the *Hull House Bulletin* explained, in advertising Collson's services, needed "help in finding employment, others encouragement and sympathy to keep them steadily at work." The officer alerted teachers and truant officers to be sure the school-age children got an education; and if youngsters fell back into "tendencies which cause anxiety," she would counsel parents and use her authority with the court to help them reform the child.[11]

The diversity of her work, Mary Collson recalled, was a source of grim amusement for one of the settlement's doormen, who noted that her evening callers, largely children, came on "business" ranging from their parents' drunkenness to the death of an alley cat. "The spindle on my desk," she wrote, "was commonly well filled with calls for assistance, and a policeman detailed to Hull House accompanied me if the places to be visited were deemed dangerous." A phone call or messenger "usually meant that the pay-envelope had been left at some saloon . . . there was apt to be wife-beating and child-beating . . . and I needed my colleague's company on such visits."[12]

By her own admission, Alzina Stevens' successor had come to Chicago knowing "practically nothing of the life in the poorest districts of large cities," but it did not take her long at the job to become well acquainted with urban poverty. What she saw on her rounds through the neighborhood slum, and the impact it had on her, can be imagined from her casebook notations.[13] Harry _____ was living on Liberty Street with his disabled mother and younger sister: "Home in very bad condition. Garbage heaped up in corner of room" (197). Mandel _____ had been cut on the arm by an exploding bottle at work, had continued on the job, lifting crates, and was now lying sick in bed in his family's apartment over a stable (161). A call to see how John _____ was getting on brought more bad news: after twice reporting to Hull House, the youngster had disappeared. "I had thought he was a fine little fellow," Collson wrote in disappointment; "boy can scarcely be blamed for running away from so poverty stricken a place" (219).

Sometimes slum parents whose offspring were an unwanted burden to them thwarted Collson's attempts to help the children. Louis _____, for example, fourteen and small for his age, was doing his best to stay at his work for a peddlar at a quarter a day, yet his stepmother complained to authorities that he was eating too much and repeatedly asked that the boy be sent away to the John Worthy School for delinquents. "I think it unfair," the probation worker objected, quite futilely as it turned out, "Just at this time when he seems to be trying very hard to do better" (92).

At the other extreme, and no less frustrating, there were parents like the Caracellis on Ewing Street, who were fiercely intent upon keeping their family of eight together in their two-room flat. After two of the couple's six children were found in the street one November evening, barefoot and insufficiently clothed, the Bureau of Associated Charities asked Collson to help place the youngsters in a foster home where they would have better care. When the case came up, nearly all of the building's Italian residents appeared in court to protest the proposed separation of the family. Neighbors testified "that the Caracellis treated their children well and were even extravagant in having two beds in the house for eight persons." The Court agreed to the unpromising compromise of giving the little ones to the care of an uncle, who lived in the same tenement. He believed he could care for his nephews, as well as his own five children, since he had all of three rooms, whereas his brother had only two.[14]

While the official reports that were prepared for the legislature spoke of "gratifying progress" in the state's new program of juvenile reform and estimated that 85 percent of the children paroled were being "saved," the ledger in which Mary Collson followed the lives of her charges week after week was a cheerless chronicle, whose bleak chapters gave little promise of happy endings:[15]

Fred _____;	father carpenter, mother not living at home. Boy says he's 16. Arrested for trying to steal copper lightening rod.
July 26	Reported July 14. Spent evening. Fred and brother 14 yrs. Wants work, asks for something to read. Treated boys to watermelon that evening. All

seemed to have a good time. Came in last evening to play games. I'd like to get Fred a job. He especially wishes to go to country.

Aug. 24   Sent Fred Aug. 22 to answer call for boy to work in country. Return[ed] today with note from Miss Johnson saying boy seems anxious to please and willing to work but is unable to do the work required. They want a man to do a man's work for $5.00 a month. Fred is greatly disappointed. What chance do these poor boys have.

Nov. 26   Fred is now in John Worthy [reform school] (191).

Stanley _____

Sept. 6.   Brought in by father because he would not stay home nights. Home clean, well kept. Stanley not at home. Working. Mother didn't know just where— in some kind of iron work.

Sept. 15   [Stanley] reported. Noticed that boy was hoarse. Inquired—found he was working in atmosphere filled with filings. Also find his hands are blistered three times across. I tell him I must find him another job.

Sept. 24   Gave Stanley letter to go to work at Morgan Wrights. Mr. Walling reports firm not violating law.

Nov. 26   Stanley in J[ohn] W[orthy] (235).

John _____   caught stealing corn out of freight car.

Aug. 27   Called to see why John had not reported. [Mother] living upstairs rear, dark, stuffy place, 3 rooms. Husband killed working at docks, defective machinery. She has suit but cannot get her lawyer to act. I advised her to go to Women's Protective Agency for assistance. Mrs. _____ seems very industrious. Goes out working 3 and 4 days a week. Keeps children neat and clean doing all her sewing by hand.

Sept. 8	Mother and John reported. Mother went to see Women's Protective Agency.
Nov. 26	Called. Mother not home. Children said John was in school (he doubtless was not). Mother out working. Children trying to get dinner. Nothing but black coffee without even sugar, and bread without butter.
Dec. 21	Notice that John was arrested (211).

The social worker now understood what distinguished her own poverty in the rural Midwest from that of the city's slum dwellers. Back in Iowa there had been "ways of escape and hope had a reasonable foundation," but in Chicago the masses of people employed in fundamental industries—the textile workers, miners, garment makers, and unskilled laborers of all kinds— invariably lived in a state of hopeless poverty "that stultified all that was best in human life."[16]

"In illustration of what I learned and how I came to learn it," Collson wrote, "I recall the case of one 'bad boy' of whom I grew to be very fond." Joseph loved animals and had stolen a couple of pigeons from a gunning club that used the birds for targets. Faced with the problem of feeding his pets, he had gone to the freight yard and siphoned off less than a bushel of corn—by jiggling a wire he had poked into one of the bins—when he was caught, arrested, and charged with "breaking into a sealed car." On hearing the case in court, Mary Collson asked to be put in charge of the boy.[17]

Since state law required that children of Joseph's age attend school, the parole officer's first thought was to get him enrolled. At the school she was told that every seat in the building was filled, and that due to the lack of room, most of the children were there for just half a day. Nevertheless, a place was somehow made for the youngster, and Collson went away satisfied that he would now get at least "a little nibble at education." Shortly, however, a teacher sent word that Joseph was misbehaving. When the case worker met with the teacher, she learned that although a state law provided free texts for needy children, the boy had never been given any books because "there were no books to give."[18]

Soon after this revelation the city announced that its school fuel fund had been exhausted and it would have to start using faculty salaries to pay for heating the buildings. This news so aroused the teachers that they organized a Teachers' Federation and launched an exhaustive investigation.[19] When Mary Collson read of the widespread corruption the study brought to light—the rake-offs on contracts for coal supplies and school book adoptions, and massive sums lost to the city through tax fraud by at least five city utility companies—she thought of Joseph immediately:

> The very corporation that brought the arrest of [my] small boy for the crime of stealing corn for his pigeons had been cheating the city out of taxes to the amount of two million dollars or so. Two million would have built a fine school building in the nineteenth ward . . . would have permitted the children compelled by law to attend school to actually have a school to attend. This corporation—which was only one of many—had actually stolen from these unfortunate children [the right to] an elementary education, yet it was composed of highly respectable citizens who were probably very patriotic and among the very pillars of law and order; but poor little Joseph was a criminal and on his way towards helping form a criminal class.[20]

II

While Mary Collson's venture into social work during her Iowa ministry had given a practical dimension to her interest in economic theory, her revolt at what she saw in Chicago rapidly transformed that interest into intense political commitment. No matter how scientific and enlightened her casework might be, the positivist approach aimed at individual rehabilitation was having little impact on society. If the world were to be improved, reforms must above all be directed at institutions and political systems. In college, her exploration of *Das Kapital* and class struggle, and her energetic discussions of the single tax

and Bellamy Nationalism had all been largely academic flirta-
tions with urban problems. Now, "with Experience as a
teacher, the words of Karl Marx sounded like the words of a
great prophet," and her rarified view of labor organization took
on a more pragmatic cast.[21]

At Hull House there were any number of ways to translate
prolabor sentiments into action. With the capitalistic system
refusing their demands for reform, settlement workers got into
the labor movement "as a matter of course."[22] Many of them
joined the picket lines routinely, despite the perils. Dr. Alice
Hamilton usually volunteered for the early morning shift, when
the police were much less in evidence. "I was in mortal fear of
having one of them seize me and drag me about," the physician
later confessed. "The fact of arrest was not as bad as the way it
was done."[23]

The settlement's cofounder, Ellen Starr, was far more
aggressive in her support of striking workers. While others
shunned the violence, Starr could often be seen leaving the
settlement art gallery or studio, where she worked, to join the
picket lines at the height of the demonstrations. Indeed, Collson later remembered Starr as a kindred spirit, who was "always dashing about with a great hustle and bustle from morning until night," prompting others to wonder what she feared
would happen if she were not there.[24] Deeply committed to
labor reform, she was often impatient with those who courted
compromise in such matters. Collson remembered Jane
Addams as the person most given to compromise. Less "intense" in her approach, Addams charcteristically urged greater
calm and restraint, and her "air of moderation" often "irked" the
probation officer, who became increasingly passionate in her
work.[25] The director's composure struck the new resident as an
affront to the poor, who, as she knew from her own history,
could hardly afford to be serene when struggling to survive.

Since Collson's job with the Juvenile Court prevented her
from joining the pickets and risking a confrontation with the
law, she threw herself all the more zealously into the work of

the settlement's labor groups. She attended meetings of the
Tick Sewers' Union, helped formulate strategy for organizing
women through the Dorcas Federal Labor Union, and accepted
the presidency of the Textile Workers' Association. The
Women's Union Label League, which Alzina Stevens had
started at Hull House in 1899—for the purpose of building a
sense of solidarity among union members by having them ask
for the union label on the goods they purchased—asked Collson
to take on its leadership as well. "Whenever I could be useful,"
she summarized, "I assisted in organizing women wage earn-
ers and did some speaking on the history of the struggles of
labor and on the part played by organization."[26]

Collson's new quest for political remedies was more radical
than that of most of the workers she helped to organize. Generally, union members were content to seek better conditions
through the existing, capitalistic framework. They were willing
to let the Democrats lead them to the great American dream. At
Hull House, however, supporters of labor were generally part of
that small minority—principally middle-class Marxists, radical
intellectuals, and a smattering of skilled union workers—who
mocked those who thought they saw some relation between
deteriorating conditions of the poor and the rags-to-riches fable
that bolstered belief in free enterprise. These reformers had
been active in Nationalist Clubs a few years before; now they
worked within the growing socialist movement. The Federation of Social Justice, an independent club founded "on the
brotherhood basis to further the inauguration of the cooperative
commonwealth," met at Hull House regularly. The editor of
The Workers' Call, a weekly created expressly to support the
Socialist Labor Party, spoke at the settlement. Others lectured
on Marxist philosophy, socialism and education, "The
Treachery of Old Party Issues" and "New Political Ideals."[27]

The socialist voices Collson heard agreed that the coming
century required a new political consciousness, one intent on
eliminating the inequities of capitalism by replacing it with a
national system of collectively owned public industry. What

Marx had foreseen was now coming to pass: first a series of internecine struggles, like the current Boer War, beween the ruling powers of nations fighting to capture world markets; then the economic crises following the wars, and their reduction of the prosperous middle class until it disappeared; finally, a great proletarian revolution by the vast, impoverished majority who had nothing more to lose. "It was an awful picture," the new social worker thought, "and the worst feature of all was that I began to see that we were moving in exactly that direction. Of course beyond disaster was the New Day, but the region we must pass through was terrifying to me."[28]

Among the numerous "independent" socialist groups Collson encountered in Chicago were the Christian Socialists, who sought to achieve a social commonwealth but avoid the class struggle by bringing all social, political, and industrial relations into harmony with God through the teachings of Jesus Christ. Although Mary Collson became a close friend of this group's frequent spokesman, J. Stitt Wilson—a former Methodist minister and later mayor of Berkeley, California—her previous study of Marx and her liberal theological training set her against "the inconsistency of their position:"

> I knew how fragmentary all the record of Jesus is . . . though it is evident that he really expected the kingdom of God to come in the immediate future. Doubtless he expected to be rescued from the death on the cross . . . [But] he had no ideas at all on the subject of production and distribution of wealth. His supply was from voluntary and commandeered gifts. Once secured, he shared his resources equally. He had no interest in production. He took his followers out of productive activity. . . . To connect our economic problems of a scientific age with the legendary history of an oriental mystic who taught the eternal truths of man's spiritual being, but who was not interested in even the economics of his day . . . does not encourage either intellectual or spiritual integrity.[29]

The Socialist Labor Party "was in for revolution right away" and therefore equally unacceptable. For though her style was in-

tense and passionate, Collson was still a born-and-bred pacifist
who abhorred violence for whatever reasons. The best course of
action, she decided, was to join the Social Democratic Party,
whose motto was "Socialism through evolution, not revolution." The SDP hoped to avert the bloodshed of massive wars
and to mitigate the crises of economic change by inaugurating
immediate reforms.

"I was not a bona fide socialist because I could not accept the
full import of the materialistic conception of history," Collson
acknowledged, "but I did accept the economic foundation of
society and was a very devoted worker, so I was in good standing in the Party."[30] By the summer's end she was totally im-
mersed in the SDP and gave it all her leisure time. It was a
presidential election year, and in an effort to crystallize a
national movement, an uneasy alliance of socialist parties
nominated the popular and flamboyant Eugene V. Debs for
president. Debs deplored the Republican platform—summed
up by its slogan of "Prosperity galore, give us four years more"—
as the worst kind of self-congratulation by a dominant captialist
elite. He ridiculed the Democratic plank as "the wail and cry of
the perishing middle class," and offered his own party's resolution as "the clarion voice of economic freedom." On election day
the socialist ticket received almost six thosand votes in Chicago, and nation-wide more votes than ever before in a major
American election. Collson had canvassed the Hull House district and was delighted when she delivered 123 votes from a
ward that belonged to the Democrats. In fact, she was so
encouraged by the returns that she set up an SDP branch at
Hull House. Her chapter promptly appointed her one of its
delegates to the city-wide convention, and there she was
elected to the resolutions committee. By the year's end Mary
Collson sat as a full-fledged member on Chicago's Central
Committee.[31]

Not the least of the socialist movement's attractions for Collson was its parties' official positions on equal rights for women.
When the Republicans and Democrats had nothing to say on

such issues, socialist platforms persisted in calling for universal suffrage without regard to sex, equalization of women's wages for the performance of equal services, and the prohibition of female labor wherever "detrimental to health and morality."

But Collson quickly learned that the socialists' attitudes towards her sex were not always as agreeable in practice as in their platforms. She understood entirely what one disgruntled sister in the party meant by the observation that woman was "just as much an afterthought with the average Socialist as she was with the Hebrew god," and that "Socialists, just as strongly as non Socialists, are imbued with the absurd idea that man is the race, woman his appendage."[32] Socialist newspapers were condescending in their treatment of women's issues and tended to reduce their importance by subordinating them to the larger "labor question." The press admitted that its tone might seem patronizing; it regretted that women were thought to be narrow-minded, weak in organizational ability, and unconcerned with improving their lot; but it defended these estimates as justified and said it expected "that most thoughtful women" themselves would admit to their validity.[33]

Mary Collson, for one, disappointed this expectation. Her legacy of feminist loyalties and assumptions of equality, enhanced by memories of her father, made her bristle at any sign of male chauvinism or exploitation of women. Her criticism of George D. Herron, whom she knew as a prominant figure in Chicago's party unification, was typical. It was not Herron's ideology that offended her. She admired Stitt Wilson, for example, who shared the same ideas. She was offended by what she considered Herron's smug male egotism and odious treatment of women in his private life. Even many years later what she remembered first about Herron was that he had "divorced his faithful wife" to marry a wealthier woman, and used her money to go abroad and live as "a rich Christian Socialist."[34]

It was disappointing to find that the socialist movement was not, after all, producing a superior community of men who could treat the opposite sex respectfully as equal human beings. Yet socialism did offer benefits Collson could not find anywhere else: an official party commitment to equal rights for women that gave her the sanction and political apparatus to work for her sisters' special interests. To make the most of this opportunity, Collson started the Socialist Woman's Club, which began holding meetings at Hull House in the Fall of 1900 and brought in such speakers as Charlotte Perkins Gilman.

Gilman had lived at Hull House briefly in 1896, and remained an enthusiastic admirer of the work being done there.[35] Many of her ideas for communal household and child-care arrangements, which she hoped would relieve women of domestic responsibilities, were based on experiments she had seen working at the settlement. Collson, like most of her co-workers and clients, firmly believed in keeping the traditional family unit intact and opposed dissolving women's homemaking role, as advocated by radical feminists like Gilman. Collson believed that if most women had the option, they would choose to be wives and mothers, rather than workers employed outside their homes. Yet as a caseworker, she realized that under the present conditions, where poor women had to work, the public kitchens, cooperative boarding clubs, and nurseries Gilman proposed would support, not subvert, family life.[36]

When Collson herself spoke before SDP branches and women's clubs, on topics usually related to education and juvenile reform, she took the position of most of her comrades, who claimed they did not want to limit females' roles, but still did not like to see women enter the work force. Capitalism, of course, was here again marked as the villain. By paying the menfolk too little to support their families, the argument ran, the system forced reluctant wives and daughters to go outside to work. This, in turn, caused the prostitution, suicides, illegitimacies, and divorce that were bringing American family life to ruin. Socialism, women were promised, would recover their right to stay home.

Besides this pledge, Collson offered the women suggestions on how they could hasten the arrival of a new social order, even without the right to vote. In Sunday schools, they could cull out the lessons' capitalistic teachings and devise ways of supplanting them with the socialist ethic. Clerks, bookkeepers, and factory workers could put aside the envy and contempt that divided them and together pursue common goals as workers and women. Those employed in the classrooms might impress upon their students that "a good character is more to be desired than great riches" and agitate among the other faculty for free textbooks, transportation, lunches, and clothing, and for educational reform.[37]

For her part, Mary Collson was doing her best as a social worker to make her relationships on the job exemplify socialist principles. "I never talked socialism in connection with my work," she wrote, "but I did endeavor in all my contacts . . . to live up to my ideals." It was not hard for her to establish a rapport with her working-class neighbors, and before long the women in the ward felt so comfortable with her that they asked to borrow her clothes, as they borrowed each others':

> My wardrobe could not be considered very extensive since it consisted of but two outfits, a serge coat suit and a relic from my days in the ministry: a dress-up dress which I donned when speaking about my work before Women's Clubs or for other social occasions demanding a proper garment. Some of my neighborhood friends had evidently seen me wearing that dress-up dress and one day a buxom young Italian matron approached me for the loan of it. In tears she told me of how her cousin had died and here she was without a decent dress to wear to the funeral celebration. If I would be so kind as to loan her that dress which she had heard about it would go far to assuage her grief. So that dress started on its career as a loan garment. . . . I told my friends that thereafter they were welcome to borrow this dress whenever occasion demanded. Henceforth dressing up for me meant pressing the worst wrinkles out of my serge suit and combining it with a fresh shirtwaist.[38]

Even the children soon understood where Collson's sympathies lay. When she came upon one of her eight-year-old charges hustling papers during school hours, the boy, knowing how to soften the woman's displeasure, pointed out that he was only handling the prolabor *Chicago American* and could be trusted never to sell "a 'scab' paper" (263). At Christmas, the caseworker's neighborhood friends expressed their affection and thanks. Collson never forgot how one poor woman, who scarcely ever had enough to eat, and certainly possessed no such luxury herself, had somehow found the money and time to crochet an Iceland-wool scarf. Nor did she forget the life-size wooden Indian head that came as a startling token of love from a young parolee who worked in a nearby cigar store.[39]

However, as the holidays passed and the winter wore on, Collson began to feel the effects of her overexertion and unrealistic expectations of what she could accomplish. She also suffered, as Addams once noted, from too great a sensitivity to even the mildest criticism. She was easily stung, Addams told her, because she took "admiration for granted, and if, in any instance . . . failed to get it . . . was amazed and hurt." When Collson asked her coworker Amanda Johnson what she thought of Addams' comment, Johnson reassured her, "Well, the Lady Jane falls for you herself," and her spirits went soaring again.[40] Yet Collson's need of praise and reinforcement remained and made her all the more vulnerable to the inevitable letdowns and disappointments in social work.

The more Collson saw of human suffering, the more it wounded her spirit, and the harder she tried to live as she thought a good socialist should. Now she gave herself "as a friend" not only to her wards and their families, but to other unfortunate people whom she met through her regular assignments. One of these was the aunt of a boy who had been parolled to her. A prostitute dying of syphilis, she was "a most unwelcome member" of a family of five that occupied two small rooms of a rear tenement. "Her disease made her condition very loathesome," Collson recalled:

She was almost blind and lay coughing and cursing on a filthy bed when I made my first visit after the boy in the family had been paroled to me. . . . A few days later when I called especially to visit with her, she told me that she swore these awful oaths because she was afraid to die. This attitude of defiance seemed to give her courage, and the greater her need of courage, the greater her defiance expressed in the most terrible language. I made many visits to see her. I succeeded in getting her somewhat cleaned up and although my own faith was growing dim and flickering, I was able to overcome her fear of death, as I myself never at any time feared death. Toward the end this poor girl was quietly anxious to die.

The day before the young woman finally lapsed into a coma, Mary Collson sat with her, singing over and over a hymn from the Western Unitarian Hymnal, which she had used routinely as an opening convocation when she was in the ministry:

I had told her about this [hymn], so she asked me always to sing it the first thing when I came to see her. She said she did not want any pious words of hypocrites but she liked this hymn, so that last afternoon . . . I sang these words:
Come Thou Almighty Will,
Faint are our spirits till
Thou comest with power;
Strength of our good intents,
In our frail hour defence,
Calm of faith's confidence
Come in this hour.
She said that perhaps if she had been taught to pray like that when she was younger her life might have been different.[41]

Frequently now, Collson started her day's work in a state of exhaustion she hoped would wear off as she trudged through the neighborhood making her calls and attending court sessions. It was ever more difficult for her to meet her evening obligations—the endless round of socialist meetings and frequent speaking engagements—but all through March she managed to do so, continuing as a member of the central committee and secretary of the Hull House SDP. She kept commitments to speak at chapter meetings in the 15th and

28th wards and to address the Socialist Educational Club. But by mid-April she had sunk into an immobilizing depression and was sent to the country to rest. The Socialist Ladies Auxilliary, who were to have heard her lecture, used their notice of the meeting's cancellation to wish her a speedy recovery: "Glad she will take a vacation and soon be herself again."[42] Unfortunately, Mary Collson's vacation did little more than postpone the end of her career as a social settlement worker. Upon returning to work, she found that very little had changed, except that there was now a backlog of casework and two months' salary lost. The corruption, the frustrations, and the human wreckage all remained; and as before, they filled the woman with a sense of revolt so intense that she lashed out against them with all the strength she had left.

It was when Collson took on the problems in the home of two small Jewish boys that her ultimate defeat became imminent. The father and daughter in this particular family eked out a living making knee pants for twenty-five cents a dozen on two old manual sewing machines. The pale-faced boys had rebelled against the work and run away, and the mother lay at home dying of stomach cancer. The caseworker found the woman to be a person of intelligence and refinement and was sympathetically drawn to her:

> The story of her life was like a Greek tragedy with its chorus of defeated hope. It was pogroms in Czarist Russia; hope of America, land of milk and honey, ending in the East Side Ghetto of New York; hope of the Golden West, ending in sweat shops in Chicago; slow torturing death, with pride crushed in the dust by the thought of herself as a charity charge and her sons as social delinquents. . . . [She] was in a bed of rags on which the July sun beat mercilessly . . . through unscreened, uncurtained, cracked and broken window panes. The two sweltering rooms were very dirty and the clatter of machines and the buzzing of flies filled the air. . . . I, too, was very hot and tired, and, as I stood in the door looking at this scene, I felt a rush of impotent rage that such things could exist. I vowed that come what might, I would get that sick woman out of that hell.

With Jane Addams' help, Mary Collson was able to get the family some financial aid, but there was still the problem of finding the mother a place to stay. Hospitals could not take terminal charity cases. The Home for Incurables was full and had such a long waiting list that Collson was sure the people on it died "of old age, if of nothing else," before getting in. At last, arrangements were made with a convalescent home in another city, and Collson took the sick woman there by train on a cot in the baggage car. She got her settled, and left her in what seemed a fairly good frame of mine. Before long, however, the manager of the rest home notified Hull House that they could not keep Miss Collson's friend any longer. More dependent than they had expected, and having to be left alone a great deal, she was frightened and homesick and cried most of the time. The social worker had no other choice than to bring the woman back to Chicago, though there was still no decent place to take her:

> Her own home seemed impossible, so I took her home with me. I said, just for the night—on the morrow I hoped to find [something better]. Everyone protested against my sharing my room with so sick a person, but I could see no other way to do. When I could find [no accommodations for her] the next day, nor the next, I got the little daughter to come help care for her mother during the day; and with the aid of the doctor's sleeping powders, I thought I could care for her at night.[43]

However, Collson soon learned that the simplest help was too much to expect. Being vacation time again, nearly all the permanent residents were away from the settlement. The nurse who was there as a summer replacement was "more romantic than professional" and seemed never to be around when Collson needed her. The doctor who was supposed to be on call also gave the probation officer the distinct impression of having "no real interest in problems of sickness among the poor." Collson suspected that these young women had only come to Hull House because "doing 'settlement work' was then quite in vogue." Whatever the case, they gave her "absolutely no assistance," she recalled bitterly, "not even effective opiate" for her suffering friend.[44]

Meanwhile, her boys continued to bring her disappointments daily. In a single morning she learned that one had lost his job, another had run off, and yet another had been sent back to reform school for violating parole. Contributing further to her despair, Collson's own financial problems were mounting and putting a strain on old and valued relationships. To be sure, she had realized before ever taking the job with the Juvenile Court that what it paid would not allow her to clear old debts or help support her mother. She would earn only sixty dollars a month, part of which she would have to give back to the settlement for her room and board. Yet the chance to move out of the ministry, where she felt misplaced from the first, and join the inspiring family of women at Hull House had been more compelling than money. She had persuaded herself that she could put off repaying her debts a while longer and that her old friends would surely understand.

Predictably, some did not. Eleanor Gordon, angered and hurt by her protégée's desertion, had quickly contacted both Jane Addams and Jenkin Lloyd Jones in the hope that they might send her back. She explained that Collson still carried more than six hundred dollars in college debts, while her destitute mother was forced to live in the home of "an undesirable son-in-law." "As I look at it," she told Jones, "Miss Collson has no business to give herself to the work she is doing until she has kept her faith with those people who have loaned her money and until she has provided a home for her mother." Gordon urged her colleagues to keep this in mind if asked to advise the young woman about her future. "We have no right to offer ourselves on the 'altar of humanity' until we belong to ourselves," she reminded them.[45] Collson was still on Gordon's mind some months later when she warned Jones that Collson would "do conscientious work wherever she [was]—but not always wise work."[46] In the year that followed, the criticism had become a familiar one to the Sisterhood's wayward disciple, and now the defeat she faced on all fronts seemed a crushing validation of it. Her attempts to accelerate progress by reforming society's laws and institutions, instead of uplifting souls, had turned out to be worthless and not "wise work" at all.

One morning in August 1901, following a sleepless night with her friend, Mary Collson went down to her office exhausted. At the sight of the long line of people who had brought their problems to her, she at last recoiled, body and soul, from hearing "a single word more which added to the . . . awfulness of the world." She collapsed at her desk, and with head on her arms, wept uncontrollably until another resident, passing through, saw her distress and took her upstairs.[47]

CHAPTER IV

Leaving the Brazen World

I

Those who came to live at Hull House generally did not stay long. In fact, the turnover was so rapid that at the time Mary Collson moved in, residents had to promise to remain at least six months. Many who joined the settlement did so primarily for a season of excitement and intellectual stimulation. Some of the transients merely enlisted long enough to advance their careers by collecting data and making useful contacts. Others who came to Hull House were still looking for purposeful occupations and made the settlement one of many stopovers where they tried out different kinds of work.[1] But even among the more committed residents there was little longevity. The limits of a worker's psychological tolerance frequently eroded her aspirations for reform. After only three months at Hull House in 1896, Charlotte Gilman, who was planning to open another settlement on the North Side, caved in under the stresses produced by the "noisesome neighborhood" and the settlement's "flux of disconnected people." While she thought it "magnificent" that "wonderful Miss Addams" could handle it "all so well . . . meeting the thousand calls upon her so gently and effectively," it was not the comfortable life in the country she really enjoyed, and she had to concede, "it tires me very much."[2]

The tolls of life in the 19th ward were much greater for the new full-time rank-and-file social workers at Hull House than for either free-lance reformers like Gilman or staff administra-

tors like Addams. It was one thing to wage war against deprivation by holding classes in art history in the quiet of the settlement's classrooms, or even by lobbying for legislation in orderly
conference halls and club parlors, and quite another to confront
the enemy day after day in the tenements, hospitals, sweat-
shops, and jails. The survival rate among the Juvenile Court's
probation officers—who were overworked, underpaid, and constantly met by defeat—was predictably poor.[3]

To prevent Collson from becoming another casualty of the
court program, Addams again sent her to the country for several
weeks' vacation, but this had little effect. Only "a search for a
remedy" had "made life in the slums bearable" for the caseworker, and now, she wrote later, she had "no enthusiasm and
no hope. I did my work without expectation of results," and
Socialism offered no solace. "I saw only the agonies of deca-
dence—the increased poverty, the wars and crises. The New
Day was so far in the future that I could no longer visualize it."[4]
Without appetite, the already slight woman lost even more
weight. Her head ached constantly, and she went about her
duties mechanically. The other residents did what they could to
lift her depression, urging a change in diet and more recreation
and rest, but Collson's condition did not improve.

Then came an unexpected gesture of sympathy from a
volunteer worker who sometimes served as the Hull House
receptionist. This woman was a recent convert to Christian
Science, the mind-cure religion that had become a serious
competitor with regular medical practice among the middle
class. With the popularization of recent medical progress, people were less inclined than they once had been to forego scientific medicine for sectarian ministrations. Yet in the wake of the
germ theory, medical men were indifferent to the influence of
the mind in causing and curing physical ailments; and in cities
like Chicago, Christian Science was successfully exploiting the
vacuum left by this disregard of psychosomatic disorders.[5] Indeed, there was such great activity among Chicago's Scientists
at this time that the sect's founder, Mary Baker Eddy, had come

to the city from Boston to address her flock and personally teach
a course in her therapeutics. Chicago's growing number of
Eddyites supported four branch churches and several societies,
which held regular Sunday services, Wednesday evening testimonial meetings, public lectures, and jointly provided a Reading Room downtown.[6]

Noticing how unhappy the parole officer had been of late,
and eager to share the means of relief she had found for her own
problems, the Hull House receptionist offered the ailing
woman a card with the name and address of her Christian
Science practitioner and urged her to pay him a visit. Collson
listened vacantly as the proselyte witnessed to her new faith,
and being reluctant to prolong the conversation, made no effort
to explain that she already knew quite a bit about Christian
Science herself, having had several more than casual encounters with it in the past.

Mary Collson had first heard the term "Christian Science"
more than twenty years before, while still a child. At the time,
mental healing was just coming into vogue, and a Chicago
woman publicizing Dr. Warren Felt Evans' latest book on mind
cure came to speak in Humboldt.[7] Evans was touted as having
developed a scientific method of treating physical ailments by
utilizing the power of the mind to control material phenomena.
His promoter claimed that Evans' procedures had cured her of
"strawberry hives" and astigmatism, and urged all who could to
send off for the book.

If mind cure, as the woman contended, was about to make
regular doctors and their ministrations obsolete, most people in
Humboldt during the early 1880s were well prepared for it. For
despite the advances since 1830, medical practice on the frontier was still in a primitive stage. The average pioneer doctor
starting out with a medical school education "had not seen an
amputation, had not attended an obstetrical case, had ex-
amined no cases of disease, had seen no fracture," and "knew
nothing of asepsis or antisepsis."[8] Rather than subject themselves to physicians' noxious drugs and dubious procedures,

the Collsons' neighbors, like many Americans, took health matters into their own hands. They stressed preventive hygiene,
temperance, wholesome foods, and sensible dress. Some had
long since emptied their medicine chests and turned to "water
cure" for relief. Others, homeopathic converts, took their drugs
in attenuated doses and consulted doctors only in the most
extreme cases. Still others, the Collsons among them, relied on
a battery of home remedies. "Onion poultices," "hot corn
packs," and "swathings of peppered salt pork on red flannel"
were Martha's favorites, and her daughter complained that
they caused as much discomfort as the ailments themselves.
Since Mary was the member of the family most often abed, she
was all for converting to mind cure immediately.[9]

Her elders, if more cautious, were also aroused by the possibilities of the new health fad, whose transcendentalist overtones gave it a special appeal. As Unitarians, they had long
preached the intimacy between a divine source of power and
the human spirit. They had dwelt on Emerson's affirmation of
the Eternal Spirit "shining through all commonplaces and
all mysteries, enlightening man from within," making him
healthy, happy, and good. Now Evans' mind cure appeared to
present itself as a way of giving practical scientific expression to
the liberals' religious heritage.[10]

In further pursuit of this new road to health, a couple of
Humboldt's most prominent women had gone to Chicago to
study mental healing, and when they returned, they
announced that they had been through a formal course which
qualified them to give instruction themselves. These classes,
Collson remembered, were greeted enthusiastically, and she
had considered herself "most blest" to have been allowed to
attend one of them. However, when none of the graduates
could get results from the techniques they were taught, the
town handed down a verdict against mental healing.

The matter would have rested there, had not one of the
teachers scandalized the community by deserting her husband
and returning to Chicago to take up "an advanced form" of

mind cure called Christian Science. Mary Baker Eddy had
developed Christian Science from teachings of other mind-
curists of the day, most notably Phineas P. Quimby, whose
work was being popularized by Evans. She insisted, however,
that her "discovery" was a unique scientific religion, and she
took pains to explain how her system was different from all the
others.[11] Evans had emphasized the magnetic power of the
hands and other mesmeric devices as important features of the
healing procedure, and his writings exalted the human mind as
a beneficent influence upon other minds. On both counts,
Eddy maintained, Evans' system was "the opposite of Christian
Science, which rests on the divine Mind as the healthiest and
holiest influence over the human mind and body."[12] The for-
mula for her own therapeutics was codified in the so-called
"scientific statement of being":

> There is no life, truth, intelligence, or substance in matter. All is
> infinite Mind and its infinite manifestation, for God is All in all.
> Spirit is immortal Truth; matter is mortal error. Spirit is the real and
> eternal; matter is the unreal and temporal. Spirit is God, and man is
> His image and likeness; hence, man is spiritual and not material.[13]

As reports of their former neighbor came down from Chicago, Humboldt's citizens became convinced that the practice
of Eddyism was unhealthful and foolish. It was said that the
woman would not heat her house in the winter, and that she
permitted her children to run about out-of-doors when they
were ill. Since the liberal community lost patience with new
ideas when they undercut common sense, their bias against
mind cure was transferred to Christian Science. Young Mary
had accepted this view as her own and assumed it was final.

That assumption, it turned out, was premature. A few years
later, in 1886, shortly after the schoolgirl had moved to Fort
Dodge, her oldest sister, Emma, fell critically ill. After the
doctors had given up hope for Emma's recovery, and the rest of
the family had been summoned, an acquaintance, Lucy P.
Lincoln, who had recently converted to Christian Science and

had gone through the formal program of instruction, offered the Collsons her services as a metaphysician. Martha Collson was at first averse to accepting the woman's offer, as it seemed to her a sacrilege to engage such dubious methods when her daughter's life was at stake; but when the doctors predicted the patient would not live through the night, her mother reconsidered. As Mary remembered it, the practitioner came at once, and upon her arrival declared that Emma was not really dying and would not die. She asked to be left alone with the patient "and with God," and all through the night could be heard singing cheerfully and reading aloud. The next morning Emma was not only alive, but vastly improved. Whereas she had been in constant pain before losing consciousness the day before, she was resting in a normal sleep when the family next saw her; and although she had not taken solid nourishment for weeks, upon awakening she asked for food and ate well. Her recovery was rapid and complete, and she had been in good health ever since.

Emma herself apparently gave little thought to the process involved in her healing. At least she never became at all interested either in mind cure or Christian Science. It was Martha and Mary, who had been in closest attendance upon the sick woman, watched her condition deteriorate, and were convinced she would have died without the practitioner's aid, who were profoundly impressed by this experience. In some manner they did not yet understand, some mental or spiritual force had resuscitated or reinforced the vital functions.

"As a born and bred evolutionist," Mary was hardly prepared to accept this occurence as a miracle, but was set upon finding "a full and logical explanation" for it.[14] The little that she had salvaged from her short course in Dr. Evans' mind cure a few years before seemed likely to afford some clue, but Mrs. Lincoln repudiated that branch of the movement as false. Although the healer had only been studying Christian Science a few months and had gone through class on very short notice, as one could in those days, she was alert to the need for keeping Eddy's "re-

vealed" mental science from being contaminated by other curist cults. Recently, Christian Scientists had been displaying so
great an appetite for all kinds of metaphysical literature, that
their leader had started issuing warnings against indiscrimi-
nate reading and urged her students to clear their minds of "the
cobwebs which spurious literature engenders."[15] As a dutiful
apostle, Lucy Lincoln insisted that if young Mary Collson
wanted to reach an understanding of the practice, she would
have to limit her reading to the authorized Christian Science
literature—Mrs. Eddy's textbook, *Science and Health*, and the
Christian Science Journal—available for loan or for sale in her
office. Further, she recommended, as insurance against dis-
traction, that the teenager burn all the other books she had in
her possession, even those she was using to prepare for college
entrance. The lurid picture of her valuable texts going up in
sacrificial flames effectively deterred the girl from any further
investigation of Christian Science for a number of years.

It was more than a decade later, after her nervous breakdown had forced her to take a leave from her pastoral duties in
Ida Grove, that Collson had her next encounter with Eddyism.
Reunited with her mother and sister in Fort Dodge, she found
that the prescribed rest and daily constitutionals were not relieving her depression, but only giving her more time to worry
about her unpaid college debts and her fitness for the ministry.
After some weeks, she began to think back on Emma's healing,
and remembering Mrs. Lincoln, decided to ask the practitioner
for treatment. After just three visits the patient felt fully re-
stored and ready to go back to work.

Collson's attempt to give Christian Science due credit for her
speedy return to the parish caused "some little unpleasantness"
over the subject, for most of her congregation and colleagues
looked askance at the movement. Even in most liberal clerical
circles hostility toward Eddy's therapeutics had been rising
correlatively with the rapid growth of her organization.[16] Unitarian ministers like Andrew Preston Peabody and Cyrus A.
Barton, who befriended the Scientists in the mid-1890s, or

James Henry Wiggen, who became Mrs. Eddy's literary advisor about the same time, were the exception, not the rule. Attempt- ting to deal fairly with the Christian Science sect, as with all religious movements, *Unity* allowed that there was "a generous amount of reality" in the Eddyites' belief "in the immense potency of mind over matter, and the metaphysical element which enters into the healing art." However, the publication deplored Eddy's "disposition to ignore coordinate truths and the failure to recognize the hurting power of dogma and the dogmatic spirit." Persuaded that Eddy was shrewdly exploiting the public's awesome regard for science by calling her system "scientific," the great majority of Unitarians in the late 1890s rejected Christian Science as "quackery." In an age that had the benefits of the germ theory, serums, antitoxins, and disinfectants, no one of any intelligence, *Unity* declared, could entertain a system of healing that dispensed with "the homely grace of common sense."[17]

Besides its questionable hygienic practices, what was seen as the narrow and intolerant character and emerging ecclesiasticism of Eddy's new orthodoxy offended Unitarians. One liberal, writing in the Iowa Conference's *Old and New*, conceded that imagination and belief often effected surprising cures of nervous and mental disorders, but she saw no reason to suppose there was any "supernatural interposition in answer to prayer to account for those results." Strong faith in one's recovery from disease, and in prayer as its means, was often enough to restore health. Yet some of the theories which were "seriously presented as finalities of thought under the name of Christian Science" were, this writer argued, mere *a priori* speculations which only obscured the facts concerning the power of suggestion in the treatment of disease. Before physicians and psychologists could discern the real value of these facts, they would have to isolate them from the "unfounded" claims of the curists.[18] On all these counts, Mary Collson's associates regarded Christian Science as dangerous. But the issue of her involvement with it became moot as she soon lost interest in *Science and Health* and put it aside half-finished, happy to let the matter rest. The following year, when she fell ill again after the Christmas holidays, her parishioners and colleagues rushed forward with every kind of assistance to aid her recovery and protect her against her weakness for Christian Science.

II

By 1901, however, Mary Collson had left the ministry, and with her Unitarian friends no longer at hand to restrain her, she went to see the practitioner the Hull House receptionist recommended. The metaphysician, who seemed to have been briefed about his new client, did not inquire into the nature of her specific problem or mention physical healing at all, but talked instead about the unreality of the world and its misery. He said that human existence and its material surroundings were actually delusions, the outgrowth of a false state of consciousness, while the only real world was spiritual and perfect. Mortals had but to grasp or "realize" this perfection to make it manifest. The patient must see herself as "a child of God" and therefore happy and well, and all of the world's apparent wickedness and suffering would dissolve. Eddyism's denial of human suffering was precisely what Collson wanted to hear, and she left the practitioner's office feeling better than she had in many months. "I again was on the track of an all-right world," she wrote later; and because it was metaphysical, "entirely beyond the reach of the human experience to destroy or alter in any way," this healthy, harmonious world "was secure."[19]

As in the past when she flirted with Science to find an escape from the problems at hand, Collson was lured by the echoes of sages whom she had long cherished and trusted. Long before Eddy, Emerson had captivated her by proclaiming the power of positive thinking. In his "Divinity School Address" she had read that "all evil is so much death and nonentity," while "benevolence is absolute and real." "The sentiment of virtue" was "divine and deifying," making man "illimitable" by "showing the fountain of all good to be in himself." Then, too, in its postulation of the absolute as the only reality, Christian Science bore some resemblance to Plato. "Having early been taught by Emerson that 'Plato is philosophy, and philosophy, Plato,' this similarity was a great recommendation to me," Collson later explained.[20]

What also sold Collson on Eddyism was its "scientific" packaging. The system appealed to her positivist standard by claiming to be presenting God's science in terms human beings could understand. Its teachings were said to provide a set of rules for demonstrating universal divine law, and the founder stressed the importance of strict obedience to "every statement . . . laid down." Eddy claimed that her method was exact and infallible, that the student who took care "not to break its rules" could not "fail of success in healing."[21]

More importantly, Eddy-Science attached itself to the scientific vogue—and adopted a concept of science close to the popular view of it as demonstrable power—without accepting the scientific point of view. Christian Science claimed to explain everything, but explained nothing in a scientific sense; that is, empirically. For reform Darwinists like Collson, who had been overwhelmed by the world's inexplicable contradictions of good and evil, Eddyism offered a welcome release from the rigors and frustrations of the scientific approach. One Harvard-trained liberal who converted to Eddyism to free himself of the troubling influence of empirical thinking explained his great longing to be possessed by a strong, if blind, faith that would lead him gently to a "scientific explanation of spiritual reality."[22] Mary Collson's experience was essentially the same. "In the bafflement of defeat," she wrote later, "I accepted Christian Science through the exercise of the will-to-believe and not [through] the exercise of reason." "I submerged myself in [its teachings] in order to escape from my world, which had become too difficult a proposition for me."[23]

There was also the appeal of Eddy's religious context and organization, features missing from the secular New Thought circles of metaphysical healing, which otherwise should have attracted someone with Collson's background and interests. While many radical, anti-ecclesiastical Unitarians were drawn to New Thought by its very absence of dogma and institutional structure, Collson, whose rationalistic training had never unseated her mystical theism, felt most comfortable when science and reform were championed by religion. Moreover, as she had always been deeply involved in denominational work, she was grateful that Christian Science had a church she could join and serve. In short, Eddyism seemed to have everything Mary Collson wanted: a "scientific," church-centered faith, whose vocabulary was tailored to express her most ardent hopes, and whose formulations worked to elude the facts that defeated those hopes.

For those who embraced it as the scientific religion it claimed to be, Eddyism was linked not only with spiritual uplift, but with reformative currents that found in Darwinism a metaphor for society's betterment. It was hardly anomalous that a woman like Collson, who took its teachings to heart, would view Christian Science as an ally of social reforms. If others were troubled that this orthodoxy not only sought to improve the material world, but denied that it existed, Collson, worn out by futile efforts to "save the race," as she put it, ignored the lapses in logic and eagerly turned to Christian Science "as an easier way." In fact, as her depression gave way to this new enthusiasm, the metaphysical appeal of Christian Science ceased to excite her as much as did the possibilities for its practical application. Above all, Collson wanted to see the results of her "right thinking" in her work at the settlement. She never considered abandoning her efforts to help the poor: "Simple as it may sound," she later wrote, "I was exactly that simple. I expected great economic changes automatically to follow the declarations of Truth and practice of the religion of Love."[24]

The first check to the convert's zeal came when, wishing that she could "help with Truth where help was so badly needed," she asked her practitioner if he would work on behalf of several particularly difficult cases in her neighborhood. To Collson's surprise, the man bristled at this request, which, he said, was totally inappropriate. Christian Science was a religion, not merely a method of healing disease and solving personal problems. Such results, he said, were "the fruits" which attested to the divinity of the doctrines, while the doctrines were the real empowering factor in the work. Moreover, since the people in Collson's immigrant district were almost all Roman Catholics or Jews and hardly prepared to give up their religions, it would be useless to try to do anything for them through Christian Science. No matter that the social worker had been unaware of their theological differences or any religious separation between them. When she insisted that "these folks had been just human beings" to her, the metaphysician dismissed her claim as either self-deception or affectation. From his point of view, there was really no common ground at all between her and non-Scientists. The wretched immigrants, he said, were not receptive to the Truth and could not have it forced upon them.

Having grown up in a Unitarian enclave surrounded by Trinitarians, Collson had often experienced the divisive nature of religious conviction. She had never before been instructed in it, however. Her previous training and persuasion had been "on the all-inclusive side," and these new Scientific teachings, offered so dogmatically and bordering on bigotry, made her uneasy. Yet her "need of illusion" at this time persuaded her not to question, but to accept what she was told as part of a system of thought she could not yet grasp. She supposed she would have to work patiently to acquire that understanding, though secretly she still wished that she could help her neighbors by giving them the Truth, however partial her comprehension and doubtful their state of readiness. It was this wish that led Collson into her first "demonstration" of Science.

Late one afternoon, upon returning home from her rounds, the case worker found a note summoning her to an outlying district, where an elderly woman had been running amok through the streets and terrifying the neighborhood. Although Collson hastened to answer the call, by the time she arrived the police had already taken the woman away. She found the husband, a semi-invalid crippled by rheumatism and helpless without his wife, alone in their flat and greatly distraught. At his urging, the social worker agreed to see if she could help and went down to the police station. The woman had been put in an ordinary cell, where she was pacing back and forth and beating the bars. Collson arranged to have her sent to a detention hospital, where she could get better care until she was judged fit for release, and then went back to see the old man, who told her more about the family's situation.

The couple, it turned out, were English coat-makers. The woman delivered the garments and did the handwork, while her husband ran the sewing machine. When Collson asked if he used the crutches that were propped up in the corner, the man explained that he himself was not able to walk at all, but that his wife had been lame for years and needed the crutches for support. Collson had just seen the woman running around in her cell at the station, and this new information came to her like an epiphany, that suddenly made her feel the enormous power of healing:

> Something came rushing over me which made me see clearly that it was all unreal and the woman was no more insane than she had been lame. I was bathed in a sense of joy that made the room seem to grow light. Then quickly it was gone and I was once again wishing that I knew how to help these people. . . . I had done my part of the work on the case and heard no more for several weeks until I chanced to meet a visitor from that neighborhood. She told me that the couple were getting along better than usual, which meant that the old lady was home. The hospital commission had found the woman perfectly sane, and furthermore she was no longer lame.[25]

Looking back at this incident through a vista of thirty years in mental healing, Collson was still not sure what most prompted her joy at the insight that the old lady's maladies were illusory: the intimation that the woman would be free of her afflictions, or the illustration of what she had been struggling to believe through Christian Science. However, she was certain that her joy had been the motive force in the woman's recovery. The event demonstrated the principle that emotion was far more communicable than any calmly intellectual "realization" of Truth. As she analyzed it retrospectively, her great desire to help another had somehow acquired a "healing and energizing grace" by making contact with "some great reservoir of creative vitality."

At the time, however, the neophyte had no explanations for the experience, though she did suspect that it bore out the principles of Eddy's teachings. At the risk of being rebuked for reaching out to the heathen, she told her practitioner about the coat-makers and was elated when he confirmed that their healing had indeed been accomplished through the Scientific denial of error's reality. With this glimpse of what could be done— where social programs and politics failed—through a command of the Eddyites' higher science, Collson decided to devote herself to getting that mastery. She submitted her resignation to Addams, settled her affairs, and moved back to Fort Dodge, where her mother was living with one of the older daughters. It was now the fall of 1901.

III
The moment the Iowa Sisters heard that their wayward disciple was back, they swooped in, determined to reclaim her. More than half of their fourteen pulpits were standing vacant now, and they needed able ministers more than ever.[26] Collson, for her part, was happy to be reunited with her old friends and soon reappeared on the Sisterhood's circuit. In November she attended the wedding of a girlhood companion in Humboldt,

where Gordon was called to perform the ceremony. From there, the two women went to Cherokee for a supper celebration of the church's tenth anniversary. She joined the large gathering of all the Sisters in Sioux City just before Christmas, when Mary Safford had her fiftieth birthday. At the year's end, Mary Collson was again conducting services as interim minister in Ida Grove.[27]

The woman was still attached to her friends' Unitarian theology and their positivistic view that their efforts to understand God's laws placed them on the same track as modern scientists, not at cross-purposes. Just recently, Eleanor Gordon had explored this relationship in a paper where she noted that in "the modern view," "society" meant "the individuals that composed it, *plus* certain forces that produce a general result beyond the province or power of any one of its component individuals." The sociologists' "present vague grasping" after their so-called "plus forces" seemed to her identical with the religious teachers' "vague groping" after "spiritual forces." "It is simply the discovery, in each instance, of a unity binding human actions together in a realm of law and order, that transcends our will and final control," she said. Gordon was willing to let the sociologists and theologians argue out between them whether the higher laws were intelligent or blind; the important point in her view was that it was "just as metaphysical" to speak of "plus forces and social laws" as to talk about "Spirit or God."[28]

With her own enthusiasm for mental healing, Collson was also pleased to see in the liberal congregations a growing interest in psychology and what they referred to as "modern menticulture." Unity Clubs were now studying topics like "Health and the Mind," "The Realm of the Sub-Conscious," "Visions of the True Self," and "Character Building on Modern Scientific Principles." Their reading lists ran the gamut of New Thought, with such writers as Swedenborg, Henry Wood, Horatio Dresser, Ralph Waldo Trine, and William James all represented. Mary Baker Eddy, of course, was the notable omission, most ministers being unwilling to give her cult any recognition. Christian Science, the liberal clergy objected, was unscientifically rigid; it was set in "fixed articles," and its cannon was closed. "Let it alone," was the recommendation, "and study philosophy and psychology as scientists, giving our congregations the results of the best scientific thought." The phenomena of healing in Christian Science were not new in human experience, and science had taken note of such events. But because the liberal church's method was genuinely scientific, Unitarians took their time to investigate carefully before drawing any conclusions or arriving at a theory. They sought to avoid the "hastiness . . . that comes of acting upon emotional impulses and the desire for preconceived results."[29]

Intellectually, Mary Collson agreed that this was the best approach, but she lacked the emotional stamina to wait any longer for answers. The swift and certain cure promised by Christian Science was for her an irresistable alternative to the Unitarians' slow, patient search for as yet obscure forces that might help eliminate sickness, corruption, and poverty. Consequently, when Eleanor Gordon accepted a call to a new church in North Dakota, in March, 1902, her protégée, left free to wander again, returned to Eddy Science.

From the time she moved back to Fort Dodge, Collson had been trying to find a job that would leave her more time for study and pay her enough to clear her debts once and for all. For the first few months, she had worked in a small café, taking turns as a dishwasher, waitress, and cook, except on those weekends when she agreed to serve at the Ida Grove church. Then early in the new year, a more attractive position came along, and, in the parlance of Science, her "demonstration was made." This blessed "demonstration," as she later noted wryly, happened also to be "a calamity" for a public school teacher whose eighth grade class had driven her into a state of nervous exhaustion that forced her to resign. The Fort Dodge school board, some of whose members knew the Collson family and remembered that Mary had recently worked with the Juvenile Court in Chicago, asked her if she would step in and fill the vacancy.

Mary Collson's class was largely composed of gifted children from well-to-do families. Many had skipped lower grades without mastering the basics for more advanced work or learning to accept the discipline needed to acquire fundamental skills. As a result, with the school year more than half gone, almost none of the pupils had made any significant headway in their eighth grade studies. Instead, they had perfected an extensive repertoire of antics designed to divert the teacher's attention from the lesson plan. When they were sent to the blackboard, there erupted a real "class war:" "From the noise of slamming, banging and battering one might think that I had ordered the demolition . . . of the room," Collson wrote. "Presently the violence of the turmoil subsided and forty-two smiling faces were looking at me from places at the blackboard. . . . [They had been] scrambling and fighting to gain [a] favorite place . . . and cleaning the space and all of the erasers within reach after the claim had been preempted, chalk-lined and defended. The inequality of the spaces marked off bore the earmarks of a highly competitive . . . culture."[30] When they were seated, the youngsters confronted the teacher with such a barrage of questions that very few return volleys could be put through. On the side, they circulated an encyclical of jokes and decorated the ceiling with cloisonné patches of paper wads and gum. So for the first few weeks, quite as the class intended, the new teacher was kept busy working out strategies for subduing her young antagonists.

Throughout the ordeal, Collson sought guidance from the Christian Science textbook, which lay open on her desk at all times. When she finally gained the upper hand by winning the class's respect and affection, she attributed the victory to Eddy's metaphysics, rather than to such human elements as her store of good feelings and the students' capacity to respond to them.

The next year's work at school was much easier, giving the teacher more time to study and practice Christian Science. Already known in the local church as a promising Scientist, she was occasionally asked by other members to help them deny the reality of their illnesses or problems. Even so, Collson was not quite ready for an appeal that came from a church acquaintance one morning during the height of a flu epidemic. This caller said she felt ill and wanted Collson to take her case. The novice suggested the woman might do better engaging an authorized practitioner—one who had been "through class" and was listed in the *Christian Science Journal*—but the woman refused to call anyone else. God was no respecter of persons, she said.

With no other choice, Collson agreed to begin mental treatment at once. Unsteadily, she looked through *Science and Health* for guidance, tried to clear away all erroneous thoughts, and prayed as the leader instructed. Then she "went to work in earnest, denying error and declaring the Truth," using every minute available until it was time to leave for school. At noon, the patient called again to report that she felt even worse then before, was certain that she had come down with the grippe, and had had to go to bed. Collson repudiated the "error" of all these statements and spent her lunch hour trying to "realize Truth," but when she went to the woman's home after school, she found her patient tossing in bed with a high fever and pain and afraid that she was going to die. The embryo therapist tried desperately to increase the intensity of her work by "knowing" more forcefully that this human misery was unreal:

> I read the Bible, I read the Textbook, I endeavored in every possible way to draw near to God, seeking to get some inspiration and realization of the Truth which would heal this suffering woman. Every time I asked her if she felt any relief, she woefully replied that she felt a little worse. I was completely dismayed.
>
> I felt unspeakably sad that I could do no more. The room in which we were was lighted, but the shades were not drawn and the darkness outside looked very dark. As the poor woman's moans

sounded in my ears, I drew my chair to the window and peered into that darkness. Despite all of my struggles to the contrary, this woman's suffering seemed very real to me and I was obliged to admit this to myself. I humbly and deeply regretted this fact, for I believed most sincerely that the right understanding of God as the only reality would have healed this misery, but I did not have that understanding. With chastened spirit I thought the black emptiness into which I was looking symbolized my ignorance of God. "Oh! If I only knew him better!" I thought, and my head bowed low. Suddenly I was aware that the moaning had ceased. I feared that this woman had died while I was lost in reverie. I turned quickly and to my astonishment, my patient was getting out of bed. She said she was healed and was going to get dressed and go downstairs and have some supper.[31]

The next day the woman was up and about, and the following day she felt fully recovered and no longer in need of treatment. She credited her teacher friend with her healing and insisted on paying her generously. It was Collson's first payment as a Christian Science practitioner, and the money seemed so sacred to her that she consecrated it to the purchase of one of Mrs. Eddy's books.

Some three decades later, Collson reflected on the dynamics of this healing and others that followed:

It is now one of the many experiences which convinces me of an unseen environment which, though it is psychical, is just as real as electricity or any of the other imponderable forces with which we are able to deal only in terms of effect. We may explore these interpenetrating influences, but this exploration can only be wholesomely undertaken as an extension of our human experience, which must always be taken as our basic reality so long as we remain on this earth. As soon as we abandon the known for some unknown hypothetic basis, I believe we lose what little we have already acquired in the way of ethical charts and compass and are soon floundering about in superstition and sentimentalized mystery.[32]

At the time of the healing, however, the novice curist was sure that her patient's sudden recovery, like her eighth graders' reform, could be explained by the metaphysics of Christian Science. Indeed, this case of healing only increased her desire for more understanding and reinforced her decision to go to Boston for formal "Class Instruction" as soon as the school year was over.

At home, the schoolteacher's family were receptive to her plans. Her mother, who always approved of whatever her daughter wanted to do, had herself been quietly interested in Christian Science since Emma's healing through its apparent influence. Martha had taken up a casual study of it along with Mary, who always remembered her mother's "unvarying support and approval" at this time as "a source of great comfort to me."[33] Frankie, the next oldest daughter, with whom her mother and younger sister now lived, while unenthusiastic, was willing to let her small son accompany his grandmother and aunt when they went to church.

On the other hand, the reaction from the convert's old friends was less benign. At Hull House, where all sorts of ideologies and schools of thought were heard, and a code of tolerance respected, at least outwardly, those who had kept in touch with Mary Collson were privately shocked by her growing involvement in "the Eddy craze," and they urged her to shake herself loose from it. In their opinion, no movement could have been more remote from the down-to-earth social gospel that activated the life of the settlement.[34] Christian Scientists maintained no parish houses, conducted no philanthropic service; they had no hospitals, no orphanages, no missions in the slums. As one social-minded minister summed up their sentiments, Christian Science was "a humbug" in professing to relieve human suffering:

> Blot out all knowledge of sanitation, of anesthetics, of surgical skill, all knowledge of the human body, and you have multiplied the pain which humanity would be compelled to endure. . . . Christian

> Scientists lavish their wealth on buildings of stone and adorn them, that they may gratify their own esthetic tastes. And why not? Squalid poverty, with its cry of sick children in fetid atmospheres, dying for lack of an outing in the country, has no existence. The sickness, the pain, the impure atmosphere and the dying child are illusions of mortal mind.[35]

The Iowa Sisterhood used more than rhetoric to discourage the prodigal from pursuing what they disdainfully called "this cult." They thought she "was just plain crazy" but might have a chance of recovery if she could be prevented from getting any more deeply enmeshed. Accordingly, when they learned of her plans to visit the Eddyites' church in Boston and be authorized as a mental practitioner, they mobilized their forces to thwart the pilgrimage. They had reared Mary Collson to recognize Boston as the Mecca of Liberal religion and were not about to allow her to make it her Mecca of Christian Science.

It was agreed among them that the woman who had paid their protégée's college fraternity expenses should now ask to have that money returned immediately. "I was well aware," the renegade wrote of her benefactor's action, "that this was . . . only a desperate effort to prevent me from taking what to her was a very foolish step."[36] Through great economy, Collson had saved enough to cover the cost of the trip to Boston and the one hundred dollar fee charged for going through class, and she sent her patron this money. However, she vowed to teach another year and save what she needed again, hugging close to her heart her Leader's counsel that the greater the adversity, the purer one's love must be:

> I went about loving everybody with great purity in those days. It mattered very little what people did or didn't do, what they were, aspired to be, or failed to be, I poured forth my love as pure sunshine. . . . This was the most genuine stage of my attempt at "reflecting divine Love," since it was the zenith of my delusion. I imagined that if I saw anybody and everybody as a "child of God," forthwith they would manifest just what I had "realized" for them.

It took me many years to separate what seem to me now elements of truth, sophistry, and of downright harm contained in this doctrine. The year of postponement effected by my friends passed quickly and happily, and I could scarcely believe that "the demonstration had been made" when I found myself actually entrained for Boston.[37]

CHAPTER V

Entering the Boston Galaxy

I

Mary Collson's new ministry was dominated by women. When she set out to join their ranks at the turn of the century, the roughly 2000 female healers listed in the Christian Science *Journal* outnumbered the men by more than 4 to 1. Health care and religion had long been traditional female preserves, and women had seen good reason to extend their prerogatives into the public sector. With justification the distaff regarded the medical profession as an intrusive male agency, intolerant of weakness and impersonal in its dealings with them. In the middle and upper classes, where female invalidism was epidemic, conflicted women whose protest took the form of hysteria were often regarded as malingerers and subjected to medical treatments that verged on the sadistic.[1] There was real foundation for the feminist claim that male physicians did more to degrade females physically than to improve their bodily health.[2] Most female metaphysicians, like their regular medical counterparts, entered the field convinced that as women, naturally more sympathetic and nurturant than men, they could minister better to other women, especially to those who suffered from nervous and sexual complaints.

Eddy practitioners almost always turned to Christian Science, as Collson had, on another woman's recommendation and as a last resort in seeking a cure for some disabling medical problem of their own.[3] Finding relief, they stayed in the movement, setting themselves up as curists, and thereby exchanging chronic disabilities for healthy social roles. As a professional opportunity for women, Christian Science healing was attractive and accessible. With just a few weeks of formal training, curists could list themselves in the *Journal*, stock their home or rented offices with authorized books for sale, take subscriptions for church periodicals, and see paying clients. Along with the income and entreprenurial satisfactions, the curists' work brought them influence and prestige within their church communities.

Mrs. Eddy's doctrinal elevation of womanhood also did much to give these women a new sense of importance and worth. In the process of "discovering" Christian Science, Eddy had taken over the curist Quimby's theory that man was more creatural, and woman more spiritual. According to Quimby, "the mind of the female" contained "more of that substance required to receive the higher spiritual development of God's wisdom."[4] Eddy had made this idea explicit in her writings, most notably in the early versions of the Christian Science "Platform" included in *Science and Health*.

Of course, by 1902 the "strong, clear masculine voices" of Eddy's advisors had shown her the need for demythologizing such statements, whose intent was being misread in human terms as a claim of the female's superiority over the male. Such a belief, the barristers warned, could only foster "mental malpractice" and have a "repressive effect on the progress of men in scientific endeavor." Once alerted, Eddy took pains to make clear that "woman" and "womanhood" functioned impersonally in her prose as generic symbols for an abstract principle or a state of mind. To dispell any further suggestions that either her doctrines or church government gave her own sex preferential treatment, she emphasized that she had "uniformly associated man and woman," even giving "the preponderance to the masculine element" in her organization.[5]

In taking up Christian Science practice to meet their needs as females, Eddy's women healers showed a marked independence in certain respects. They had freed themselves from an ineffectual male medical establishment, and turned their backs on disapproving orthodox clergymen. When, as frequently happened, their new religious allegiance created dissention at home, and meant their going to church alone or not going at all, they willingly parted ways with their menfolk on Sundays. Yet for all their assertiveness in seeking good health and religion, Eddy's female followers did not object to the male "preponderance" at the higher levels of her organization.[6] While they were led into Science by distinctly female needs, few seem to have experienced feminist discontent with male domination and gender-based inequities in society. In fact, most were married and traditional in their domestic arrangements. Their main concern with achieving good health, prosperity, and peace of mind for themselves and their clients turned their attention inward and not to political activism. Instead of working for women's rights, they complied with their leader's directive that members confine their campaigns to denominational causes. When both the husband and wife were sufficiently trained to teach, only one of them, the man, was permitted that prestigious position, and the woman remained in the lower ranks as a healer.

To be sure, Eddy had on occasion spoken out against sexist discrimination. In her *Miscellaneous Writings* she had refuted the notion "that women have no rights that man is bound to respect," and in *Science and Health* she had been even more specific: "Our laws are not impartial, to say the least, in their discrimination as to the person, property, and parental claims of the two sexes. . . . If a dissolute husband deserts his wife, certainly the wronged, and perchance impoverished, woman should be allowed to collect her own wages, enter into business agreements, hold real estate, deposit funds, and own her children free from interference."[7]

Not surprisingly, statements like these aroused the interest of some hard-core feminists like Susan B. Anthony and Phoebe Cousins, who in the late 1880s took a short course in Eddy's

Science in Washington, D.C.[8] And again, not surprisingly, these reformers had come away from their class unconvinced. Christian Science was not for them, they concluded. Its emphasis was too much on abstract doctrine, Anthony said, and its practice deliberately inattentive to the world of human experience. While Eddy might urge her female apostles to "work as the industrious Suffragists . . . shoulder to shoulder" to advance their own reforms, her textbook's wobbly endorsement of the vote for women betrayed the primacy of her interest in spiritual correction, metaphysically achieved.[9] "If the elective franchise for women will remedy the evil without encouraging difficulties of greater magnitude," Eddy hedged, "let us hope it will be granted."[10] Anthony said she simply could "not see through . . . Christian Science . . . or any of the other theories," and would just "have to go on knocking away to remove the obstructions in the road of us mortals while in these bodies and on this planet;" she would leave it to those who had "entered into the higher spheres, to revel in things unknown" to her.[11]

Mary Collson, on the other hand, still bruised and disillusioned by her attempts at reform in the here-and-now of Chicago, preferred to believe that Christian Science was the best approach. The neophyte chose to accept Eddy's words that "God equalizes the sexes" as an expression, at a higher level, of the principle underlying the movement for women's rights on the human plane.[12] If all good was being advanced by this higher science, Collson reasoned, its founder would certainly champion sexual equality before the law no less here on earth than in heaven. She was satisfied that its teachings raised womanhood to great new heights and bestowed new dignity and privileges on her sex. The very fact that its founder was female seemed affirmation of this. Collson was further heartened by her new religion's concept of God as both divine Mother and Father, and by its leader's assertion that God's androgynous principle made the sexes equal. Even if Eddy had not yet made any women trustees or directors, and gave the men preference when choosing First Readers and officers of the church, her organization seemed to have gone far beyond most other churches in placing women side by side with men in the pulpit, as Second Readers and lecturers. Moreover, in opening up to practitioners the vocations of healing the sick and reforming the sinner, she provided her sex with a well-paying occupation, whose advantages Collson had quickly recognized.

Collson's early impression of Christian Science as an ally of women's rights was undoubtedly strengthened by the movement's male apologists, who emphasized that the founder had corrected the Pauline injunction against women being vocal in the church. A number of men in the fold praised Eddy's work for ushering in "woman's hour," a time when she was beginning to enjoy her "emancipation from all that limits her mental growth and her position in the world, socially, civilly, and religiously."[13] Predictably, however, it was one of the organization's seasoned women, not one of the men, who did most to swell the new Eddyite's feminist expectations of Science.[14]

Annie Macmillan Knott, one of Eddy's most faithful and favored disciples, was a rising star in the movement when Mary Collson first heard her speak in Fort Dodge in 1903. A diminutive woman with a large, commanding voice, Knott had entered the faith in the 1880s after a brief and unfortunate marriage ended in divorce. She had quickly built up a large healing practice in Detroit and was soon earning a good living as a prominent metaphysician. In 1888 Knott was among a select few enlisted by Eddy to hold public meetings and preach "the Christ healing," and shortly after she became a charter member of The Mother Church. More recently she had been honored with a place—one of just two Eddy gave women—on the church's prestigious and highly remunerative Board of Lectureship.

"All of this preferment," Collson would later admit, did much to inflate her "expectations of some peculiar spiritual illumination from her instruction."[15] The neophyte was particularly impressed by Knott's apparent independence and feminist consciousness. It was common knowledge that when she first joined the circuit, she rarely received engagements, though her remarkable baritone could be heard anywhere in a lecture hall. The public had simply preferred to have a man on the platform as speaker.[16] Knott had met the challenge by rising "to the attitude of true womanhood" and she proved that her sex could declare the Truth as well as any man.[17] Eager to have this woman as her teacher and counselor, Collson began corresponding with her and received a promise that there would be a place for her in Knott's class whenever she was ready to enroll.

II

"From an early habit of thought," as Collson later wrote of her choice in mentors, her "motto was always 'Ladies first,'" and it came as a great blow to her when she learned, on arriving in Boston in the summer of 1904, that the woman whom she had come to study with was no longer teaching. The explanation was that Mrs. Eddy had had Mrs. Knott suspend her classes indefinitely so that she could devote herself to the church periodicals. Knott recommended that her would-be student contact Alfred Farlow, another established teacher whom she described as a particularly gifted and highminded metaphysician. There was no one, she said, with whom she would rather see such a promising Scientist study. Since Collson's chosen teacher had been ruled out, "the next best thing" seemed to be to visit the man suggested as a substitute.[18]

Farlow's credentials in the movement were indeed impressive. Coming into Science in the 1880s, he had studied under its founder at her Massachusetts Metaphysical College, receiving the C.S.D., or Christian Science Divinity degree, upon completing the brief course. Farlow, who went on to become a teacher and lecturer, told Eddy that God had given him "the ability to simplify the Truth to beginners," and his mentor seemed to agree.[19] Indeed, Eddy was so impressed by her student's alacrity and skill in defending her cause against public criticism, that in 1901 she established a one-man Committee on Publication for The Mother Church and gave the position to

Farlow. His job, the establishing bylaw said, was "to correct in a Christian manner" any false views of Christian Science or "injustices" to Mrs. Eddy imposed on the public by the press or other media. As chief spokesman for The Mother Church and supervisor of all state Committees on Publication, Farlow had quickly become the Christian Scientist best known to the general public, save for Mary Baker Eddy herself. In fact, in 1901 it was rumored that he was the Founder's chosen successor; and while the church's matriarch denied this, she continued to elevate Farlow, eventually adding to his offices the presidency of The Mother Church. To the public eye, certainly, Alfred Farlow was very much Mr. Christian Science when Mary Collson first met him in 1904.

The details of Farlow's personal life, on the other hand, were scarcely known, though over a period of years, Collson was able to piece together his occasional disclosures about his past. Born on a farm in Knoxville, Illinois, Alfred Farlow had been the eldest of eight children:

> He was too proud to evaluate his father below par, but I gathered from things he dropped now and then that this father was more fecund than efficient. At least from an early age my teacher had borne the greater share of the burden of support of this large family, and at the time of my acquaintance with him, he had a houseful of them. He one day told me of how he had dreamed of being a lawyer, but "of course," he said, "the family circumstances made it wholly impossible for me to obtain the necessary education." With [perfect candor] he continued, "But for Christian Science my life would have been a flat failure."[20]

Collson disliked Farlow from the first, and it is easy to see why her relationship with him got off on such a bad footing. For one thing, it had been thrust upon her on the rebound of Knott's abrupt sabbatical, and for another, it was contained within the authoritarian framework Scientists deemed appropriate for their student-teacher relationships. "In his times of honesty I really liked the man," Collson later wrote, "but such times were seldom and brief. They were rare intervals when he seemed to have forgotten his place in the ecclesiastical order and, upon recalling it, jumped hastily back onto his dias."[21]

As the chief public relations man, Farlow maintained a kindly and undogmatic bearing in all his official correspondence and dealings with the press. As a highly placed member of the ecclesiastical order, however, he was expected to conduct himself in accordance with Eddy's system of stratification. Because the *Manual* dictated that rank, which was supposedly aligned with one's degree of spiritual attainment, be respected absolutely, the greatest metaphysicians felt obliged not only to look up to the Founder with meek obedience, but to exact full respect and compliance from the horde below: the teachers, lecturers, practitioners, class-taught and self-taught students, and patients.[22]

It appears, moreover, that Farlow had an inordinate need for recognition from his subordinates, that having been scarred by early poverty and thwarted ambitions, he required constant reassurance of his power and position. The man's lack of a college education was a particularly sensitive point, no doubt aggravated by Eddy's tendency to make an issue of it when his work displeased her.[23] Collson considered Farlow to be "very quick in thought and uncannily shrewd." She thought "he wrote well. His style was concise. His arguments were well put, although facts troubled him a little." But like Eddy, she found him "quite innocent" of any knowledge in the liberal arts, where her own background was extensive.

Given Collson's own makeup, the clash with Farlow was inevitable. Her considerable education, evident culture, and pride in her learning could only have grated on him, as did her assertive and independent nature. She was hardly cut out to accord the man his customary adulation. Not only had she been raised to expect equality in all human relationships, but her father's failure to give her support when she was a girl made it all the harder for her to accept and respect male authority.

What impressed me about this distinguished Scientist was his air of extreme self-importance and an evident expectation of great deference and admiration in appreciation of the audience granted. I had been priviledged in my life to have some association with a number of people who were truly great men and women and I found myself comparing this man with them and their invariable modesty, simplicity, and immolation of self to work. I felt it rather absurd to be seeking spiritual enlightenment from this man of common, if not coarse, fiber, so crudely bristling with self-satisfaction.[24]

Towards the end of their first meeting, Farlow announced that he already had a waiting list of more than five hundred names, and that a new bylaw, preventing teachers from holding more than one class a year, restricted his yearly enrollment to thirty students. By a quick calculation, Collson could see that the people on standby would keep Farlow's classes supplied for sixteen years, "provided there was no impatience or mortality among the applicants." With genuine relief, she told him that she would just as soon not be put on the list, but to her surprise and discomfort, he insisted on taking her name anyway.

Within a few weeks, Collson had lost her enthusiasm for class and had gone through most of the money she had saved to pay for it. She was virtually alone in the city and "had no one with whom to talk," for Knott was absorbed in her work and remote, and at The Mother Church, where attendance was large, no one spoke to her. Collson spent her days wandering aimlessly or sitting in the Christian Science Reading Room trying to get some direction. At last she thought to place a notice in the *Boston Transcript* and thereby found free lodging with an elderly woman who kept a summer cottage at the shore and agreed to exchange room and board for light housework. But Collson needed something more permanent and returned to Boston almost daily to look for work.

The job she eventually found came along when, quite by chance, she ran into an old friend from her social settlement days, a woman with whom she had worked in the Women's Union Label League. At the time, their efforts with this group had largely been given to setting up social halls for the men, maintaining workers' relief funds, and promoting the use of union-made products.[25] But little had been done to improve the lot of wage-earning women, and impatient reformers like Collson and her friend had often urged their working-class sisters to organize more effectively on their own behalf. The distaff's need for a strong federation had become so insistent in the few years since Collson had left, that a coalition of union leaders, women laborers, and settlement workers had created a nation-wide labor reform alliance for women. The National Women's Trade Union League was formed in 1903 "to assist in the organization of women wage workers into trade unions" and thereby help the distaff get decent pay and working conditions. A branch was established in Chicago the following January, another in New York in March, and a third had been started in Boston a few weeks before Collson met her old comrade-in-arms.[26]

Collson's friend was apparently now connected with the Denison House settlement, a center of women's union activity where WTUL operants in Boston were devising strategies for relieving the plight of unemployed textile workers. She had just returned from Fall River, the mill city to the north, where a series of sharp wage reductions had forced the employees into a lockout, closed down the cotton mills, and thrown the community into a state of disaster. Daily, scores of laborers were migrating to other mill centers, leaving behind empty tenements and stores and rapidly deteriorating neighborhoods. The local religious organizations had taken the lead in relief work, preparing lunches for school children, sending out dinner pails to the destitute, and collecting warm clothing and shoes for the families in the cold months ahead. Some additional help was provided by the United Textile Workers of America and the AF of L, but it was not nearly enough, and life for the workers was steadily growing worse.[27]

To help the situation, and give the new League visibility, Collson's friend had conceived the idea of recruiting some of the girls and younger women laid off at the mills for domestic service in Boston and other nearby cities. She had been looking for someone to assist in this venture when Collson turned up. The woman's plan was to go to Fall River, where she had reliable contacts, and pick out the couple hundred workers best qualified to be housemaids. Collson would meet them at the railway station in Boston, take them to an employment agency that had volunteered to help, interview the prospective employers, and generally see to the details of placing the young women properly.

The pathetic picture of the mill workers' situation touched Collson deeply, and she consented to enlist in the relocation effort. To get financial backing, her partner approached one of the wealthy labor sympathizers in Boston who were being asked to help underwrite the costs of transportation, food, and lodging connected with the maneuver. When told about Collson, the man agreed that she was "pure gold," but pledged just a paltry eight dollars a week to defray her expenses. It was an abysmal quotation of what such a precious metal would bring on the market, but since there was no other financial support for Collson's end of the job, the woman had to accept it.

Collson knew that to make ends meet on so small an allowance, she would have to remain at the cottage, and she wondered at first how well her staid employer would like the idea of her maid's becoming involved with a convoy of unemployed laborers. However, the elderly woman not only gave her approval to the arrangement, but showed an active sympathy with the cause:

> At first she was a little afraid of the girls—afraid that I might bring home some vermin or disease, but I assured her that these girls were as self-respecting and clean as I. A number of times I could not place all the girls who came and I felt obliged to stay the night with them at the Salvation Army lodgings. Then to my very great surprise and delight, she remembered some cots she had stored in her attic and she offered to let me put them in my room and bring home

the occasionally left-over girls. I dearly loved this little old lady before we parted.[28]

During the summer several hundred young women were brought from Fall River to Boston and placed in domestic service, but this massive relocation of workers did not improve their situation:[29]

> The strike was lost. The workers went back to attend more looms and receive less pay. Every one of my girls went back. They were so lonely in their work as housemaids. We had a hall where we all met for as good a time as we could possibly give them on Thursday afternoons and evenings, but the homesickness of the girls was pathetic. All of their lives they had been accustomed to working in groups with a feeling of social equality among themselves, and when transplanted into an isolated place in home life, it was very hard for them. So we did not make any very valuable contribution to the solution of any problem, but we certainly did our best and helped a little perhaps by doing just that.[30]

Collson was asked to stay on with the WTUL, whose people were determined to make the new federation credible through successful activities on the city and national levels. Articulate women with her command of the language were needed as publicists, to keep the workers' struggle in the public eye and to get their side of the story to fair-minded, uninformed citizens. There was also demand for mature and experienced staff to train the younger sisters just coming into the movement. A common League tactic was to send working girls who were "little more than children" to ask the male unionists for their moral and monetary support. Here again, the organizers believed that during these "trying expeditions," the fledglings should have "a woman to turn to" for "motherly care" and comforting "oversight." Then, too, personnel were always being sought for such jobs as soliciting funds, securing lecturers, arranging business meetings, and setting up evening classes or recreational events.[31]

The League was naturally eager to recruit someone with Collson's experience, and a few years before, Collson would have readily joined this group. These were admirable women who, with but token remuneration, were "standing ready to mother [every] new little union" that was born, "to help out in difficulties, counseling the impulsive," "encouraging the timid," and "daring to go out and picket in freezing weather" if necessary.[32] But while Collson still had her old sympathies, she had lost her faith in political organization. Moreover, she had caught a glimpse of what seemed an easier road to reform that could also lead to greater professional and personal rewards. Thus she returned to the Reading Room, where she had left word of her need for work, and there learned of just the opening she wanted.

A housewife up in Amesbury who had recently come into Science was looking for another church member to move into her home and help in the care of her nine-month-old daughter. In return for this work, there would be a wage of five dollars a week, plus board. In addition, and quite outside the terms of the contract, Collson would get her first lesson in a darker aspect of Christian Science doctrine: belief in "mental malpractice."

III

In Eddy's system, the idea that thoughts could be marshalled to heal was accompanied by the grim corollary that thoughts could also be used to inflict injury. In the years of Collson's novitiate, as now, students of Science referred to such evil employment as "mental malpractice," though more commonly as "Malicious Animal Magnetism" or "M.A.M.," and were taught to guard themselves against it vigilantly. Their venerable leader had warned her fold that "committing the bare process of mental healing to frail mortals, untaught and unrestrained by Christian Science," was just "like putting a sharp knife into the hands of a blind man or a raging maniac, and turning him loose in the crowded streets of a city."[33] A false practitioner, she cautioned, "whether animated by malice or

ignorance," would "work mischief" and could "disastrously
affect the happiness of a fellow-being—harm him morally,
physically, or spiritually." Although malpractice found no place
in, and receive[d] no aid from the Principle or the rules of
Christian Science," Eddy discussed the dynamics of M.A.M.
extensively in her writings.[34] In fact, she was so preoccupied
with the threat of malicious mental attacks on her personally
that she drafted a number of loyal students into her home to
keep "watches."[35]

Mary Collson's employer in Amesbury shared this same fear
of mental malpractice and decided to implement Eddy's
strategy of installing a vigilant student of Science in her household. This woman believed that her family's wealth and prom-
inence in the old town made her home an easy target for the evil
released by neighbors and gossips who were skeptical of her
religious practices. She was especially fearful for her baby, an
only child who had arrived late in the parents' married life. For
having been "born in Science," the little girl never received any
medical treatment, and everyone in the community seemed to
be watching darkly to see if the child would survive in such
perilous circumstances. Plainly, the woman's own obvious
fears that the worst would happen had stoked her neighbors'
doubts about the child's welfare.

In turn, the mother's anxieties had been fed by her attentive
practitioner who, Mary Collson surmised, "had been very
strong on Animal Magnetism." This curist had been "engaged
in intense cultivation of her patient's already fearful nature"
when, as if to give her warnings added authority, she had
suddenly died, leaving her client convinced that she was the
victim of mental "assassination." Such pronouncements had
become commonplace among Christian Scientists since 1882,
when the Founder attributed the death of her last husband, Asa
Gilbert Eddy, to an estranged student's malpractice.[36] Yet up to
now, Collson had not been aware of this phase of Christian
Science, having "lightly passed over the chapter on Animal
Magnetism" in the textbook, and never studying the lesson on

that subject any "more than necessary." She was therefore amazed at her employer's fear, and further amazed that the woman's practitioners encouraged it:

> She was afraid to have their former family physician pass the house for fear his thought might fasten a law of disease upon the child because no medicines were being used. She was afraid of some of her friends who were childless and who, she imagined, might be jealous that she had this child. She was afraid to "give thought" to the child's feeding and afraid not to do so. She was afraid to keep her very efficient maid because she was a Catholic, but she was more afraid to let her go.[37]

This last anxiety introduced Collson to yet another of the more arcane features of Christian Science: the notion that the Roman Catholic Church was among its most dangerous enemies in the raging war of mental malpractice. Although Eddy wrote almost nothing that leveled the charge directly, she observed in her correspondence that "the Catholic priests" were "afraid of the power of Christian Scientists and would exterminate the Leader."[38] Her students also gave ample evidence of this belief. Edward Kimball, a prominent teacher, saw fit to devote a part of his class instruction to the problem of "Romanism" and its "claim to bestow a curse," with "all the machinery through which the curse operates."[39] In the same way, the practitioner who was counseling Collson's employer considered the Catholic housekeeper's presence in the Amesbury residence to be lethal and pressed for the domestic's prompt dismissal. When the husband, who was "more indulgent than devout," settled the question by stating that he liked the maid's cooking and wanted her to stay, the fear of what this disobedience might incur preyed upon the mother's mind, adding further to her anxiety.

Though perplexed by the fear that filled the home, Mary Collson was not yet sufficiently schooled to be susceptible to it, and she actually found a great deal of pleasure in working for the family:

The mother was willing that I take the baby out in her carriage, and when the snow was deep, we had a warmly upholstered sled. I took her on long rambles all over Whittier-land. We climbed the hills sturdily with the pines and ran down hill lightly with the little birches. The baby was too young to understand what I talked to her about, but she felt the fun and laughed merrily. She was altogether too sober a baby when I first came there, but now she was growing happy and rosy-cheeked, and I found the experience delightful.[40]

Then, to her surprise, Collson received word from Farlow that he had decided to let her take class with him in the session about to convene. Replying at once, she explained that she no longer had the enrollment fee and understood, from her earlier correspondence with Knott, that a student should not consider herself ready to go through class until she could make the demonstration to pay for it. Farlow, she trusted, would agree that she ought to postpone her study. To her even greater surprise, however, Farlow did not agree. He saw no deterrent to her enrolling, since "all rules had exceptions," and he fully expected that with the spiritual powers he helped her develop in class, she would soon be able to settle their account. The Reading Room librarian also overruled Collson's objections. Speaking as a veteran Scientist, she assured her new friend that her reluctance was nothing but animal magnetism trying to obstruct her advancement. She urged her not to pass up this rare opportunity and invited her to be her houseguest in Boston for the two weeks the class was in session. Since "it all seemed decided," the novitiate acquiesced.

Collson got off to a bad start in Farlow's class. As she remembered it, her first mistake was in thinking that he would be open to questions, when actually he seemed to take all queries as criticisms. "He replied by pointing out the obvious fact that he and not I was teaching the class," she recalled. This rebuke, though lightly administered, was her first hint that "all teaching in Christian Science" was "merely instruction in *what to think*" and "in no way spiritual education."[41] The basis of

Christian Science instruction had been devised six years before, when Eddy set up her Board of Education. At that time she
ruled that teachers of Primary Classes must confine their material to "Recapitulation" in *Science and Health,* a chapter which
used a question and answer format to enunciate the tenets of
the faith. The only other specific requirement, that the pupils
be fortified with lessons in self-defense against mental malpractice, was the principal order of business in Collson's class
under Farlow:

> My teacher, being a superior instructor, gave vivid and vigorous
> instruction on this subject. I was bold to complain. I said, "This is
> the worst form of evil that I have yet encountered." I added, "You
> have talked this thing up until I am . . . actually getting scared." He
> laughed and replied, "I have talked it up to teach you to talk it down.
> . . . Evil," he said, "wishes to remain hidden. It does not want to be
> brought out into the open and dealt with." This puzzled me. How
> can evil have a desire if it is nonexistent?[42]

During the first week of class the student and teacher
clashed on this subject so often that Collson nearly dropped out
altogether.[43] As best she remembered, "twelve lessons constituted the course, and in disgust I absented myself from three."
Her librarian friend, whom she respected, convinced her that
she was still "being used by M.A.M. acting through pride in
human intellect" and, this being the case, that she was demonstrating the force of the very evil she denied. Here was a total
reversal of her rationalist legacy. Where she had always been
taught to trust reason, she now was told to suspect it. Her
hostess handed her Eddy's article, "Ways That Are Vain," with
one passage bracketed for special attention:

> Certain individuals entertain the notion that Christian Science
> Mind-healing should not be two-sided, and only denounce error in
> general,—saying nothing, in particular, of error that is damning
> men. They are sticklers for a false, convenient peace, straining at
> gnats and swallowing camels. The unseen wrong to individuals and
> society they are too cowardly, too ignorant, or too wicked to uncover,

and excuse themselves by denying that this evil exists. This mistaken way, of hiding sin in order to maintain harmony, has licensed evil, allowing it first to smoulder, and then break out in devouring flames.[44]

In her state of uncertainty, the admonition sufficed. "I meekly went back to class," Collson wrote, "resolved to exercise my intellect as little as possible." Each morning thereafter, before she left for the day's instruction, she had her friend read Eddy's article aloud. This worked to silence her until she had finished the course, and it made her more receptive to what was being taught. Indeed, by the time the ordeal was over, the unwilling student was haunted by the feeling that evil was not only real, but much worse than it ever seemed in Chicago. "I resolved to do the best I could to keep the teachings I liked in the foreground and let them shy the bogies off," she later explained. Without reckoning on the effect the group's thinking would have on hers, she believed she could stay in Science and still have her private opinion on M.A.M.[45]

Back in Amesbury, the Christian Scientists now treated Collson with deference. Her employer, elated to have a certified healer in residence, took it upon herself to set her up in practice. She rented an office for her, even furnishing it with some family antiques, and offered to let her divide her time between caring for the baby and seeing her patients. The arrangement seemed too good to turn down, but Collson accepted it uneasily. "It troubled me," she later explained, "that I could not see where I had been spiritually benefited in the least by going through class. I wondered if I did have sufficient spiritual understanding to set myself up as a practitioner."[46]

For all her doubts, no sooner had Mary Collson, C.S.B., put out her shingle than clients, most of them middle- and upper-class women, began to stream in. The new therapist attributed the demand for her services to "right thinking," though women's widespread reluctance to use male physicians and their consequent willingness to try unorthodox cures for their troubles, were far more obvious explanations. Many of the women who came to the Amesbury healer did so because they had trouble communicating their intimate problems and fears to men. In the thirty-five year old female metaphysician they found a motherly figure who could provide the quiet sympathy, gentle assurance, and protective guidance they yearned for. Though women could sometimes bypass the "assaults" of male physicians and find sympathetic treatment by going to one of the few women doctors, Collson's patients obviously preferred the ministrations of a mental healer, whose claims of matter's unreality offered them an escape from the entire burden of physiology.[47]

The remedies in the healer's metaphysical pharmocopoeia had great appeal for those with problems related to sexuality. At a time when pregnancy, childbirth, and abortions brought women acute anxiety, pain, and isolation, the Christian Science therapist could offer her patients the comforting news that gender and sex did not exist, that marriage ought to unite hearts, not bodies, and that it was the wife's privilege to refrain from sexual intercourse.[48] Eddy said celibacy was "nearer right" than physical union, since "spiritual unity" was the real "scientific *morale* of marriage."[49] In fact, the Leader hoped for the time when the race would no longer marry or even bear the distinctions of sex, but would be "equal unto the angels" and "wedded to the Lamb, pledged to innocence, purity, perfection."[50] These teachings, and Collson's natural gift for inspiring confidence, reportedly made her patients more receptive to therapeutic suggestions and helped a good number of them regain their health. The practitioner, for her part, greatly enjoyed this mothering ministry, for it produced none of the gender conflicts that caused her to break down when she was a Unitarian pastor.

While Mary Collson was settling comfortably into her promising new career, Annie Knott was looking for a lieutenant whom she could dispatch to the Midwest to handle a problem that had developed there. On learning of Collson's advancement in the field, Knott approached her about relocating and told her a little about the situation. A student whom she had expected to build a respectable Christian Science organization in Evansville, Indiana, had instead become a divisive force in a "dinky little movement." Although the man in question had been in her class some years before, he was, from a Scientific standpoint, still her responsibility. Under the bylaws, certified teachers were obliged to promote their students' progress by counseling them "persistently," not only during the class term, but thereafter, and "to watch well" that they proved "sound in sentiment and practical in Christian Science."[51] Students, for their part, were expected to seek their teachers' advice in all matters affecting their activity in the church or their practice and to accept the teachers' authority without dispute. Collson was flattered that Knott should ask her to carry out such a mission. Moreover, after having been in the East for almost a year, she was homesick and warmed at the thought of moving back nearer her family. So with Knott's assistance, though without the obligatory consultation with Farlow, she packed up and traveled westward to Indiana.

CHAPTER VI

The World of Christian Science

I

Glad to be back in the heartlands again, Mary Collson could not have been less prepared for the hostile reception she found in Evansville when she arrived in the fall of 1905. In the Hoosier state, as in much of the country just after the turn of the century, public censure of Christian Science was so intense and widespread that a newly arrived practitioner had a hard time merely finding a place to live. The religious movement had entered Indiana quietly enough in 1889, when a few of Eddy's votaries in Indianapolis formed a study group. It had taken another eight years to establish the state's first Church of Christ, Scientist, and even now there were fewer than two thousand Christian Scientists statewide.[1] Yet orthodox churchmen were alarmed at the cult's entrenchment in the principal cities, where it was drawing communicants away from established denominations and allowing Eddyites who retained their established church connections to contaminate the rest of the flocks. Not a few of the clergy interpreted Eddy's teachings as a diabolic mariolatry and saw in the movement's advance a harbinger of the antichrist.[2]

It was the medical fraternity, not the ministry, however, that led Evansville's opposition to Christian Science. Doctors and health officials, who had been working to upgrade professional standards and implement public health programs, considered Scientists dangerous fanatics who trifled with human life and disregarded sanitary practices at the city's peril. Having recently worked hard to put through legislation to regulate the licensing of physicians and standardize requirements for graduates of the various medical schools, they were not receptive to the Eddyites' claim of immunity from such controls on the grounds that Christian healing, as demonstrated by Jesus, needed no college diploma, but rather spiritual credentials that were far more difficult to attain.[3]

The medical men, who were frankly disturbed by the curist competition, found in Christian Science "much charlatanry (by which many honest fanatics are decieved), much to surprise reason and common sense, to offend good taste and the proprieties, to outrage justice and the law, and to mortify the pious." Moreover, "this cult's ghastly masquerade in the garb of Him that prayed in the Garden of Gethsemane" was deplorable, they said.[4] Nor did these guardians of public health—who sought to combat epidemics and control communicable diseases—take kindly to Mrs. Eddy's wisdom that "when there are fewer prescriptions, and less thought is given to sanitary subjects, there will be better constitutions and less disease." They cringed at her advice that "the less we know or think about hygiene, the less we are predisposed to sickness."[5] Since "materia medica," as the Eddyites called it, was regarded as a conduit for mental malpractice, believers were also warned against medical examinations on the grounds that "physical diagnosis of disease . . . tends to induce disease."[6] Determined that public health safeguards not be undermined by fanatic religionists, the Hoosiers' medical association insisted that all mental healers who were likely to take the place of doctors be brought under the same statutory controls, and that Scientists who failed to comply with the sanitary codes be held in violation of the law.[7]

The press joined the crusade by making the public aware of the tragedies for which Christian Science treatment was held responsible. In November 1904, for example, the Evansville papers reported the death of a twelve-year-old Connecticut boy who succumbed to diptheria after five days of Christian Science treatment. Neither the child's parents nor the curist had notified Health Department officials or put themselves under quaranteen, and at the time of the boy's death, his two siblings had contracted the disease, as had the metaphysician's own young child.[8] Another typical item picked up by the papers the following March told of the arrest of a Christian Science therapist whose elderly patient was found in critical condition, "and not expected to survive."[9] One story told of a Denver man who killed his wife and himself, allegedly after having been driven mad by the woman's cultic devotion. Yet another reported the case of a New York Christian Scientist who became too disoriented to care for her children and had to be institutionalized.[10]

An especially harmful assault on the cult's reputation in Evansville came when the wife of the local Scientists' First Reader died just before Mary Collson arrived. The local press headlined the story in bold type and gave all the un-Scientific details of the woman's untimely passing.[11] When one of the congregation wrote to the *Journal-News* trying, not very successfully, to correct the "false impression" left by the paper's obituary, the Eddyites' image was damaged all the more.[12]

While the public's hostility toward Christian Science might have united a different group, it did not even slow the perpetual fighting in the Evansville congregation. The battlelines were drawn for Collson to see the first evening she went to the church to hear the weekly testimonials. The new practitioner stayed for a special session afterwards, which had been called by the First Reader, "who was virtually leader," for the purpose of censoring "a very shallow and sensational type of novel that was flooding the field with a sort of pseudo-Christian Science propaganda." The works in question were novels by writers like Clara Louise Burnham, Mary Hornibrook Cummins, and Catherine M. Yates, who wrote sentimental stories Collson characterized as having "a tinsel glitter of optimism" and "a fantastic assortment of miraculous healings."[13]

These books had a natural appeal for Christian Scientists. Eddyites were typically first generation public school graduates whose new literacy had engendered a keen, if unsophisticated, enthusiasm for reading. Scientists enjoyed their religion, in part, precisely because it was a bookish religion, unique in its almost exclusive reliance on the printed word. The Bible and *Science and Health*, from which Readers presented the church services, were the congregation's "only preachers." Eddyites happily spent many hours each week alone with their authorized books, reading them with a simple acceptance, free of any reflection or probing that might give license to "mortal mind." The Christian Science novels, which entertained and reinforced the faith without provoking dangerous critical thought, met the special needs of many of Eddy's book-loving communicants.

Unlike the Evansville leadership, Boston officialdom took no offense at these books. To be sure, Mrs. Eddy complained that "literary commercialism" was lowering intellectual standards "to accommodate the purse" and "meet a frivolous demand for amusement instead of improvement." Although she deplored "nauseous fiction" as well as other "tangled barbarisms of learning,"[14] the popular novels did not fall into this category.[15] Mrs. Eddy herself enjoyed the stories and even recommended several "to all lovers of truth."[16]

Even so, Mary Collson, with her love of good literature, saw nothing wrong with putting a quietus on the proliferation of the "silly reading matter," and she was ready to pledge her help in discouraging its consumption until it became clear just what form of action the First Reader had in mind:

He proposed converting the destruction of this "threatening error" into a social event. His idea was a gathering of the congregation at some stated time on some selected spot outside the fire limits and consigning to the flames of a bonfire all novels of this sort that might be in the possession of the members of the audience. Immediately the gentleman beside me arose from his seat . . . and marched toward the door, whereupon the friends of the exodus swelled the movement, and in less time than it takes to tell, I found myself the only seated member of the congregation. Since most of the offensive volumes were the private property of the offended and now absent group, there appeared to be no further incentive for the speech, and the speaker unceremoniously stepped over to join his supporters, who had risen to their feet to view the backs of their fellow Scientists. . . . I went to say good night to the conferring remnant and to commit myself as a supporter . . . without exactly sponsoring the bonfire . . . and thought that I effected a rather diplomatic exit. When I got outside I found an open air conference going on. To this assembly I did not mention the object of the meeting, but merely stressed my appreciation of the rapid action of the drama . . . and we parted in laughing good humor.[17]

Here, then, in full view, was the problem Annie Knott had assigned her lieutenant. Her student, Louis Vallade, the recently bereaved First Reader of the Evansville church and the city's sole practitioner, had not only failed to unite his congregation at a time of intense public criticism, but had become a principal agent of the internal strife that was jeopardizing the little church's survival.

Mary Collson's belief that she could be friendly with both factions, mend the fracture, and avoid criticism herself was characteristically naive and brief. Vallade quite naturally resented the new metaphysician, who had seemed to appear on the scene for no other reason than to infringe upon his professional territory. As the new healer's popularity and practice grew, and Vallade's income and authority declined correspondingly, his sense of her threat forced him into the role of archobstructionist in all church proceedings supported by her constituency. For her part, she learned to dislike him just as intensely, not only for his incompetent, dictatorial management of church affairs, but for his conduct as a family man. Soon after his first wife's death, she told a friend, he married "a rich widow—from whom he was reported to have obtained a horse-whipping, some alimony, and two beautiful diamonds."[18]

Vallade's domestic record alone would have set Collson against him, for it triggered old hostilities toward men who did not fulfill their responsibilities to women.

The Evansville church required unanimous endorsement of anyone who wanted to join, purportedly to prevent any discord from infiltrating the church, so Vallade's dissenting vote was able to keep his competition off the roll for more than a year. Ironically, it did not prevent her from being elected without membership to replace him as the congregation's First Reader.

As the new leader of the Evansville church, Mary Collson spent much of her energy trying to thwart the physicians' campaign against Christian Science healers. Intent upon protecting her livelihood and professional rights, as much as her patients' freedom to choose their own religion and therapeutics, she wrote to one of the organization's experts on such matters, George H. Kinter, C.S.D., of Chicago. Kinter, a one-time railroad man, was one of Mrs. Eddy's favorites and frequently served as a metaphysical worker in her home. Some years before, when legislation inimical to the practice of Science seemed imminent in New York, Kinter had joined Alfred Farlow in lobbying against it. Unlike his associate, however, he had passed up a career with the Boston organization, preferring to set up a healing practice with his wife, also a C.S.D., and caring for his association of students.[19] Collson's correspondence with Kinter, who advised letter-writing campaigns, not only elicited the tactical help she sought for defending the Cause in Indiana, but initiated an instructive friendship with two influential Scientists.

While Collson worked for supportive legislation, she also tried to create a more favorable climate for the church by bringing in some of the organization's most prominent personalities to deliver free public lectures. She had Judge William G. Ewing come from Chicago to answer the recurrent criticism that Christian Science was neither Christian nor scientific.[20] When the celebrated "Next friends suit" against Eddy intensified the public's curiosity about the elderly matriarch, Collson called in Septimus J. Smith, The Mother Church's former First Reader, to explain how the religious leader had been "maligned and misunderstood."[20]

Mary Collson also made it her job to scan the local papers for articles seeming to compromise or cast aspersions on Science. Whenever she found such an item and thought a response would be efficacious, she alerted the state's one-man Publication Committee. Thanks to her vigilance, an unfavorable series of syndicated reports run by the Evansville papers in 1906 was followed by a lengthy rebuttal from the Eddyites' public relations man for New York, where the stories originated. The press, the official protested, had been amassing false information and pressing it upon its readers in order to prejudice public opinion. This inaccurate news reporting punished Christian Science for the mistakes of other systems, when actually Scientists condemned the dubious practices incorrectly ascribed to their faith. "Christian Science," the official declared, "does not foster quackery in any form, nor does it breed fanaticism, and its adherents will not consciously tolerate such acts."[21] Collson also ferreted out articles that classified Christian Science with faith healing, mesmerism, Hindoo wonder-working and other dubious systems considered effective only in treating hysteria and neurasthenia. According to Indiana's state Committee on Publication, Mrs. Eddy's religion was "not thus limited." In its forty-year history, he said in a letter to the Evansville *Journal-News,* the practice of Christian Science had resulted in the healing of practically every known disease.[22]

As Collson conceded later, her public relations work probably did more to keep her own criticisms of Science in check than to arrest outsiders' attacks on it. For one thing, her attempts to reach the community as a church apologist were severely handicapped by a social aloofness which, she soon learned, was expected of Eddyites. The Leader's opinion that right-thinking persons should take "no time for amusement, ease, (or) frivolity," precluded the kind of sociables that had fostered congenial relations among different groups when

Mary Collson was in the ministry and social work. Demanding undivided loyalty, Eddy had declared that God supplied "within the wide channels of The Mother Church dutiful and sufficient occupation for all its members."[23] Since the congregation were not supposed to join any charitable or social groups other than those church-related organizations specified in the *Manual*, Collson's contacts were largely confined to the Christian Science sector, further hampering her missionary efforts.

Yet within the strict limits imposed on her, Collson was a highly effective representative of the faith, if the experience of a cub reporter named Edward Meeman was at all typical. Meeman, who later gave his account in an autobiography, first met Collson while covering church news for the *Evansville Press*. He had gone to her office to do an interview, fully expecting to come away with a story about oyster suppers and bazaars. Instead, he had left with a feeling of great respect for the self-assured therapist, whose idealism seemed to speak from clear blue eyes that sparkled beneath her crown of braided hair. In fact, the young journalist had been so impressed by the woman and what he decided must be her "higher order of religion," that when he began to suffer from depression a few months later, he returned to her for professional help.[24]

While Meeman found *Science and Health*, which he read on the curist's recommendation, as crude and disjointed as she had first found it herself, he drew much benefit from Collson's counsel and words, which even now owed more to Emerson than to Eddy. Sensing the woman's religious independence, Meeman saw in Collson a soulmate, a passionate mystic and theological liberal, who could teach him how to practice Christian principles scientifically without also requiring him to accept as fact what he regarded as biblical fiction.

The practitioner's past involvement in the Socialist Party and continuing sympathies with the labor movement broadened the foundation for a friendship that quickly developed between her and the young journalist. Meeman's first real exposure to urban poverty during his first few months on the union beat had affected him in the same way Chicago's slum conditions had affected her: it so aroused his moral indignation and reforming instincts that he had become a socialist and a vigorous leader in the party's local chapter. Collson's visits with the young man and his working-class family, almost the only contacts she had outside the claustrophobic church community, kept her from forgetting completely her secular obligations. She always displayed the union "bug" on her professional calling cards and quietly sent checks to philanthropic and reformist groups.

Still, the metaphysician's restricted interaction with the community, and consequent inability to meet its hostility head-on, so magnified her congregation's importance to her that its thinking took unexpected control of her own. "A practitioner was dependent on her group in times of attack by pulpit, press, or law," and therefore had to feel "unshakeably certain" before criticizing the church's "established *modus operandi*," she later explained. Laying aside all personal objections to what Farlow taught her in class, she joined the fight against animal magnetism. "Henceforth I very faithfully protected my work against malicious malpractice and entered into full unity with the entire teachings" of the church. "For a time I enjoyed the peculiar satisfaction of being in a state of perfect orthodoxy."[25]

Mary Collson found that "along some lines it was not at all difficult . . . to adopt Christian Science ideas and ideals." Despite their supposed denial of matter, the metaphysicians and teachers she met in Science were affluent people, who gave every evidence of their wordly prosperity. Supported by well-paying practices and student associations, they formed their own wealthy class. Mrs. Eddy's palatial homes and lavish furnishings, fine clothes, and army of servants, while loudly condemned by non-Scientists, inspired her followers. Collson saw her colleagues with some "wonderfully fine stones," including the largest diamond she had ever seen outside of a museum.[26]

The first time the respected Scientists George and Elizabeth Kinter invited the Evansville therapist to their Chicago home, they astonished their guest—who expected from them the high degree of spirituality said to accrue from close association with Mrs. Eddy—by their preoccupation with the subject of status and "bountiful supply" for the Cause and its representatives. They talked about Turkish rugs at length and convinced her she needed one for her office. They also showed an intense interest in finances and fees, and argued that Collson ought to be charging her patients much more than she was. Following Mrs. Eddy's recommendation, she was asking the same rates as most of Evansville's medical doctors with general practices. But Kinter took the position that with all the work she was doing, she ought to be taking in twice as much.

It was true that besides tending to her large practice and serving the church as First Reader, Collson was on the local board of directors and supervised virtually all church activities. Yet her income, if less than her friends thought it should be, was still so much more than in the past, that she already felt rich and successful. Nevertheless, she was now to learn to value the material rewards of church work as much as she had always valued the recognition it brought. Only later would she condemn this orientation as hypocrisy: "At this time, when I was supposed to be most spiritually correct, I regarded people with an alert consideration of their social position and their worldly goods and chattels." To manifest the truth that "God does not see His children in poverty or sickness," she "assiduously avoided any inconvenient evidence of poverty" while trying to prove "the unreality . . . of all things material and human."[27]

Collson had never before had the means or the inclination to live like the gentry. The Transcendentalist idealism in which she had been raised stressed egalitarianism and spiritual, as opposed to material, wealth. Growing up among western Unitarians, she had always heard women's "excessive concern with fashion" criticized for its "criminal" waste of money and energy. Her liberal mentors, trying to perpetuate "the Browning spirit," had taught her to "leave social emulation and display behind." "Fancy telling Susan B. Anthony or Clara Barton or

Jane Addams that their first duty is to be beautiful," they
chided.[28] As a minister in poor farming towns and as a settlement worker in the slums of Chicago, Collson had always
studiously avoided any display or behavior that would have
implied superiority to other people.

The persistence of these old habits irritated her Evansville
associates. In her new field, with its veneration of rank and its
accoutrements, she was bitterly criticized for taking Negro
patients and for insisting that they be allowed to attend the
church services (even though she "compromised on segrega-
tion in a row of back seats").[29] She was also criticized for not
dressing more in accordance with her prominent position in the
church. Their Leader, she was reminded, "was always beauti-
fully groomed, and . . . Jesus wore richly embroidered robes—
so costly that the soldiers cast lots to obtain the valuable garment that he wore."[30] Collson remembered one church member
in particular, a native Kentuckian who "had that peculiar deep-
seated Bourbon pride of the Southern aristocrat," talking
"glibly of humility" as a Christian Scientist, yet objecting to
Collson's belief that "as children of God all are equal" and
criticizing her for lacking the pride of "a lady." "I often reminded her," Collson noted later, "that I was of very humble
origin," but this woman was determined to give the First
Reader more class.[31] She took it upon herself to look after
Collson's wardrobe personally, and even bought her a trunk to
replace her old telescope suitcase.

It had only been five years since Collson had managed nicely
with a serge coat suit, some shirtwaists, and the solitary dress-
up dress that circulated through the Hull House neighborhood.
Now, prodded by her constituents, she "endeavored to wipe out
all 'sense of limitation' and accept the doctrine that 'nothing is
too good for a child of God.' " Swallowing her disappointment
that in matters of race Christian Scientists were no farther
advanced than any other denomination in Evansville, she
bought all the clothes she had time to buy, and commissioned
more from a dressmaker. "Through our united efforts I found

one summer that I had fifteen very pretty white dresses," she later recalled. "Although this may not have seemed like an exorbitant number to some people, it did to me when I compared it to any wardrobe that I had ever possessed up to this time. . . . I bought no jewelry, but I had some pretty pieces given to me. . . . Worldly prosperity was a new experience for me, and I enjoyed it."[32]

II

By the end of her first year in Evansville, Collson understood enough about the idea of abundant supply to see that the Scientists needed a more impressive place to meet. They had been using Evans Hall, an old civic auditorium badly in need of repair and unsuitable for either a proper Sunday School or Reading Room. Moreover, being public, it was also used by the Spiritualists and other blue-collar groups with whom the bourgeois, class-conscious Scientists did not care to be associated. Collson and her followers agreed to rent a flat as a first step toward greater respectability. They furnished it attractively and called it Christian Science Hall, borrowing the name their Founder had given the temporary facilities her congregation had used while awaiting completion of The Mother Church. Unfortunately, the new meeting place was located over the *Evansville Journal*, whose presses below sometimes drowned out the services, and Collson decided that her church must have a building of its own.[33]

This ambition was to eventuate in a new church on Mulberry Street, but first it produced an open split between the congregation's warring factions. Already strained relations ruptured over the selection of a building site. According to Collson, Vallade had recommended the purchase of an old wooden structure once used by some defunct denomination. He claimed that his choice was inspired, but Collson's contingent was unimpressed. They could hardly see how the purchase of a dilapidated property would demonstrate their "abundant supply." Enraged at this rejection, Vallade declared that the meeting was mesmerized by "human personality," and he stalked out with his supporters behind him.[34]

Within a matter of weeks a Second Church of Christ, Scientist, appeared in Evansville. For the record, both sides stated publicly that the split was "not the result of any differences over the building of the new edifice of worship, but simply an expansion of the faith in the city."[35] But outsiders sensed that all was not well among the Eddyites when Collson's parent church took the "additional step toward perfecting the [organization]" by filing articles of incorporation that insured its supremacy and status as the city's "First Church."[36] Feeble at birth, Second Church soon expired. Vallade had a falling-out with his group soon after it broke away, and he watched his followers straggle back to his rival's congregation. From the tales they carried with them, Collson realized for the first time that the man really feared her as a demon who was using the black art of M.A.M. against him. He "actually believed," she later mused, "that I and my wicked smile—and not in the least his own character and behavior—were responsible for all the misfortunes that were befalling him."[37]

While Collson laughed at these stories at first, she was gradually taken over by the very same primitive fear of mental malpractice. Indeed, she would not have welcomed back the straying members so cordially had they not willingly repudiated their fallen leader's teachings as spurious and joined the chorus condemning his methods. Vallade never returned to First Church in Evansville, but moved to another city where, Collson surmised, "he was better appreciated and perhaps better behaved."[38]

Meanwhile, the brief appearance of Second Church in Evansville had repercussions all the way to Boston. Although she had entered the Indiana field secretly bearing Knott's aegis and had tried to carry out the woman's wishes, Collson had never quite understood the battleplans or her part in them. Her commander in Boston assured her that she herself was "handling" Vallade's malpractice—which she could do effectively, since he was turning to her for help, but she seemed to have little influence over his conduct, and certainly no more with Collson as a deputy in the field. Only after the fact did her agent understand that the idea was to work undercover through metaphysical means, while "keeping the mantle of harmony adjusted properly at all times." Such a job seemed to Collson "more on the order of hiding an elephant behind a fan," but her failure to perform the feat so angered Knott that she broke off their relations, forcing her hapless lieutenant to return to her own teacher for protection.[39]

Quite predictably, Farlow was outraged when he heard of Knott's "unscientific" intrusion into the affairs of one of his students. He made no attempt to conceal his low estimate of her spiritual fiber and marvelled aloud at her rapid ascent in the Boston operation. Collson later recalled that though he also reproved her for moving her practice to Evansville without consulting him, he said he would forgive this instance of lese majesty and promised henceforth to give her the closest possible supervision. Needless to say, abject dependence upon her teacher was not at all to Collson's liking. Reared in an environment that had fostered independence and a love of intellectual freedom, she had never, not even in childhood, felt compelled to conform out of fear. Yet now she was under strict surveillance and made to mind her p's and q's by force of believing that the cerberean monster, M.A.M., was on call in case she disobeyed.

Farlow applied his coercion with a pretense of goodwill, but his tight grip made Collson bridle. After all, this man, who appeared to bask in the warmth of a vast adoring public, admonished her for being fond of people as mortals, for caring too much for social life, and for allowing her patients to make too much of her personality. "In fact, according to him," she wrote later, "nearly everything I did exposed me to gusts and gails of mental poison."[40] On one occasion, she found herself asking him if he thought it safe for her to go out to dinner with some friends. She was warned against it. Farlow said he himself had not gone out socially for years, and he simply could not protect his students from animal magnetism if they refused to exercise the same prudence.

By now the woman respected animal magnetism sufficiently to accept most of Farlow's logic without dispute. Periodically, however, when her rational powers broke free, the arbitrary and even sadistic nature of his advice so infuriated her that she wrote him long letters challenging his dictatorial rights, ridiculing his superior posturings, and defying the wiles of M.A.M. Invariably, this boldness triggered such fear of its consequences that she would shortly dispatch self-effacing recantations, replete with lavish expressions of gratitude for her teacher's guidance. Collson knew full well that any break with her teacher would be her professional undoing, the end of her livelihood and her role in what she still believed was a sound religio-therapy. As a leader in the church, whose job it was to maintain respect for the ecclesiastical order, she would be condemned and immediately deposed if it were even suspected she had been disloyal to Alfred Farlow.

Collson interpreted her fitful behavior in terms of a normal human conflict between the desire for freedom and the reluctance to pay rebellion's price, but Farlow preferred a more colorful reading. He saw his student's instability as an awful psychomachia in which the ubiquitous villain, M.A.M., was trying to seduce his victim to shed Truth's protective influence, thereby leaving malpractice free to destroy her. This script always renewed Collson's outrage, as it seemed to her just another ploy to frighten her into cringing servility, and the cycle of letters to Farlow would start all over again. At last, in despair of ever changing the situation by mail, the woman went to Boston to see if things could be straightened out.

But in Boston Mary Collson was greeted by a new and startling explanation for her mercurial conduct: she showed, Farlow said, all the inconsistencies of a woman madly in love, and obviously, a woman in love with him. He regretted that this was the case, he went on, since his devotion to her was strictly spiritual, and he could not reciprocate her romantic feelings. Collson's immediate reaction to this scenario was indignation, but she was also determined to get at the root of her problem and not let false pride interfere. Therefore, she tried to think of her case as an instance of what Eddyites described as animal magnetism "reversing the Truth," and for a moment or two it even seemed plausible that this machination of M.A.M.'s had inverted a deep affection for her teacher in a way that made her feel it as antipathy. But the disjunction between this reasoning and what Collson genuinely felt was too great, and her thoughts would not stay in line.

Overcome by a sense of the interview's total absurdity, she suddenly had a new insight into Farlow's psychology. It struck her that his treatment of her involved not only simple paternalism, but an effort to gain a mastery over the opposite sex, which he felt he needed to prove his manhood. Because she refused to contribute "to the general atmosphere of adoration in which he lived and moved and over-fed his enormous appetite for glory," he put forth a special effort to subdue her. Collson knew that "he had large crowds of women of all ages and degrees of comeliness worshipping at his shrine." She also knew that he was responsible for a large household of brothers and sisters, and that this arrangement by itself was a deterrent to marriage. Yet Collson guessed it was Farlow's unwillingness to jeopardize his following and their sublimation of his personality that prevented him from ever "stooping to marry." Only when a student refused, as she did, to "honor where honor was due," would he willingly "stoop to conquer."[41]

When it came Collson's time to respond, she suggested "as tactfully as possible" that since she was proffering an unwelcome affection, it might be best if she went to another teacher for help in her work. Farlow vetoed this proposal, however, on the grounds that it would be a capitulation to error and invite mental malpractice against him. M.A.M. already trailed him twenty-four hours a day, he complained, and it needed no such encouragement as the airing of this difficulty. He considered himself quite capable of taking care of his students, he said, and Collson saw the door of this exit close.

The demands on Alfred Farlow during these years were indeed enormous. His job as chief Committee on Publication, just one of many assignments, would have been sufficient to occupy him full time. It required that he rectify all published "injustices" to Mrs. Eddy, and these he perceived as numerous. To outsiders, they seemed to arise from any release of information that reduced the Founder's exalted image to merely human proportions. What made Farlow's job all the more taxing was that the church leader was now an old woman, well into her eighties. Her sufferings from the "claims" of physical disease and the fear of M.A.M. had caused her to withdraw from the prying eyes of an often hostile public, and her seclusion merely stimulated an even more aggressive curiosity. Each assault on Science required its own deliberate response from the adroit Publication Committee. For example, when the popular Mark Twain wrote a series of critical essays discrediting Eddy's claims to a divine power and stature, Farlow had several long talks with the writer and sent him, for balance, some copies of his own articles on Eddy's work.[42] A more alarming exposé by Frederick W. Peabody had called for the stronger offensive of a nation-wide boycott against the book's publisher and its distributors.[43]

Yet despite demanding responsibilities elsewhere, Farlow managed to keep a close watch over his wayward student. Indeed, his attention was so constant that she felt her life was no longer her own, and by the end of 1909 was ready to try the only means by which she could still attain her freedom amicably. She would apply to go through the Normal Class taught by the Scientists' Board of Education, and by ascending to her teacher's rank, become entirely independent of his authority. The Board's Normal Class was held only once every three years, and admission was highly competitive, but the Kinters had frequently recommended that Collson take the course, and

George had even offered to endorse her application. The Evansville therapist realized that she would need Farlow's signature too, but she also knew that if he were willing to give it, her endorsements would mean virtual acceptance.

With new hope, Collson again took the train to Boston. Farlow greeted her with his customary cordiality, and when he learned that she wanted to apply for the Normal Class, he said he thought it a fine idea and would gladly give it his backing. At once, Collson had misgivings that "it was coming too easy;" yet when Farlow asked from whom she intended to get her second endorsement, she told him "with Little Red Ridinghood simplicity." Only when she saw Farlow's peculiar smile at the mention of Kinter's name did she remember that the two men had worked together as lobbyists in New York and still saw each other a good deal whenever Kinter was called back East. From that moment, Little Red Ridinghood knew she would never go through Normal Class.[44]

Nevertheless, before she left Boston, she made out her application, secured her teacher's endorsement, and sent the form to Kinter in Chicago. She waited more than two weeks for a reply, and when it arrived, she found the application had come back without a signature. Instead, there was a long and elaborate apology for the delay, explaining that Collson's letter had been forwarded to Boston, whence Kinter had been summoned quite unexpectedly. This call to duty, he explained, had prompted him to reconsider his previous offer to endorse his friend's application. It had led him to see that using his name in this way would amount to exploiting the privilege of serving Mrs. Eddy, since it was this work in her home that made his signature valuable. With no other friend who was qualified to sign her papers, Collson realized that her move had been thwarted "scientifically."

The woman returned to Evansville feeling she was a prisoner for life, and without the slightest hope of renewal, watched the New Year, 1910, arrive. She brooded over Farlow's reminder that she "would forever be his student" and that "even his death could not change that relationship since it was spiritual."[45] It was a devastating situation for her after having spent almost four decades trying to learn to be her own master. As a girl, she had sought to put her father out of mind, for having failed to realize his own dreams, he had tried to regain his dignity in the home by discouraging hers. Ever since, in her quest for independent womanhood, she had instinctively avoided male authorities, whom she readily suspected of trying to keep her subservient in order to make themselves feel strong. Her identity and self-respect depended upon her freedom from male domination. Yet she was again bound to a "failed father," to a man who, by his own admission, had been "nothing" outside of Christian Science, and who had undermined her hard-earned freedom in order to reassure himself of his success.

With all exits blocked, Collson's fear of Farlow grew tremendously, as did her fear of malpractice against her. She worked feverishly to protect every treatment she gave, and "if things went wrong," she assumed she had not kept ahead of the reversals wrought by animal magnetism.

At about this time the Evansville church sponsored a public lecture by a prominent Scientist, and Collson sought to unburden her fear by speaking with the man confidentially. With great circumspection, she told him that M.A.M. seemed to be raging in the city. The lecturer replied that it was the same everywhere, though probably a little worse at Collson's church because of her high degree of spirituality. To remind her of what she could scarcely forget, he repeated their Leader's warning that "looms of crime" were hidden in "the dark recesses of mortal mind" and were forever weaving "subtle webs" to ensnare faithful workers for Truth.[46] He urged even greater protective work and left Collson with the ominous thought that "the devil knows it enemy." If this was intended as high praise, the woman, more anxious than ever, was unable to enjoy it.

An accident only a few days later served to realize Collson's worst fears. The daughter of one of her best friends fell on the ice and was paralyzed. It came as an almost prostrating blow to the metaphysician, who had developed a motherly fondness for Isabelle and now found herself powerless to help her. "There was not the slightest symptom of improvement," the curist later admitted "although at times we tried very hard to think that we did see some slight gain on which to build hope."

At last, in desperation, Collson decided to write to Farlow. "With utter disregard for myself . . . I begged him to forgive any disrespectful or foolish thing that I may have said or done and implored him to do everything in his power to help this beloved and unfortunate young lady." Farlow replied that he could do nothing. He had warned her against the error of "inordinate affection," but she had ignored his advice until her indulgence in human attachment brought disaster upon her friends. Having shown such marked attention to Isabelle and her mother, he said, she had singled them out to their metaphysical enemies, while she herself, protected from M.A.M. by her teacher's faithful work, had escaped the assault directly. This was too much for Collson. Seeing in Farlow's reply "nothing less than the sadistic cruelty of jealousy," she rebelled with her "entire being against such superstition and truly devilish doctrine," and decided to leave Christian Science.[47]

III

Mary Collson decided to take the year of study abroad she had dreamed about as a girl, and then return to the Unitarian ministry. Without telling anyone of her intentions—for fear of being thwarted by her enemies' mental assaults—she quietly arranged church business so that things could go on without her and left with the simple announcement that she was off on a vacation. After stopping off in Iowa and Chicago to get in touch with old friends, she sailed for Europe supplied with letters of introduction mapping an exciting return to the world

outside Christian Science. The first stop was Oxford, where
Collson's hometown minister, Marian Murdock, had gone to
study. Being ineligible for regular admission to the exclusively
male university, and uninterested in pursuing a degree at any
of the women's colleges, Collson, like Murdock, simply enrolled
informally in classes that promised to get her back on an intellectual track: some history, some literature, and a refresher in
Kant taught by Manchester College's Lawrence Pearsall Jacks.

During her first months in Oxford, she was absorbed in her
studies and thought little about Eddyism. But one afternoon
toward the end of the term, curiosity steered her into the Christian Science Reading Room on Cornmarket Street. "A short
hour of reading and looking over the periodicals, a little chat
with the librarian, in which I heard the old stock phrases of 'the
new tongue,' and my aversion to all things Christian Science
was back again in full measure," she later wrote.[48] It was clear
that emotionally the fugitive from M.A.M. had not broken free
of her Scientific conditioning. Indeed, within a few weeks she
had begun to feel that her pursuer was again gaining ground.

Not the least of Collson's satisfactions in her clandestine
departure from Evansville had been that it was all accomplished without her teacher's knowledge. "He was among the
last to hear," she wrote, "so well had I profitted by his example
. . . of working by indirection."[49] However, in her renewed anxiety, she decided to follow the "safer policy" of repairing the
fractured relationship, even though she had no intention of
seeing Farlow again or ever returning to his organization.
Accordingly, she sent off a letter explaining her decision to
study abroad and find a new means of livelihood after her return
home. With well-practiced self-deprecation, she stated that she
was obviously not suited for Christian Science metaphysics,
but wished nonetheless to remain on friendly terms with her
former associates, to whom she was indebted for many kind-
nesses.

As so often before, the woman regretted making this concession to irrational fears as soon as she received Farlow's reply.

"His letters," she explained, "always made me aware that I was defeated no matter what it was I tried to do." This time he wrote that he thought her decision a good one and agreed that she probably was not advanced enough spiritually to practice Christian Science, though someday she might be equal to it. He assured her that in the meantime he would look after her wherever she was, in whatever work she chose, and would do all he could to promote her spiritual growth.

Though Collson renewed her pledge to forget Christian Science, her interest in it persisted. When the term closed at Oxford and she went to London to see the sights, she could not resist looking in on the Eddyites too. There were four branch churches in London, but it only took visits to two of them for Collson to see that M.A.M. flourished abroad as well as at home:

> At the second Wednesday evening meeting that I attended, there was an exhibition of it. The First Reader endeavored to check a speaker who was attempting to give a testimony. . . . The speaker was none other than a former First Reader who had been accused of allowing her banner of Truth to become soiled by "mad ambition," and [as] her badge of orthodoxy was alleged to be seriously faded, she had been requested to keep silent in the meetings. But on this occasion she started, continued, and finished her animated testimony despite all protest. The performance was politely conducted, both on the part of the just and the unjust, but those in the audience who were initiated into the ways of M.A.M. felt mental assassination in the air. I had no desire for any additional experience with Christian Science in London.[50]

In Paris it was much the same story. A nasty feud within the congregation had recently erupted, producing a second branch church and filling the air with mental malpractice. Thinking it best to avoid the unwholesome climate, Collson left quickly and spent the rest of her time on the Continent leading tours for Americans, who happily showed no interest in Christian Science.

The exile returned to the States early in January 1911, and spent most of the month with old Unitarian friends in New

England. Although her past failures had moderated her zeal for social crusades, experience had also convinced her that there could be no legitimate religion without the benevolent motive expressed by those who espoused the social gospel. In London she had spent part of her time "poking around" in the slums, and her visits to the settlement houses there had renewed her appreciation of genuinely philanthropic enterprises. Her reexamination of Kant at Oxford had also promoted a reaffirmation of faith in Christian service. With a sense of its indisputable truth, she had pondered Kant's proposition that the only good in the world is the will to follow moral law, not as a means, but as an end, regardless of profit or loss for oneself.

By Kant's definition, morality was not the doctrine of how to make oneself happy, but of how to make oneself worthy of happiness. Kant further contended that churches and doctrine had value only insofar as they assisted in the development of this morality. After assessing her difficulties with Christian Science in terms of Kant's critique, Collson concluded that Eddyism was really "a philosophy of getting," where the motive for action was always the desire for gain, whether the object be perfect health, worldly prosperity, or some other commodity of the good life. It seemed to her that "the hope of getting the good things" was probably what produced that "buoyancy of spirit" which "was commonly mistaken by the Scientists themselves for spiritual joy." Yet with Kant, she doubted that it was possible for a philosophy of "getting" to foster the "character traits essential to human progress and ethical well-being."[51]

In reaching for an ennobling base and a way to resolve her reformist dilemma, Mary Collson looked again to Jane Addams. She was grateful for the woman's gentle and unconditional friendship, and revitalized by her model of service to humanity. As she told Addams in a letter, she valued "the bigness" of the woman's love "and her generous manner of helping struggling, floundering creatures." After running the gamut of solutions to the world's problems, she was convinced that the settlement leader's spirit, her secular saintliness, was the best guide. "I one time thought we would have the millenium if we could only manage to get everybody fed and housed," she explained. "Then again I thought we would surely establish the ideal state if we could get everybody to putting 'God first' in the order of their lives. Now it seems to me the only thing I really have faith in is a large *human kindness*, and so my dear Miss Addams, I find myself turning back to you as 'the Great Apostle' of this creed."[52]

But Collson was still not impervious to the attraction of Christian Science as the means of improving individuals' lives. Even while she was taking steps to return to the Liberal ministry and its social gospel, she felt a pull from patients and friends in Evansville who, having heard she was back in the country, asked her to come back to them. The heavy mail from Indiana cited all sorts of crises and threats to the church's welfare. No doubt, Collson found it painful to think of what it might do to her patients if she discredited the system on which she had taught them to rely. Moreover, as she later conceded, "this influence from without had an advocate within—for in my heart I did not wish to give up Christian Science." Whatever her reservations about the Eddy organization, she still believed in mental healing as useful work, and she clearly enjoyed the income and social status that went with it. Surely, she told herself, she would be able to follow the creed of human kindness by making her "demonstrations" Scientifically.[53]

This wishful thinking, however, was quickly shaken. For during her year away from the field, Collson had removed her professional listing from the official registry of practitioners in the *Journal*, and Farlow refused to approve its reinsertion. Resolving to bring the conflict out into the open once and for all, she boldly requested a hearing before the board of directors in Boston and was granted an audience with its chairman, Archibald McClellan.

McClellan seemed sympathetic and agreed that Farlow had exceeded his authority as a teacher and dealt with his student unfairly. But then, to her bewilderment, he advised her to move her field to New York City where, he said, she would have more quiet and leisure. This seemed a strange recommendation in view of the well-known factionalism that had been wrecking havoc in the New York organization. Indeed, had she not been so eager to make a display of cheerful compliance to prove herself worthy of the director's support—or so reluctant to readmit her doubts about officialdom's purity—she would have caught the man's intent and the irony of his words. As it was, she returned to Evansville confident justice would be done. She said farewell to the clients who had called her back to Science, and without even waiting to see her new church's cornerstone laid, moved her healing practice from Evansville to Manhattan.

It was an expensive step and came at a bad time. The practitioner's savings had been depleted by the trip abroad, and the sudden death of her married brother had recently put a new financial burden on her. Much to her chagrin, she had been forced to borrow money, and her indebtedness made her all the more anxious to build up a practice again. As she might have foreseen, however, the board of directors now notified her that they could not, after all, list her card in the *Journal* without her teacher's permission. Memories of the Kinter affair came rushing back at her, and she winced as she remembered what Farlow had said when she threatened to take her case to higher authorities: "If I did some of the things I see done over there," he had snapped, "I should expect you to condemn me." At the time, his student had taken this warning as nothing more than spite, but now she was certain "they all had something to cover up" and were afraid to defy the formidable Committee on Publication.[54] Evidently Farlow had seen McClellan before Collson's hearing, and the men had conspired to purge her from the movement by moving her from her power base and setting her afloat in strange and perilous waters.

To appreciate fully the gravity of Mary Collson's position, it is necessary to know something about the New York organization and its long-time leader, Augusta Stetson. The flamboyant Mrs. Stetson was one of Mary Baker Eddy's most devoted students, but also one of her most powerful and unsettling competitors. A brilliant fundraiser, she built for her followers lavish churches, which not only rivaled The Mother Church, but drew much public censure for their excess. At last, when Stetson's attention to material symbols of spiritual wealth became an embarrassment to the organization, and worse, she announced that all signs and portents were pointing to her as Eddy's successor, the directors condemned her as a heretic and cast her out of the church. When the eighty-nine year-old Eddy died in December, 1910, just month's after the excommunication, Stetson was naturally held responsible by her enemies, as she was from then on whenever there was an illness or death among church officials.

After her eviction, Stetson had formed her own Christian Science Institute in New York, where she had dominated the field for twenty-five years and watched her students swell the ranks of the city's practitioners. Since those who remained loyal to her now shared their teacher's anathema, it was crucial that all faithful Eddy healers, especially in New York, be listed in the *Journal* to avoid being taken for Stetson heretics. Without anchorage in this turbulent new field, Collson was at a severe disadvantage without a *Journal* entry.

There was no more direct communication between her and her teacher, but word came from Boston that he was determined to see her again and have her acknowledge the "error" of her appeal to the board. This ominous report convinced her that Farlow was intent upon her destruction and was malpracticing to dislodge her from her New York base. Her terror of losing the metaphysical fight expressed itself in an obsession with staying within the city limits. This unreasonable fear was encouraged by Collson's own practitioner, who counseled her colleague and client to resist her teacher's devilry by devoting all her energy to remaining where she was.

At just this time, however, Collson heard from her sisters that her mother was critically ill. Although her love for Martha had been salient throughout her life, her fear of witchcraft was now more compelling than her filial devotion. She suspected that this new crisis might be a channel used by "error" to separate her from the work God wanted her to do in New York, and so she delayed a visit to her mother. Instead, she employed a practitioner to help treat the patient "absently," and sent extra money to make sure that Martha had fresh flowers in her room. Finally, one of her sisters wrote: "Mother repeatedly excuses you when we say you ought to be here. She thinks you do not know how sick she really is or you would come."

> This broke the spell and I hurried to my mother's bedside and was shocked to see how frail she looked. I then scarcely left her day or night and as I saw that the end must be very near, my regrets of delay pierced me deeply. She spoke of my devotion to her through the years and of how great a comfort it had been to her and that only increased my sorrow that I had failed, or almost failed, at the end. . . . On the very last day one of my sisters insisted that I must lie down to rest . . . and my grief was deepened that while I was sleeping my mother passed into a coma from which she never roused.[55]

Grief-stricken, Collson spent days reliving this experience. In her bereavement she blamed her teacher's malpractice for her refusal to respond at once to her family's call. Convinced that he, like her father, had deprived her mother of the comfort she deserved, she again transferred to Alfred Farlow all the anger she felt toward Andrew Collson.

At the same time, Collson feared Farlow's power in proportion to the misery she believed it had caused her. She dreaded returning to New York, but she held leases on her office and apartment and felt she had no other choice but to resume her fight with M.A.M. Not surprisingly, the practitioner's mental condition deteriorated rapidly after her return to Manhattan, where the environment and routine threw her into old grooves of thought. As she later explained, "the monotonous repetition of statements which I employed to ward off the evil influences of my teacher soon put me into a state of superstitious anticipation . . . exceeding anything I had previously experienced."[56] Her mind became so riveted on animal magnetism that she could no longer conceive of a realm of life extending beyond the pale of Christian Science influence. It was only a matter of months before this mental set became so unwholesome that it set off the mechanism for its own destruction.

One morning, Collson set out for her office by subway, as was her custom, when suddenly she felt as if she were suffocating in the dank air. At the first connection, she left the underground transit and caught the Fifth Avenue bus, but she found breathing there no easier than she had underground. Moreover, as the bus approached Forty-Second Street, where she had to get off, she was overcome by such an aversion to going to work that she could not move:

> Since I seemed unable to make the effort to get off the bus at this point, I decided that if I rode around the loop, perhaps I could make it on my return. The result was that I spent hours repeating this trip, for every time I caught sight of my office building I felt glued to my seat.
>
> I said the Lord's Prayer and the "scientific statement of being" over and over. I repeated the "definition of God" and everything else that I could think of as statements of Truth with power to exorcise animal magnetism. I declared that this experience was unreal, that it was a dream, and I repeated these declarations until, as in a dream, the bus began to appear to be floating along, rather than rolling over the pavement. It was almost like a phantom bus, and with the Ancient Mariner I could easily have said that Death and Life-in-Death were casting dice for my soul.[57]

Then, in recoil from the horror of this travesty, Collson grasped the railing on the bus. It was real, and as she held it she proclaimed that the whole material world in which she lived was a real world. "In detail I declared the buildings were real— made of real brick and real stones—and the people about me were real human beings, right-minded, sensible people going about reasonable tasks in a sane and normal manner." She pulled the buzzer, got off the bus, and took the subway back home. Exhausted, she threw herself on her bed and slept until the next morning.

Awakening to the aftermath of the previous day's grotesque episode, Collson set to work readjusting her thinking. In large part, she accepted responsibility for her near nervous breakdown, acknowledging that she had allowed herself to be controlled by the very sort of dogmatism she had deplored all her earlier life. She had sought an escape from her problems by accepting as absolute the authority of Mary Baker Eddy—"a human being no different from myself," she realized—and in so doing, she had let herself be reduced to a state of humiliating submission to a man for whom she had no respect. She also decided that her hysteria had been induced less by her relation to Farlow than by her gradual acceptance of the doctrine of animal magnetism. The preoccupation with M.A.M. had alienated her from the rational world of empirical experience, with the result, not uncommon among Eddyites, that she addressed her problems through "unreasoning superstition instead of with practical understanding of natural causation." On the Fifth Avenue bus, some instinct toward survival had changed the direction of her thinking, and that, she believed, "had saved the day."[58] Without further postponement, she sat down and wrote to The Mother Church asking to have her name dropped from the membership roll. Glancing at her calendar and dating her letter carefully, she marvelled that time moved so swiftly. It was already February 12, 1914.

CHAPTER VII

Freedom and Heresy

I

Once Mary Collson had fought the last of her metaphysical battles with Farlow, she noticed that thousands of other women in New York City were fighting a down-to-earth war for suffrage and women's rights. Ever since the state's legislative session of 1913 had passed a women's suffrage amendment and agreed to submit it to popular vote two years later, the New York Suffrage Association, the Women's Political Union, the College Equal Suffrage League, and other profranchise groups had been planning appeals for the vote and deploying their forces throughout the boroughs. By the winter of 1914, canvassing squads had swung into operation, and bonfires, open-air meetings, and weekend parades were becoming familiar events. There were plans for street dances on the lower East Side and rallies in every immigrant neighborhood, and to finance it all, sandwich sales on lower Broadway and teas on Long Island. Collson reached out to make contact with this world of activists as instinctively as she had reached out for the hand railing on the bus; it returned her to a healthy, concrete reality, through which she could reaffirm her progressive ideals.

One of the several reformist fronts on which she positioned herself was the Women's Political Union, where campaign organizers seized on her talents and experience to help their ladylike volunteers overcome their verbal inhibitions and teach them not to shrink from public gaze. It was no easy task bringing women out of their parlors and into politics to mingle in rowdy crowds and address perfect strangers without the shield of polite introductions. Nor did the soft, accommodating voices of well-bred females carry well, and effective loud speakers had not yet been invented. Suffragist leaders were therefore on a constant lookout for veteran speakers like Collson to organize street meetings and give their new recruits on-the-job training.

Carrying the suffrage evangel to all corners of the city, Collson's troops marched on public parks, Wall Street banks, post offices, medical centers, court squares, and college campuses. Their speeches were sometimes delivered from the back seats of motor cars, and even the seasoned orators had to learn how to keep their balance while they called out to passersby from their unsteady platforms.[1] Often there was at first only an audience of a small boy, a dog, or a few loafers, but the unusual spectacle of the campaigners would soon draw a full crowd, and then, as Collson learned, the real difficulties arose. There was likely to be "considerable heckling," and she was "not so good at handling that sort of thing," despite her many years facing the public.[2]

Collson also spent some time with the campaign's socialist flank after meeting some of its women members at the Henry Street settlement. She agreed heartily with their argument that universal suffrage was not just a feminist goal, but a farther-reaching reform that would strengthen all society by giving women a means of attacking the capitalistic system, which was even harder on them than it was on men.[3] Collson helped organize pro-vote meetings for the Socialist Party's Women's Committee and labor unions supporting the vote.

With the outbreak of war in Europe that summer, Collson's commitments to women's rights and socialist ideals both came to focus on the cause of peace. Jane Addams, who was preparing to come to New York for an antiwar meeting, considered the preservation of peace women's special responsibility and called upon her sisters to start waging war against the war. Charlotte

Perkins Gilman was also urging New York's distaff to protest
the "Pan-European slaughter" by staging a massive demonstration. "Everything that makes for solidarity among women is
good," Gilman said. Because "the women of one nation" cared
"deeply for the sufferings of other nations thousands of miles
away," the moral effect of their unity would be felt around the
world. "Let the women wear mourning," she urged. "There is
cause for it. And let them march by the thousands."[4]

Heeding the call, Mary Collson was one of the small but
impressive army of 1500 women who assembled at Fifty-
Seventh Street on a Saturday afternoon in late August. Dressed
in black, she marched to the cadance of muffled drums down to
Union Square, while an immense crowd lined Fifth Avenue
and stood silently. Some of the marchers carried the peace
banner or funeral bouquets. Others wheeled babies in car-
riages. There were women of foreign nationalities dressed in
their native costumes, a division of nurses in blue uniforms
from the Henry Street settlement, and a large band of socialist
women wearing red badges or armbands over their gowns.[5] "I,
for one, felt as doleful as I looked," Collson remembered.[6]

The activity of the summer and fall of 1914 revitalized Collson. It reacquainted her with the world beyond Eddy's metaphysical one and helped meet her long-stifled need to be a
useful part of it. But the war in Europe quickly extinguished
any new sparks of interest she had in reform through political
means. Having seen social reformers' "cherished hopes and
high ideals tumbling in crashing wreckage," she was persuaded to go back to mental healing and individual
counselling.[7] Therapeutics, she reasoned, if unencumbered by
church politics, would surely enable her to make a better world
by making people better. Then, too, mental healing had always
provided a good and ready income. Even now, many of her old
patients still called on her for help, some even writing from
Boston and Evansville for "absent" treatments by mail. Having
made her decision, she left New York when winter came and
settled in Brookline, Massachusetts, and there she resumed her
practice.

Collson now steered clear of Christian Science officialdom entirely and had no qualms about working outside the organization. Nor were her patients concerned about her independent status. They continued to enlist her services and still recommended her to their friends. But the therapist was disturbed by her lack of a non-Scientific explanation for the metaphysical healing that had become a "decided fact" in her life.

Having regained some distance, she could now analyze the polar shift that had taken place in her religious position. Before embracing Christian Science, she had believed, with Comte, that "as people improved upon themselves," they became more capable of comprehending good, and their concepts of God evolved correspondingly. "I accepted, even as I had been taught, that it had taken thousands of years of human experience to transform in the Hebrew thought the cruel and jealous Elohim into the God of the prophets, and yet longer to prepare the thought for the God of Jesus."

By contrast, Christian Science had taught her that God, as revealed by Mrs. Eddy, was "the full and final self-revelation" of God to human beings. At the time she took up Science, it was not hard for her to accept the Absolute as the only reality because this orientation had Platonic overtones.[8] Furthermore, she had desperately wanted to believe. "I was equipped . . . to understand the situation . . . but I was greatly in need of illusion . . . and enjoyed accepting Christian Science for what it claimed to be, rather than what my intellectual training would have [shown] it to be." She could now see that there was "no likeness whatever between the dogmatic, deductive method of reasoning employed by Mrs. Eddy and the masterful dialectics of the dialogues of Plato." But being a positivist reformer with a Romantic legacy, she had always been torn between materialistic and idealistic approaches to reform. "Although I had been trained to think as a rationalist," she later conceded, "I was emotionally what almost every human is: a credulous mystic."[9]

Now that the mysticism of Christian Science had "landed her in the ditch," she was eager for "a more common sense" and "more modern" context for her therapeutic work. Henri Bergson's *Creative Evolution* and *Matter and Memory* provided such a context, she thought, by furnishing a reality immediately at hand. As she understood it, Bergson's argument was that "we know life by living life," and that "existence—exactly at the point of existing—is the reality . . . for that hour or moment." It was "the immediate contact with life through existence" that constituted the union of creation with its Creator;" and by extension, Collson concluded, "Man's immediate contact with the great reservoir of Creative Energy in daily living endowed him with the potential power to control his most intimate material environment, his physical body."[10] Long before this, of course, Channing and Emerson had taught her that the highest revelation of God took place within each human being, and had spoken of man's intimacy with the potent life forces in the universe. Once Collson realized how little her "new" philosophy varied from her old Unitarianism, beyond its thrust towards a practical therapeutics, she again considered returning to the Liberal ministry and finding a place for her healing practice there.

In the spring of 1917 Collson submitted an application to the Unitarians' Ministerial Union and gave the names of Jane Addams and Florence Buck as references.[11] Addams was happy to give her endorsement and verified that the applicant had lived at Hull House "engaged in protective work for children." She had been a "reader and a student," Addams said. She "spoke very well" and had done a commendable job at the social settlement.[12] Reverend Buck, a longtime Unitarian minister with close ties to the Sisterhood, had known Mary Collson in what she called a "touch-and-go fashion" for some twenty years and recently had seen her again. Buck believed Collson was "sound to the core," despite her record, which showed an "adventurous spirit" with "the usual accompaniment, lack of stability." Buck described her as "personally attractive" and "ready of speech." "Intellectually bright, quick, ready rather than profound," she accepted "an idea easily," later rejected it "with the same ease." Although "an avowed Socialist," she was "standing with the government for the war," and Buck believed she was "really devoted to her ideals" and had "fine impulses." Also noting that Collson brought with her "a belief in mental healing and in her own powers in that line," Buck predicted, "No doubt she would do some good work for us, with those who are willing to listen to her special theories and somewhat radical views, but I can imagine they might prove an element which would tend to cause division in a congregation."[13]

Reverend Buck's forecast showed her to be a shrewd judge of character, as her forecast showed. Even before a decision had been made on her application, Collson discovered that her "special theories and somewhat radical views" did indeed come between her and the majority of her Liberal brethren. For one thing, the wartime pressure to back America's military preparedness was so intense that even the traditionally dovish Unitarians were hedging their historic ideals and swinging into line. Collson's unconcealed socialist sympathies and unshakable pacifism made most of the liberal church members she met in Brookline uncomfortable.

For her part, Collson was horrified to find that the denomination's *Christian Register* was now one of the country's most hawkish religious periodicals. To justify its stand on the war, it argued that, if faced with the current threat, even Jesus would have taken up "bayonet and grenade and bomb and rifle, and done the work of deadliness against . . . the most deadly enemy." "That is the inexorable truth about Jesus Christ and this war," the paper proclaimed, "and we rejoice to say it."[14] Certainly all Unitarians did not approve of the *Register*'s militancy, but only a few, like Collson's old *Unity* friends, absolutely refused to be shaken from their pacifist moorings. When Jenkin Lloyd Jones persisted in condemning the "monstrous crime" of war and registered his opposition to this one, there being a "better way," he lost scores of Liberal friends and the hospitality of many familiar pulpits.[15] Despite the assurance of patriotic loyalty Collson had given to Buck, she shared Jones' repugnance toward the war effort and could never quite bring herself to endorse it. Consequently, even before the American Unitarian Association voted in April 1918 to withdraw support from any minister who was not "a willing, earnest and outspoken supporter" of "the vigorous . . . prosecution of the war," Collson had decided against returning to the Unitarian ministry.[16]

Collson's disillusionment with the Liberals for their stand on the war was compounded by their indifference to mental healing. Her hopes of finding a Unitarian home for her practice of mind cure had been encouraged at first by Reverend Thomas Van Ness, the popular minister of Brookline's prosperous Second Unitarian Church, whom she had met shortly after returning to Boston. When she had proposed that they form an adult class in mental healing in his Sunday School, Van Ness had agreed to the idea, for he had been interested in the subject of mind cure for most of his adult life.[17]

Although Van Ness, who had once met the woman, did not consider Mary Baker Eddy much of an intellect, and although he criticized the belief in "witchcraft" which she disseminated as the doctrine of M.A.M., he had always been willing to pass over "minor criticism of this kind." For as he followed the movement's growth over the years, he became convinced that its leader had done a great service by bringing mental healing out of obscurity, giving it "place and dignity," and "most important of all," a "truly religious basis." Unitarians had long been preaching that communion between the Eternal Spirit and the human spirit was possible, but they left it there. Eddy, Van Ness contended, had simply taken Emerson's statements literally, seizing upon the idea of equating the universal mind with goodness, health, and prosperity. As a result, whatever the faults of her organization, the woman had given "practical expression to a great and helpful truth." Certainly those who had studied her work had "something to show Unitarians."[19]

After talking with Collson, Van Ness was eager to see what interest she could generate in mind cure, and he helped her form the study group she proposed. "If ever there were a chance of interesting Unitarians, that would have been the chance," she later observed wistfully.[19] But the response had been discouraging. While most of the congregation was too absorbed in the subject of war to be thinking about supposed metaphysical struggles, those who did take an interest strongly resisted their group leader's flat rejection of medical help. One gentleman, she remembered, "pointed out that I still had the distinctively Christian Science attitude, even though I attached it to a new philosophy."[20] She had denied this and said that to act otherwise, mixing methods, would never prove anything. However, her actions soon showed that she was still thinking like a scientist.

It happened that Collson was suddenly stricken by an extremely painful illness that "resisted" her own mental work, and after several days of almost constant agony, she found herself turning again to a Christian Science practitioner. The metaphysician's sole reliance on spiritual power brought the patient peace of mind, even if a rather slow recovery. Collson concluded that this return to Eddy's methodology at a time of intense suffering confirmed her belief in Christian Science, and she decided to resume her healing practice under it aegis.

Where earlier she had resolved to divorce herself from the organization, she now vowed to remain independent of most of the church's doctrines as well:

> The teachings concerning animal magnetism were irrevocably wiped out so far as I was concerned. I also was certain that nothing could ever reestablish my teacher's domination over me; but ever since I had begun to practice mental healing, I had never for any length of time been without a practice, and I now desired to devote myself exclusively to healing work which was solely concerned

with the Life forces which constitute our mental environment. We might call the power Creative life-energy, or we might call it God, but the stand should be: "On Him we place reliance." It seemed to me that Christian Science alone took such a stand.[21]

Old associates and church officials made her return to The Mother Church easy: her application for admission was approved without Farlow's signature, and one of the directors assured her, in a letter which she preserved, that he "would be happy" to endorse her request for professional listing in the *Journal*.[22] Still, the woman could not have been more critical of officialdom had they tried to obstruct her reinstatement. Although she had intended to devote herself exclusively to the study of "life-forces" and their healing properties, she found herself looking censoriously at every aspect of the church and bristling with animosity towards those who welcomed her back.

The courtesies the directors extended her made her smile bitterly, for she knew quite well, and far better than they suspected, just why they dared to defy her teacher now. On one of the rare occasions during the years of her association with him, when Farlow had dropped his patronizing manner and allowed himself to appear before his student as a troubled human being, he had confided to her what few if any outside his family ever knew: bothered by failing eyesight, he had gone to a noted specialist and was told that his optic nerve was diseased and blindness only a matter of time. Collson remembered how startled she had been that Farlow accepted this verdict, how her heart had filled with sympathy for him, and how she had argued against the possibility of such a fate—until the impropriety of talking Christian Science to her teacher became apparent to them both. "He became his superior self again," she recalled, and without an object to fasten on, her sympathy had immediately dissolved.[23]

But now it was 1918, and Farlow's predicted blindness had closed in on him. He was living three thousand miles away in retirement on the West Coast and could no longer influence any church business outside his association of students. Collson realized that, given his tastes and disposition, her teacher's blindness was all the more tragic, and she was "truthfully . . . shocked and disgusted at the callousness of his colleagues toward his fate." Boston's official gestures of kindness toward her seemed "like bearding a blind, chained lion in his cage," though six years before she would have welcomed such treatment as a reassuring administration of justice. "I certainly deserved it much more when it was withheld," she thought wryly, "than when it was given."[24]

The authorities' attitude on her return to the church opened Collson's eyes further to one of the "peculiar effects of Christian Science teachings:" because the doctrines rejected the belief in original sin, denied the reality of evil in human experience, and presented death and suffering impersonally as error's self-destructive behavior, human misery neither inspired humility in Eddyites nor evoked their sympathy.[25]

One of the most blatant illustrations of this insensitivity was provided by the case of an eighty-year-old woman, whom Collson had been asked to help. This patient had been under treatment from various Christian Science practitioners ever since a small patch of irritation had appeared on her face several years before, but the growth had never been arrested. By the time Mary Collson was called in, it had spread over half the woman's face to her eyes and ears, which were now so badly damaged that she could barely see or hear. The patient had to be left alone for long stretches while her daughter was at work, so Collson made it a point to visit her every day during the week and devised some novel techniques for giving the treatment:

> I conceived the idea of writing in large black letters made with a carbon pencil on cardboard, since the only means of communicating with her had been to shout through a pasteboard tube placed against her best ear. She had studied the Christian Science textbook for many years, so I put what I considered Christian Science teachings in my own language in an effort to arouse new interest. The admission is also necessary that this cardboard manuscript

contained a few jokes and other extraneous matter that could not be classified as authorized literature; but the poor old lady treasured it, and her study of it constituted her only diversion when she was alone.[26]

Not long after Collson had taken the case, the daughter, at friends' advice, moved her mother to a Christian Science sanitorium. When the ailing woman grew homesick and complained that she received no attention, the manager blamed the patient's unhappiness on Collson's frequent calls. She charged that Collson's excessive sympathy toward her client had caused the old woman to expect such catering from everyone. Instead of staying at home as she should have and "working absently" to "reflect the divine love that heals the sick," the metaphysician entertained and mesmerized the patient with "human personality," while the disease only grew worse. The daughter was persuaded to engage a new therapist, despite her mother's protests and her own reluctance to make the change. The patient, however, refused to give up the valued cardboards, and they were found by their author's successor, so rife with "error" that she marvelled to find the old woman still alive. The new practitioner had the cards destroyed immediately, and after a few visits to cleanse the atmosphere of "mortal mind," did all her work "absently" and never visited the old woman again.

Even as Mary Collson's past errors were being brought to the surface, she made yet another wrong move:

I sent my former patient a Christmas card, a card pressed in relief which she could follow with her fingers. It never reached her but fell into the pile of evidence against me. It proved that I was mentally holding onto the case and retarding the healing, which allegation was utterly absurd, for I was very tired and appreciated my release, despite the offensive manner in which it was effected. While this performance was going on, the patient was drawing near to the end. . . . After the mother's death, I waited one evening after church to speak to the daughter. I tried to say the right thing and to refrain from all "mortal mind sympathy." Nevertheless, she broke down and, putting her arm about me, said, "I wish I had told mother that you sent her a Christmas card. It hurt her that you had completely forgotten her, and she worried for fear you were offended because I changed practitioners." The tears came to my eyes, too, and I thought it such a mockery to deceive this poor old woman and hurt her feelings so that the "reflection of divine love" wouldn't be interfered with by an act of human kindness.[27]

By demonstrating so clearly how the doctrine of divine love's "reflection" thwarted naturally good responses, this experience wiped out what little remained of the mystic sentimentality that had led Collson back into Christian Science.

Eddyism's denial of human needs went hand in hand, Collson saw, with its failure to function as the provable science it claimed to be. Wherever it dealt with the subject of evil, she found "contradiction, confusion, and elusiveness." Because Scientists gave evil "no actual place" in their scheme of thought and left it "without restraint of definition or location," evil became "an ubiquitous racketeer, defying all the laws of logic."[28]

Never was this more apparent to Collson than when she accepted an invitation to join a circle of Christian Science "War Workers." This elite group of church women, some of whose members were authorized teachers, and all of whom had at least been through Primary Class, met weekly to make woolen blankets for Belgian refugees. Coming directly from a year-long association with a similar circle of volunteers at the Brookline Unitarian church, Collson was repulsed by the bellicose atmosphere of the Scientists' gatherings. If the Brookline fellowship had given their tacit support to the war, most had at least shunned the *Christian Register*'s militant propaganda. However, by Collson's account, the Christian Science ladies were caught in a maelstrom of hatred. They took great relish in exchanging stories of German atrocities and listened greedily as the more imaginative conjured up spectacles of the German fleet landing in New York harbor, destroying the city, ravaging the women, and torturing helpless children.[29] The most graphic pictures of all were often produced by the group's organizer, who despite her C.S.B. and supposed metaphysical acumen, did not believe that global enemies could be dealt with Scientifically—that is, by being seen as the perfect children of God. Taking her lead from the *Monitor*, she exhorted her group to think of the Kaiser not "as any ordinary enemy, but as a madman, with gory knife in hand" who would destroy democracy unless checked by "the speediest methods," not metaphysical ones. Wartime, Collson was told, was "no time for talk."[30]

When Collson first came into Science she had assumed that God's power would be available to overcome any delusion of evil, but in time she had learned that this was not quite the case. Actually, the Founder had taught that a demonstration could only be made if the principles were honestly applied and the circumstances made it "humanly possible."[31] The fledging had been struck at once by the logical fallacy of the inference that some human circumstances were beyond the power of an all-powerful deity. But as she later admitted, she had been so desperate for a panacea that she had accepted the teaching as a handy device for explaining away the failures of mental treatment. Collson had also been troubled by the logic of the hypothesis—basic to Scientific healing and redemption—that one could actualize or produce "the perfect man" by seeing him as a reflection of God. "Although I was a very busy and reputedly successful practitioner," she wrote afterwards, "I had given up trying to think of man as 'God's image and likeness' because I had decided I did not understand the Creator"; and "if I was unable to 'realize' God, why attempt to 'realize' . . . his perfect child?"[32]

Though she was willing not to "reflect love" toward the Kaiser, she could hardly bring herself to join the shrill chorus of hatred against him or accept what she considered the speciousness of a system which could not explain why some kinds of "error" responded to "right thinking" and others did not. "I found it difficult to make out just why 'realizing the Truth' about the Kaiser was classified as something 'humanly impossible' for use in the quiet of our homes, while there were these constant reports of 'demonstrations' made by the boys on the front . . . wherein immunity from injury has been gained by 'realizing' the unreality of bursting shells and raining shrapnel."[33] The Christian Science War Workers and the *Monitor*'s editorials convinced Collson that Science offered "not the slightest assistance" in the prevention of wars because it equivocated on the nature of evil in human experience. Eddyism had turned out to be neither truly reformist nor scientific, and "with much self-pity," Collson saw herself as a weary wanderer who had returned home with wider vision only to find her family more disappointing than they had seemed when she left.

By the war's end, Collson had reduced her contacts with Christian Scientists to her practice, which continued to thrive and give her a sense of usefulness. During the flu epidemic after the war, she spent hours at the bedsides of the sick, but was never stricken herself, and saw every one of her patients recover. "I felt I came through with flying colors," she wrote: "I reported all cases and they were quarantined, but we used no material remedies." She later recalled treating one case diagnosed as double pneumonia, where a doctor had been in attendance and given up hope of the woman's recovery, but the patient "did get well, and got well quickly."[34] Unfortunately, whatever assurances these successes gave her, they were dissolved by a long run of failures that followed; and the therapist took these failures as further evidence that the doctrinal base of her practice was unreliable because it was unscientific.

The woman withdrew more and more to the fringes of the church community, where she was freer to follow the biddings of her social conscience. Disregarding the church's preferences, she kept in touch with socialist friends and their political causes. In the winter of 1919, when Attorney General Mitchell Palmer began his "raids on the Reds" and had thousands of immigrants rounded up and herded into police stations, she joined her old Hull House colleague, Alice Hamilton–who was now teaching at Harvard Medical School and living in Boston–

in protesting the mass arrests, raising funds for the Quaker feeding centers, and helping in other ways to ease the plight of the victims. While Hamilton tried to soften the postwar hatred toward Germans by speaking at various public and private functions throughout the city, Collson sheltered some of her radical friends in Boston and sent money to others in New York.[35] She joined the Friends of Soviet Russia when proletariat sympathizers, who were stirred by the famine in Russia, launched the organization in 1921.[36] She also supported the founders of the Communist *Daily Worker*, becoming a shareholder when the paper was started in 1924. Though she realized that from their perspective her religion still "stood in the way with these people," she felt much closer to them than to her fellow Scientists.[37]

Collson's postwar experience of Christian Science in Boston nearly caused her to sever her connections with it entirely. She did make "several gestures" in this direction, and in 1920 even sold all her Christian Science books, a significant step for an Eddy metaphysician.[38] But the thought of leaving a secure career at the age of fifty without any attractive alternative persuaded her that the problem might in part be geographic. To see whether a Christian Science practice would be more agreeable in the Midwest, Collson moved back to Evansville, Indiana.

III

After an absence of eight years, the onetime church leader found that the Evansville she had known was "a dream of the past." Automotive industries had replaced most of the horse-related businesses and dramatically altered the face of the old commercial district. There were also new department stores, banks, and theaters; a movie house was under construction, and even the city limits had been moved to allow residential development. The Christian Science sector had also changed in certain ways. The Eddyites now occupied the long-awaited church on Mulberry Street and their congregation was largely composed of new faces. Like the old group, however, the new one was split into bitterly warring factions. Consequently, while Collson agreed to help the Cause by becoming a member, she made this concession solely to gain firm anchorage for her practice and had very little else to do with the church.

As the years passed, even minimal contact with the Eddy community was enough to make Collson guard her independence fiercely. Having lost confidence in the church's ability to improve character, she had again become an enthusiastic supporter of social and political reform strategies. The Scientists' disinterest in civic affairs, and their willingness to let *The Christian Science Monitor* do all their thinking for them, appalled her. Collson got an inside view of this mentality during Prohibition, when Indiana's Anti-Saloon League was pressing for stricter enforcement of the liquor law. On the assumption that they would find allies among the Christian Scientists, who were doctrinally opposed to the use of intoxicants as an enslaving drug, the League wrote to all the Indiana practitioners listed in the *Journal* asking for funds to support their crusade. Convinced by her work in social welfare that such law enforcement was crucial, Collson sent a contribution and thought no more about it until a second letter from the League arrived in the mail. The organization wanted to thank her specially for her remittance, as she had been the only one of the state's numerous practitioners to have responded to their appeal.[39]

Curious to see what Boston's reaction to this information would be, Collson sent it on to the Board of Directors. She never expected the editorial that soon appeared in the *Monitor* urging support of enforcement campaigns by groups like the Anti-Saloon League, which it named specifically. However, once this endorsement came out, she was not surprised by the instant change in the attitude among her professional colleagues and fellow Scientists. In particular, Collson remembered how one of the metaphysicians at a testimonial service solemnly rose to give thanks for the *Monitor*'s editorial and express her confidence that all loyal Scientists would comply with its policy. "I knew," Collson wrote, "she had ignored an appeal for help made a few short weeks before . . . and I was conscious I was shying off in the direction of the goats when I questioned the moral strength of such support and believed that such sheeplike servility was destructive to human character."[40]

Another display of this slavish mentality and the church's encouragement of it accellerated Collson's final departure from Christian Science. Its occasion was a membership meeting at the Evansville church in 1927 where the State Committee on Publication had come to be congratulated on his successful lobbying for new legislation protecting denominational interests. Thanks to his efforts, Christian Science metaphysicians, whose legal rights to work in the state had never been secure, were now clearly entitled to practice. Now, too, Christian Scientists could have their children exempted from physical examinations in the public schools.

With genuinely good intentions, Collson stood up at the meeting and voiced her appreciation for what the gentleman had accomplished; but she made the mistake of embellishing her expression of thanks, adding that her joy at the Scientists' victory had been dampened only by the simultaneous defeat of the eight-hour-day and child labor bills. Somehow still fully expecting that everyone present would sympathize with her remarks, she was stunned when the speaker launched a tirade against "agitators for child labor laws." He was, she recalled, one of those self-made men who supposed that the only alternative to putting young children to work was to have them loafing on street corners and learning bad habits in alleys. "He contended that it hurt no child to be made to work; often weak children were made strong [as a result]. He had worked hard as a child, and there we were, eye-witnesses to the highly beneficial results." Collson had seen very different results when she worked with her young boys and girls in Chicago, and now, as the State Publication Committee made his defense of child labor, she "cringed in shame" to find herself in a position where she was obliged to support him. Granted, the man's remarks on

working children were only his personal views and not neces-
sarily representative of Boston's stand on the issue, but his
audience automatically accepted them with approval because
he was the highest-ranking Scientist present. As Collson
scanned the upturned faces of the docile fold, her hope for
social reform through Science, a hope which had gradually
grown thin and frail, "gasped one last gasp, and expired."[41]

Even in her therapeutics, Collson finally withdrew to the
movement's outskirts, having come to admit that the orthodox
curist procedures had frequently been little more than a tedious
charade. It had become "the most slavish mental bondage" for
her "to sit hour after hour, meeting a procession of distressed or
suffering human beings" with nothing more to offer them than
the same specious remedy. In fact, she acknowledged, there
were times her mind grew so weary of attempting "the impossible" that it refused to travel in the prescribed grooves any
longer.Wandering off, it would play with such frivolous questions as what kind of lace trimming would best suit a certain
new petticoat. Horrified by such waywardness, she would then
be obliged to spend the remaining time set aside for the patient's problem in keeping her own thoughts in line. "I had
patients tell me," she wrote, "of practitioners who unmistakably
dozed off while giving a treatment, and I only hoped there was
no indirection in their comments."[42]

Since returning to Science in 1918 with a fiercely critical
eye, Collson had dealt with this problem by formulating her
own "key to the Scriptures," a personal credo that fit more or
less within the program of Christian Science therapy. This was
easy enough because, as Collson later quipped, Eddy Science
used biblical phrases "like small boys fly kites—the higher up
into the air they go, the better." She was able to use the standard
quotations to convey her own, genuine counsel.[43] Instead of
talking about a perfect Creator reflected in a perfect creation,
she advised her patients that since it was difficult to comprehend God's perfection, they would probably make better progress by simply trying to prove that God's power was greater than

that of the evil troubling them. The first step towards understanding the divine influence of God, she said, was to grasp that good was a real force in itself, and one which could overcome its opposite.

While the healer saw nothing really heretical in these teachings and was able to cite Eddy and scripture fluently to support them, other points in her version of Science were risky at best. For one thing, having stopped trying to find a useful definition of existence in some nebulous "perfect child of God," she was again teaching her clients what she had believed as a progressive Unitarian, that character constituted a person's only reality and made itself manifest in a material world. No longer pretending to regard the human condition as an illusion, she presented it as the only reality mortals could understand. "Here I was straining at my tether and was well aware of it," she confessed. However, her patients seemed to benefit from her approach, and their number increased.[44]

Actually, by dint of what she did not tell her clients at all but admitted only to herself, the therapist had already broken away from Eddy orthodoxy and entered the precincts of heresy. After suspecting it for years, she was now certain that demonstrations of healing did not depend upon the practitioner's spirituality or state of consciousness, but solely upon the patient's own attitude and will to believe. This position was antipodal to the practice of Christian Science, whose founder made clear that a patient's "awakening" from a problem depended ultimately on the curist's handling of it. Just as Jesus healed by seeing man as God's perfect likeness, so the modern metaphysician was said to effect cures by holding the right idea of her patients firmly in her mind. "If the *healer realizes* the truth," Eddy wrote, "it will free his patient." Her own italics reinforced the point.[45]

The accumulation of evidence to the contrary was overwhelming, however. Time and again, Mary Collson had seen individuals recover from serious physical ailments simply because they thought they were having Christian Science treatment, even when they were not. On one such occasion, a dying man who lived at some distance from Collson but had heard of her skill as a healer, wrote to ask her to take his case. She was swamped by work at the time, however, and wrote back that she would not be able to treat him herself, though another practitioner, whose name she enclosed, would be happy to do so. Collson's reply passed a second letter from the man informing her that he had already been marvelously healed, thanks to her metaphysical work. As the therapist later explained, "About the time he judged that I had received his letter he began to feel much better, and his improvement had progressed so rapidly that at the time he was writing . . . some two or three days later—he considered himself practically well."[46]

Nor did it appear that healing had much to do with the gender of treatment administered. Here Collson liked to tell of her elderly uncle, who was still alive and active in 1932, more than forty years after being healed of a "fatal" kidney disease. It seems that one day when he was well enough to be "up and poking about," he came across a bottle of Lydia Pinkham's Vegetable Compound in the medicine chest. He sampled it, thought it made him feel better, and disregarding its intended use as a tonic for "female complaints," continued to take it until he decided he was healed and fit to go back to work. "It would have been impossible for me," Collson wrote retrospectively, "to have remained in the professional practice of Christian Science for so long a time if a large number of people had not been physically benefitted and some quite remarkably healed through my ministrations. Yet it took me a long time to comprehend that the recovery of the sick does not prove that the method employed is a vital factor in the recovery."[47]

As a matter of fact, the metaphysician had discovered that loyal Christian Scientists were themselves "mixing methods" more and more. Indeed, quite early in its history Christian Science had started drifting away from a strict reliance on spiritual power in healing. In the late 1880s, Collson had heard of a child's broken arm healing improperly and becoming deformed because his Christian Science parents had not called in a physician. A few years later she met a deaf woman who spoke bitterly of the sect, blaming her loss of hearing on her parents' Scientific refusal to care for an ear infection she had had when she was a girl. The frequency of such incidents led Eddy to encourage proper sanitary precautions, the antiseptic cleansing of wounds, and a show of "practical wisdom" in the sickroom. It had also prompted a revision in her textbook stating that "it is better for Christian Scientists to leave surgery and the adjustment of broken bones and dislocations to the fingers of a surgeon," until such time as the "advancing age admits the efficacy and supremacy of Mind."[48] In due course, Eddy handed down a bylaw allowing practitioners to consult "with an M.D. on the anatomy involved" in cases not responding to Christian Science treatment.[49]

These concessions to material aids had proved capable of almost indefinite extension, as Collson had noticed, much to her disappointment, after the war. When she entered the healing profession, it was far from Scientific for a therapist's mental treatment to go hand-in-hand with surgical operations, but such cooperation had made significant inroads upon "legitimate practice" by the time she returned to the field in 1918. While Collson herself had never treated patients who also were receiving medical help, she had always thought lesser problems of her own, such as chapped hands and even weak eyes, should be disposed of materially without undue thought to avoid a waste of mental energy. Hence her recourse to cold cream and eyeglasses. By the late 1920s, however, she was feeling the sting of her own criticisms. She realized that her therapeutics were not as pure as she had once thought, and that her "experimental" practice of Science was as expedient and deviant as the straddling of spiritual and material therapies. She told herself that since she could not believe and practice the doctrines as taught, she must stop working under the Christian Science banner.

With this intention, Collson closed her Evansville practice in 1928 and set out to find some new kind of work. She wrote to

the Quaker's George A. Walton in Pennsylvania about the possibilities of developing, through the liberal churches, self-
improvement programs—like the Oxford movement, later
known as Moral Rearmament—to help people change the
world by changing themselves. Walton was interested enough
to correspond for over a year, but "nothing came of it" and
others dismissed the idea immediately. Jane Addams thought it
impractical and suggested newspaper work instead, and also
urged involvement in the Peace Party enterprise.[50]

When Collson went to Florida to visit her old mentor Eleanor
Gordon–who was now retired and living in the Orlando home
she had shared with Mary Safford until her death in 1927–she
was told that the outlook for women seeking liberal pulpits was
bleak. Gordon agreed with Addams that journalism might be
the best field to explore, and Collson therefore set out in that
direction. Without experience, however, the only offer she had
was a job writing inspirational columns for the *Key West Sun* at
a salary that would barely have paid for her paper. With Florida's economy depressed by the land boom's recent collapse,
jobs in all fields were scarce. But Collson enjoyed the state's
climate and the ocean and was eager to stay, so she settled in
Key West, where there was a small Christian Science community, and let it be known she was a qualified Eddy practitioner.

Though still devoted to her patients and glad to have a good
income again, Collson was not happy. She felt guilty practicing
under the banner of Christian Science, conscious that the
affiliation was nothing but sheer expediency and that it compromised her integrity. She longed for the spiritual buoyancy of
her early days as a convert and wished she could somehow turn
back the clock and become a believer again. It occurred to her
that things might have turned out differently if she had studied
under Annie Knott, as she first intended. The thought so took
hold of her that, as if to test its validity, she wrote Mrs. Knott a
letter, saying that she was coming to Boston to visit The Mother
Church and was eager to see her again. Knott, who now held a
seat on the powerful five-member Board of Directors, replied

that she would look forward to renewing the acquaintance and would welcome Collson as a guest at the upcoming annual meeting of her students.

Collson left for Boston hopeful that this reunion would realign her with the Eddy church and its teachings. But as it turned out, the trip dealt the death blow to her dream of reviving her faith. She found the student association meeting "very dull," and when she met with the teacher privately a few days afterwards, Alfred Farlow's name came up, and Collson realized that Knott had actually thrown her to the wolves without a thought thirty years earlier:

> It was [Knott] who had chosen [Farlow] to be my teacher, and now I could scarcely believe my ears when I heard her saying, "At the height of his popularity, I never had confidence in that man. He certainly was not a person I would ever go to for counsel or help." . . . I was very angry. Tears of resentment and disappointment ran down my cheeks that she could conceive I had forgotten her eulogistic commendation which had persuaded me to accept him as my teacher those many years before. I excused myself as best I could, and when I gained the hall-way, I spied a place behind a large fern where I could sit unobserved while I finished my crying. My anger turned to self-pity and I wept bitterly for the wasted years of my life. I, who started out with a sincere motive to do something useful, had devoted my life to deceit, sophistry, and mockery.
>
> I do not know how long I sat there weeping. It was bright sunshine outside, then twilight and dark before my sorrow for myself was spent and I felt an inflowing compassion for everybody who has a human life to live. I saw us all—the wise, the simple, the proud, the humble, the rich, the poor, the diplomatic, the rash, the patient, and the rebellious—all in an endless procession, stumbling, plodding, dancing, mincing, dragging, creeping, strutting along, in pathetic ignorance of what it all means.[51]

While she now felt certain that she had reached the end of her journey through Science, Collson resolved to act more deliberately than in the past and wait a year before severing all connections with the organization. She moved back to Boston, not far from The Mother Church, and spent this final probative period reviewing the structures of Eddyism and her career as a metaphysician. Dictated by a deep respect for human experience—and by the "mathematical intelligence" that had made Collson want proofs for stated truths since she first studied algebra and logic as a girl—the final verdict was that Christian Science was of no use whatsoever in solving human problems, for it impeded the development of those character traits most "essential to individual and social progress." Collson reaffirmed her belief that an honest empiricism was the only satisfactory approach to life "because Nature is intolerant of pretense."[52]

By working them out systematically, Collson found that all Christian Science statements were "a repetition of the equation, 'Divine Mind equals Divine Mind,' which . . . is mathematically provable since it may be read either forward or backward." But since patients were human beings seeking help in living lives humanly, not divinely, practitioners had to "trim and quibble and explain away the obvious in a continuous effort" that led to heartless "sophistry" and "self-deception."[53]

It was now 1931, with the country reeling under a savage depression. Collson could not imagine a time in the nation's history when there had been greater mental and physical suffering. Millions of Americans had lost their jobs and their savings, and breadlines had become a standard fixture in the cities. Collson herself had lost all but 5¢ on a dollar of what she kept in a Miami bank, while her sister's once prosperous family had lost everything. Many of her patients had also suffered financially and were sick with worry about the economy's toll on their children and their marriages. To "twist or conceal" facts like these through science was indefensible.[54]

It was only after Collson stopped trying to distort experience that she felt at peace with herself. "All the years that I was considered a successful Christian Science practitioner," she confessed, "I wrestled in vain with the treatment; for no human being was ever transfigured into 'a child of God' in my sight." She had only been able to "make believe" that earthly existence was an illusion. In fact, she had known all the time that she lived in a worldly environment.[55] No longer willing to falsify life to make the facts fit the formulae at the expense of those who asked for her comfort and guidance, Collson reclaimed her "trust in the greatness of the Creative Power which is working out some purpose in the universe." With this trust, she would strive to live in the physical world, among mortals, "as nobly and fearlessly as possible."[56]

On June 22, 1932, Mary Collson wrote to The Mother Church for the last time. She requested her name be dropped from the membership roll and explained why she wished to withdraw. "It is decidedly contrary to my worldly comfort to give up my work as a Christian Scientist," she said, "and I have been in this work for so long that I am not well prepared for any other occupation. Nevertheless, I cannot honestly remain in the work":

> I want to be free from all denominational connection, for just now I am more interested in economics than metaphysics. I find no satisfaction in my "personal 'peace, harmony, health and plenty.' " I no longer think I know the solution of the world's ills and I cannot pretend that I do. So kindly give me my freedom. . . . I never could understand the old orthodox theology which made people happy at the thought of eventually going to heaven tho millions were in hell.[57]

CHAPTER VIII

An Ongoing Ministry

The final chapter of Mary Collson's story was not a resolution of contradictory elements, but a recapitulation of familiar motifs. Collson's last twenty years found her still weaving back and forth between personal and public reformist avenues in pursuit of an elusive "all right world."[1] Her penchant for economics and sympathies with class struggles persisted, and as before, these were ultimately overridden by her compulsion for social order and whatever "makes for the continuity, progress and harmony of life as a whole."[2] Collson's Transcendental reverence and mystic sense of oneness with Nature's mysterious powers endured. But so did her scientist faith in evolutionary progress and man's eventual ability to fathom these higher forces of life, which were "ever creating [the] world anew . . . and developing a human character of greater spiritual strength, higher intelligence, and broader vision."[3]

Though the woman looked forward to the future as a new and exciting adventure when she moved back to Boston in June 1931, her first order of business was to write a book about her experiences with Eddyism. Unable to bear the thought that she had wasted half her life in the movement, she hoped to salvage the lost years by "setting forth . . . the lessons" she had learned "from thirty years' struggle with the Christian Science solution."[4]

Old friends encouraged her literary venture. Eleanor Gordon, delighted to hear she was finally free of her cultic connections, urged her to move ahead with her writing. Alice Hamilton, who was teaching nearby at Harvard's Medical School, also liked the plans for a book and offered to read chapters of the manuscript. Jane Addams sent the embryo author some of her own writing—the newly published collection of memorial addresses, *The Excellent Becomes the Permanent*—as a gesture of support. But of all the old friends, the most enthusiastic was Edward Meeman, whom Collson had met as a cub reporter in Evansville.

Now a successful Memphis newspaper editor, Meeman had turned away from socialism years before, renouncing it as too militaristic and "more sinister than the capitalists."[5] However, he had never broken free of Eddyism, which he also came to regard as "one of the worst of human systems." Not only had he found the strain of trying to be a Scientist enormous for "a fluid, imaginative person," but he regarded the doctrine's attempt to divide the whole of life into truth and error cruelly artificial and "really an awful blasphemy." After reading the outline and introductory chapter of Collson's "great confession," he realized (and told her) that the authority Christian Science assumed in his mind had been placed there almost entirely by his respect for her. Now that she had "broken with it and cast it overboard, the last lingering threads of its influence" over him were severed too. As a Catholic by birth, he had always been struck by the Eddyites' talk about Rome's awful hold over its communicants. For in his own experience after leaving Catholicism, he had never had either "the slightest desire to return" or the slightest fear for his soul if he did not, whereas Christian Science dogma had controlled much of his thinking even after he sought to reject it. "I was never comfortable in trying to conform [to Eddyism]," he confessed, "and until now, I was uncomfortable because I vaguely felt my life should be nearer the Boston pattern than it was."[6] Thanks to Mary Collson, he had returned to his natural attitude, "a clear-headed mysticism" which no longer outlined any specific beliefs. "I simply have a deep sense of the wonder and beauty of life, that my individual life has a meaning, that I must do all I can for human betterment . . . without regard to any pretended divine revelation."[7]

At the same time, Meeman was a practical man, whose thrift and good management had made him wealthy and saved more than one of his Scripps-Howard papers from bankruptcy. He doubted seriously that his friend could manage her venture financially. She herself had told him her savings had grown "rather lean," and that some of her relatives were still depending on her for a share of her "meager" resources.[8] Forced to economize, she had moved from a spacious flat in Boston's Back Bay to an attic apartment made over from servants' rooms in an old run-down Cambridge mansion. She assured Meeman she still lived comfortably, just a little more simply, and that the worn furnishings and old skylight in her present quarters gave her the delicious feeling of having "attained class as a literateur." But when she admitted to being afraid of having no way to help her family, Meeman insisted that she accept his financial backing while she worked on her manuscript.[9] "I gambled a thousand dollars on an invention once," he said. "This is much more interesting. . . . If you didn't take the money, somebody else would who would have far less to show for it."[10]

Anxious that her friend see some return on his investment, Collson went out to test the publishing waters as soon as she had finished her first chapter. The old Boston house of Little, Brown liked what they saw and asked for a finished manuscript by spring. Elated, the aspiring author wrote Meeman immediately. "Just think! they say my style is 'convincing and quotable.' They also say I am unusually fair and have a sense of humor which keeps my work 'from becoming arid.' They want 60,000 words and . . . think it advisable to stick to this and get it out."[11]

By mid-January Mary Collson had finished the section which dealt with her settlement work, and sent it off to Memphis for Meeman's reading. She asked him to pay close attention to the tone, as it had been difficult to maintain a light touch when dealing with such depressing material. Moreover, she knew that her attempts at being "artistic" were often undone by her desire to be convincing, by the same tendency she had to "bear on hard and rub it in" when she was talking with people.[12]

She sent a second copy to Alice Hamilton, and a third to Jane Addams, to be sure there was nothing "objectionable" in the presentation of Hull House. "Of course I have stated nothing but facts," she assured Addams in advance, "but perhaps [I] have not stated them in a proper light. I would not want to do anything that you did not approve of." She had made every effort, she added, not "to exploit" the Hull House director's fame, or to leave any doubt that she alone had been responsible for her actions.[13] When Addams' dovishness during the war caused the public to demote her from national heroine to national villain, Collson had been her constant defender. Indeed, she had come to regard the reformer's fall from grace as a glorious martyrdom, and more recently, her failing health as a symbol of all humanity's suffering.[14] "I have lived broader and deeper because I met you," she told Addams when she sent the manuscript, "and I could have said much more than I did.[15]

Collson's surge of productivity was interrupted in February when her eyes gave out and forced her to rest for almost two weeks. She took this setback philosophically, accepting the authority of natural law: "I have never in my life had more ideas I should like to develop," she wrote afterwards, "but regardless of the abundant life of the spirit, the machinery of the human body does give out. . . . For the privilege of accomplishing more I should wish to be younger, but I have looked over the whole field and even if it were possible I do not find one single year that I feel I could spare from my experience."[16]

Meanwhile, a far more distressing development had held up word from Jane Addams, as Dr. Hamilton explained in a letter from Chicago on March 1:

You will pardon my long delay when I tell you that I came on to Chicago ten days ago because of a serious heart attack Miss

Addams had had and when I arrived, found that Mary Smith was
also in bed, with bronchitis which changed to pneumonia and she
died on the 22nd. Miss Addams is still in a pretty critical condition
and the shock has been very great to her. She has made her home
here for many years and Mary has been her closest friend ever since
she came to Chicago. I am planning to stay on for the rest of the
year—till summer, I mean.

We both think that the pages you sent on are too detailed about
Hull House, that it makes the whole episode too long and . . . reads a
little like a defense and it is not needed. Moreover your book is not
really an autobiography, it has a thesis and the Hull-House part
must not be made too prominent.[17]

Collson made some revisions on her early chapters and
finished the last four by spring, even though toward the end she
was slowed by doubts that "such an analysis of C.S." as hers
would ever "be permitted expression." She confided to Meeman, "I had a compulsion to write it and could not do otherwise,
[but] the further I go the less confidence I have."[18] Her friend
assured her that the manuscript would find a publisher, though
the church's "elaborate system" of censorship might make it
hard to get the book sold.[19]

Anticipating the worst, Collson had tried to prepare her
defense by making the book "more constructive than destructive," and weeding out, as best she could, "any trace of resent-
ment or other meanness." She had also taken the precaution of
dropping two chapters which dealt iconoclastically with the
Founder and her "divine revelation." "My thesis is the doctrine,
and nothing is gained by discussing the origin of the
teachings," she reasoned; and to suggest that Mrs. Eddy's
"discovery" was derivative would certainly "arouse activity" on
the part of The Mother Church.[20]

Collson's fear of the Scientists' "dictatorship" in the publishing world seemed well-founded after Little, Brown rejected
the manuscript.[21] Although there were clearly many factors
involved in the decision, the author was sure that fear had been
overriding. "The C.S. Publication Committee must have some

quite terrifying weapon which they brandish over the heads of publishers," she thought. Hamilton offered to use her influence with Macmillan's, the firm that was publishing Addams' books, but Collson imagined that "it would be useless as Scribner's backed down with the Dakin book and Crowell and Co. . . . cut the vital features from the Dresser book."[22] Instead she accepted Meeman's offer to contact a friend at E.P. Dutton's. The newspaper man sent off a promotional letter predicting that Collson's story would be read avidly by all those thousands of people who had come into contact with Christian Science directly or indirectly, but remained mystified by the Eddy philosophy and regimen.[23] Within a week Dutton's had written back asking to see the manuscipt.

Collson was tremendously relieved to be free of the project, which months before had ceased to be an affordable luxury. Her savings were long since gone, and during the spring she had had to cash in a small insurance policy merely to pay for new glasses and meet her day-to-day expenses. Having sold most of her large collection of Christian Science books years before during one of her mental struggles with the doctrine, she now had nothing to pawn except her watch, a little furniture, some books, and a few other items. She had always had faith, she told Meeman, that she "would be of service to the end" and had trusted that her needs would be met.[24] "If times were normal," she pointed out, "I should do as I have previously done—try to find work in the field of unskilled labor." But times were not normal and many of the old roads to earning a living were no longer open to her. Younger unemployed people were scrambling for low level jobs—one Boston doctor was now a janitor, and a wireless operator was working as a chef—and older professionals like herself simply could not compete.[25] Miss Addams had earlier invited her to Hull House as a guest until she was "on her feet" again, but she had not accepted—for reasons she now conceded were "perhaps not practical ones"— so that opening, too, was closed.[26]

Despite her resilience in the past, Collson had begun to feel "illy equipped" to make her way in the real world after having spent half of her life "dilly dallying" in metaphysical pastures.[27] Her status as a practitioner had cut her off from practical experience and isolated her from other people generally. As Eddy metaphysicians, whose standing depended on the denial of all unpleasantness and the depreciation of human personality, she and her colleagues had "never honestly" talked about their problems with each other or formed the close friendships that grow from such exchanges. "There was no social life connected with the Christian Science church," she testified, "and I personally found my relation with other practitioners to be more competitive than cooperative." "We all [thought] alike and [talked] alike and only [vied] with one another in the precision of our yea, yea, and nay, nay, and our accuracy in repeating what the *Monitor* had to say about anything and everything."[28] Indeed, the lack of solidarity among the organization's women had so disappointed her feminist expectations of Science, that when she finally left the movement, she found she had no friend "to whom to say goodbye" outside of her own clientele. "The years I should have been gaining real strength by living a normal life in wholesome contact with the affairs of the world," she lamented, "I was indulging in pipe dreams of metaphysical intoxication."[29]

Meeman suggested his friend try to find a position with some Liberal church, perhaps even as an assistant pastor in a healing ministry. But Collson was now "quite weary of churches and the ways of the churches" and vowed she was "through with all organized religion." The Unitarians seemed to her to be "carrying on in a waning light" and receptive to very little innovation. "In the Middle West," she informed Meeman, "many are closed owing to finances, and here in the East they are open but empty for the most part. The Elliots, Lowells, Cabots, and Lodges still pay for pews they do not occupy except as a special favor conferred from time to time upon the highly appreciative pastor."[30]

As for mental healing, she went on, it was not "sufficiently dependable" to interest her any longer. She was well aware that there were "a few remarkable healings—both in C.S. and out— accomplished by some sort of psychic power."[31] Yet since mortals understood "practically nothing" about this power, it was absurd for them to think they had found the techniques for harnessing it:

> My sister was healed in 1886 and I have been somewhat in touch with the subject ever since. In those 50 years I have known of exactly two cases of healing of cancer which were definite cases in advanced form. The interminable number of cases that were treated and not healed is a tale of horror in my memory. In my later work I never took cancer cases—except for a few treatments— unless they had been given up by the doctors. Then I did my best to see what hope—or some other psychic factor, perhaps faith—might accomplish. It took me 30 years to see that we are too selfish and greedy and materialistic and primatively money-worshipping to succeed in utilizing the spiritual forces that surround us.[32]

Collson knew that she could rebuild a healing practice easily, for even as late as 1936 she still had old clients asking for help with their "personal troubles . . . largely . . . problems . . . involving sex."[33] But she vowed she was finished with mind cure, as such. "I realize I must be practical," she told Meeman, "but I see no reason for going at all if one goes backward and does something one no longer believes in."[34]

One of the goals Collson did still believe in was the reform of society through the scientific cultivation of its members' moral resources. "I see clearly that emphasis on human character is what the world needs," she told Addams in June, 1932.[35] As she argued in her book manuscript, the laws governing human instincts and passions operated just as consistently as the laws of physics, and by understanding these laws, people could eliminate those tendencies that impeded their progress and disrupted the social organization.[36] Since returning to Boston, she had been studying psychology, reading extensively in

Freud—whom she evidently found useful—and the behaviorists—whom she deplored—and attending lectures, to catch up on the developments she had missed while in Christian Science. After "two years at it," she was feeling "rather well informed and up-to-date" and qualified to help others "discipline and refine" their lives "in the midst of their material environment."[37] Psychology had always appealed to her, but since it was now a recognized branch of medicine with strict professional requirements and its own licensed practitioners, she had no expectations of being able to move into that field directly.

Rather, she hoped to earn her living writing a newspaper feature, which not only would enable her to continue conselling, but would greatly increase the number of people she reached. "I should enjoy a question and answer attachment," she told Meeman. "I am self-confident enough to believe that I could deal with human problems in a more modern manner than the Dorothy Dix column."[38] Her column, called "Profit and Loss," would show how "character and human socio-economic conditions" could work together to produce "a properly balanced individual . . . and an orderly social life." Newspaper editors were not interested, however, and by 1934 Collson had bitterly abandoned her hopes of teaching "character values" to the capitalists, "with their cherished idolatry of money!" Instead, she was preparing to take another course of action.[39]

Like many American liberals, Collson had watched the economy collapse with a sense, both disturbing and cheering, that capitalism was finished at last.[40] To be sure, the brand of socialism that had once attracted her and other Social Gospelers had lost its force of persuasion, having become almost indistinguishable from social reform, which in the present circumstances seemed useless. Galvanizing the liberals' rejection of the old reformism, Lincoln Steffens, John Chamberlain, and John Strachey delivered the compelling message that nothing but revolution could change the system now.[41] Revolution, however, was just the beginning. A new way of life lay beyond. Strachey presented the communist state as the fulfillment of the same collectivist dream which had so charmed liberals a decade earlier. It was, in his view, the only system that would enable all Americans to secure an adequate standard of living. To travel from capitalist to socialist territory would be to "pass from death to life," he proclaimed.[42] Strachey's millennial enthusiasm was shared by many intellectuals who had begun to think of Lenin as their deliverer and spoke of him in such salvationist terms as "the Christ of reality."[43] Mary Collson's position was that either Lenin or Gandhi would "be pronounced the Moses of these times," though she could not guess which one it would be.[44] In 1931, when Steffens had pointed the way with his declaration, "All roads in our day lead to Moscow," Collson was sorely tempted to take that direction. "I know I should join the communists if I could be a materialist," she said.[45] By September 1934, her idealism shattered, she had no reservations about following the throngs of disenchanted Americans who were trying to get work in Russia.[46]

Inclined to agree with many Protestant radicals that the Russians, for all their ungodliness, might well be laying "the foundations for a living Kingdom of God," Collson no longer felt that her mystical faith prevented her from embracing the Communist state.[47] If anything, the Soviet Union appeared to offer the very kind of communal society the Christian ideal demanded. As one churchman put it, Russia seemed "so fast to be developing a real human brotherhood under the name of social justice, that we Christian nations [might] one day find ourselves obliged to learn anew at Russia's feet the deeper meaning of the social teachings of Jesus."[48] Of course, Collson's recent renunciation of organized churches would make her move to communism much easier: "Now I have no religion that would offend," she said. "I care as little to talk of God as they do."[49] Embittered by the failure of American capitalism, and given to romanticizing the Soviets' egalitarian system, she saw the collective way of life as the only hope for the future now and wanted to become a part of it. "I was in such despair before this thought of Russia came to me," she told Meeman.[50]

Collson thought that once she was settled in Russia she would be able to "make a sort of living" as a newspaper correspondent. She figured she had about nine more years to live ("According to family inheritance—we are usually active to the end," she explained to Meeman), and was convinced that a move to the Soviet Union was her only hope for spending these final years productively. For more than a month she busied herself with working out the details. "I can go steerage and winter rates are much reduced," she noted. "I have about $80 and I held back some tapestry and my books—Britannica Enc. and Standard Dictionary—and a Seth Thomas clock—a good wardrobe trunk—and a few other things." She would keep her typewriter, of course, but otherwise would be perfectly willing to "live in a suitcase" the rest of her days.[51]

In taking stock of her assets, Collson also reckoned in her contacts with the Friends of Soviet Russia and communists on the staff of the *Daily Worker*. "I was a shareholder when [the paper] started," she reminded Meeman; "one of my old friends is still working for the Friends of S.R.. I am sure she will remember me. I protected her during the Red Raid of Mitchell and gave financial aid. Another member in New York I helped financially during a nervous breakdown. So I believe I could get into Russia and find a cheap place, if I can only get there."[52]

Meeman, who had no affection for the Left Wing's "illiberal liberals," set out at once to dismantle his old friend's "wild dream."[53] "There was not one chance in a thousand," he assured her, that she could find work in Russia, when thousands of idealistic Americans had already tried and failed. The Russians, he said, did not welcome foreigners who wanted to help them build their country. They thought they could do it by themselves, and they were probably right. "I think you are a dear for wanting to do such a bold, venturesome thing," he added, but when are you going to stop looking for panaceas?

You found that Christian Science was not [a cure all]. Life is not so simple as that."[54]

This patronizing rebuke would have smarted enough without enclosing a letter of rejection from Dutton's. The editor did not believe that Collson's book would ever find much of a readership and dismissed the author as a weak and self-pitying female who had squandered her life seeking escapes from reality. This estimate sounded enough like Meeman's to make the woman suspect its influence, and it aroused her to speak in her own defense.

"When I wrote you that I had whitewashed my C.S. experience," she answered Meeman, "I stated the truth, but positively *did not spare myself*, and that may partially account for the gentleman's judgment of my weakness and need of 'warmth' and 'comfort.' " She reminded her critic that she had omitted her exposé on "the Revelation"—although she fully believed that the Christian Science movement was "founded on deceit" and that "the *leaders know it*"—while for her part, she had not only faced up to her mistakes, but had sought to make them public for the benefit of others. "I am not whining," she thundered. "I am the heroine of my own adventures, and to borrow Browning's words . . . 'I saw them and I knew them all. And yet / Dauntless the slug-horn to my lips I set, / And blew.' "[55]

As for the trip to Russia, Collson wanted Meeman to know that he had again underestimated her: "I really am a most unfortunately keen sleuth when it comes to propaganda," she reminded him. "I would be a successful lady in life if it were not for this fatal gift. I had no interest in taking a mere trip as a tourist. I was hoping to take the trip as a means of getting in." That issue, however, was now moot. She had been unable to get a visa for more than thirty days, and was reconciled to her defeat by reports that foreign correspondents could no longer get inside news since "everyone was afraid to talk."[56]

Alice Hamilton was much more sensitive to Collson's situation and was quick to comfort her friend. She assured her that Dutton's letter was "absurd and shallow" and had missed the crucial point that one's religious evolution was never complete as long as one lived. Hamilton also helped Collson get some financial footing by finding her a job on the social service end of the state's Emergency Relief Administration. The work was often depressing, but it was also "intensely informative" and Collson claimed she was "grateful" to be back "in touch with facts and reality." She would continue to write what she considered "real ethics" in her spare time, preferring to go unpublished than to dish up the kind of unwholesome pap that was weakening society's moral fiber. "I have an obligation," she told Meeman, "to hold on to my ideals, even in direst defeat. I cannot sacrifice my intelligence to keep my body comfortable."[57]

For a while, the fact that a few paying clients from Collson's old practice still came to her kept alive an interest in getting a job as a psychiatric assistant to private physicians. However, this scheme was also defeated by the economy, which forced most doctors to cut corners and do their own psychiatric therapy. Moreover, though Collson had come to appreciate the value of material treatment for the ill and was eager to ally herself with the medical profession, she now found herself at odds with much of the current psychology, whose views on sex seemed plainly "vicious" to her. She deplored the notion that sexual activity was essential "for balance" and feared this "perversion of the reproductive function" would do awful damage to coming generations.

"I am well aware of the 'behaviorists' theory of the feelings," she declared, "and utterly repudiate them." She considered it far more important "to learn how to act like human beings than . . . to know *why* we act like beasts," more useful "to study 'cases' of sex victims than to vivisect rats and rabbits, dogs and monkeys." "I still believe that Jesus was a virile, vital personality and he did not need to turn all his female acquaintances into prostitutes to maintain his manhood," she told Meeman. "I think the higher feelings of conscience and a longing for the higher satisfactions that accompany a sincere enjoyment of making life worthwhile are the characteristics of man as a human being."[58]

Despite Collson's idealistic faith and determination, survival was no easy feat for her. For one thing, it was nearly impossible to wrest an existence from the four-dollar weekly welfare payments allowed single women. Then, too, the physical and psychological stress of her jobs with the E.R.A., and later the W.P.A., turned out to be more than a woman of her age and constitution could weather. While serving tours of duty in adult education programs and vacation camps for the elderly, her health broke down repeatedly, and she then had to live on a reduced stipend until she could go back to work, "doing what she had to do and trying to like it."[59]

For a time, her situation made her bitter. She missed the good life, with its material comforts and social position, and when Meeman, who enjoyed both, once inquired how she was spending her time, she shot back, "You speak as though I were doing something of my own choice." When he sent her a book on Christian socialism, she told him testily, "Don't send me any more such reading matter—send me flowers. . . . Despite what some taxpayers think, the welfare does not supply us with violets. . . . I love flowers. I love all the pretty fine things of life." The Community Church she sometimes attended frequently had Christian socialists as speakers, she said, and the last time she had heard one speak, she had had to get up and leave. "His talk was so trifling to one who, trying to be truly honest, has landed on . . . welfare. . . . Those of us on the dole," she reminded the well-to-do newspaperman, "are beginning to form a sort of class by ourselves."[60]

In time, however, the bitterness passed. Because of her delicate health—"a doctor's report which I daily defy," she called it—and her "love of mental freedom," she accepted Old Age Assistance and a disability pension from the state. A Unitarian women's group and the Juvenile Court in Chicago remembered her services in the past and also gave her small allowances. Once again she was as willing to talk about God as about economics. At the age of seventy-seven, as she looked back at the Great Depression, she was as grateful to "the Creator" as to F.D.R. that she had been taken care of "so wonderfully." "I have never lacked food, shelter, or necessary clothing," she testified; and "like Diogenes I can say that it gives me pleasure to see how many things there are in this world that I can get along without and be satisfied, contented and happy."[61]

Her hostility toward Christian Science and disillusionment with mind cure also dissolved, and she returned to her Transcendentalist faith in spiritual forces and a philosophical appreciation of people like Mary Baker Eddy, who had tried to utilize them. Although she had "no desire for close association with C. Scientists" and could not bring herself "to even think of Church membership," she often walked the several blocks from the row house in which she lived in her last years to sit in the reception room of the Eddyites' Publishing House. As she watched the faithful come and go and pondered her kinship to them, she felt "a sense of unity" with "their efforts to find the living God," but also vast differences in their "attitudes of mind" and "conceptions of certainty and finality." For having been reared on Emerson and Plato, she knew that Eddyism was not a new and final revelation as it claimed, but only a restatement and fresh application of old truth.

More importantly, after spending most of her long life studying so-called "revelations," Collson was sure that nothing but faith in a power beyond oneself could ever sustain or uplift a human being. "The reason so many of us Christian Scientists were a flop as Christians," she concluded, was that "we thought we could read and be *instructed* into Truth instead of *living* our individual ways into a consciousness of God."[62] While institutional reform had come to seem remote, she believed as firmly in her old age as in her youth that one could progress individually through constructive, human relationships and loving service to humanity.

Mary Collson's last home was "a very pleasant room" looking out on a courtyard filled with trees. She had a young woman who did errands for her, and kindly, caring neighbors. Yet while her own lot had "altogether fallen in pleasant places," her ease was disturbed by the knowledge that "man's inhumanity to man" continued to make the world unbearable for a great many others. So it was that in 1952, while Americans fought in Korea, Mary Collson, now in her eighties and just months away from her final illness, continued to carry forward her ministry. She was doing what she could "in collecting clothing" to send to war victims abroad, and she tried to lift the sights of the younger generations by sharing with them the New England vision that had proved the bedrock of her reformist faith. "I find comfort in Whittier's poem 'My Triumph,' " she told Meeman in her last letter, and then, in a hand still strong and firm, she copied out these verses:

Let the thick curtain fall;
I better know than all
How little I have gained,
How vast the unattained.

Others shall sing the song,
Others shall right the wrong,—
Finish what I begin,
And all I fail of win. . . .

The airs of heaven blow o'er me;
A glory shines before me
Of what mankind shall be,—
Pure, generous, brave, and free.

A dream of man and woman
Diviner but still human,
Solving the riddle old,
Shaping the Age of Gold![63]

Notes

ABBREVIATIONS

AESL The Arthur and Elizabeth Schlesinger Library at Radcliffe College

AMA Archives of The Mother Church, First Church of Christ, Scientist, Boston

AUA American Unitarian Association Papers, Andover Library, Harvard Divinity School

CHS Chicago Historical Society

HHP Hull House Papers, University of Illinois at Chicago Circle

JPA Juvenile Protective Association Papers, University of Illinois at Chicago Circle

MTSL Meadville-Lombard Theological School Library and Archives, Chicago

MVC Mississippi Valley Collection, Memphis State University

SCPC Swarthmore College Peace Collection

SHSI State Historical Society of Iowa, Iowa City

UHA Universalist Historical Society Papers, Andover Library, Harvard Divinity School

UUA Unitarian Universalist Association Papers, Archives of the UUA, Boston

CHAPTER I

1. Mary Collson, "My Search for an All Right World," p. 21, MVC.

2. The term is used by Henry Nash Smith in *Virgin Land: The American West as Symbol and Myth* (Cambridge, 1950). Glenda Riley describes the trans-Mississippi migration and Iowa's frontier promotionalism in *Frontierswomen: The Iowa Experience* (Ames, Iowa, 1981), pp. 3–28.

3. A. D. Bicknell, "S. H. Taft: A Sketch," *Old and New* 14 (1906), p. 33.

4. Rev. Stephen H. Taft, *The History of Humboldt, Iowa: A Semi-Centennial Address Given . . . on the 11th Day of September, 1913* (Humboldt, Iowa, 1934), n.p.

5. As Julie Ray Jeffrey points out—in *Frontier Women: The Trans-Mississippi West, 1840–1880* (New York, 1979), pp. 28–29—"though family situations differed, all emigrants had to be financially solid enough" to raise the cash for the trip, and relocation, as the risks of attempting this with too little money were high.

6. See e.g., *History of Kossuth and Humboldt Counties, Iowa* (Springfield, Ill., 1884).

7. Mary Collson to Jane Addams, June 17, 1932, SCPC.

8. Collson, "My Search," p. 46.

9. Ibid., p. 96.

10. Ibid., pp. 2, 50–52. In *The Reproduction of Motherhood* (Berkeley, 1978), Nancy Chodorow argues that the early experience of being cared for by a mother produces daughters who themselves turn their energies toward nurturing. For an excellent review of recent scholarship on the effect of mothering on daughters, see Judith K. Gardiner, "The New Motherhood," *North American Review* 263 (Fall 1978): 72–76.

11. Riley illuminates the hardships of Iowa's pioneer homemakers in her chapter on "Women's Workplaces." *Frontierswomen*, pp. 29–55.

12. Mary Collson to Jane Addams, June 17, 1932, SCPC.

13. Collson, "My Search," p. 7.

14. Mary Collson to Jane Addams, June 17, 1932, SCPC; Collson, "My Search," p. 7.

15. Mary Collson to Jane Addams, June 17, 1932, SCPC.

16. Collson, "My Search," p. 81.

17. *Unity* 18 (1887), p. 264.

18. Eleanor E. Gordon, *The Second Chapter of a Long Story* (Humboldt, Iowa, 1934), p. 1.

19. Charles D. Cashdollar, "European Positivism and the American Unitarians," *Church History* 45 (Dec. 1976), p. 493.

20. Gordon, *The Second Chapter*, p. 3.

21. See William Leach's sketch of Dall's career in *True Love and Perfect Union: The Feminist Reform of Sex and Society* (New York, 1980), pp. 278–279.

22. Clara C. Helvie, "Unitarian Women Ministers" (Boston, 1929), p. 19, UHS.

23. George Willis Cooke, *Unitarianism in America* (Boston, 1902), pp. 283–284. This attitude is also documented by Charles H. Lyttle in *Freedom Moves West: A History of the Western Unitarian Conference, 1852–1952* (Boston, 1952), pp. 146–149.

24. *Star in the West*, Feb. 8, 1868. Cited by Catherine F. Hitchings, *Universalist and Unitarian Women Ministers* (Boston, 1975), pp. 4–5.

25. *Unity* 3 (1879), p. 107.

26. Gordon, *The Second Chapter*, p. 1.

27. See Carroll Smith-Rosenberg, "The Female World of Love and Ritual: Relations Between Women in Nineteenth Century America," *Signs* 1 (Autumn 1975), esp. pp. 16–17.

28. *Unity*, 3 (1879), p. 122.

29. Amelia Murdock Wing briefly mentions her work in Humboldt in "Early Days in Clayton County," *The Annals of Iowa*, 3rd ser. 27 (April 1946), p. 288.

30. Rev. Florence Buck, *Cleveland Sun and Voice*, June 17, 1894.

31. Collson, "My Search," pp. 1–2.

32. *History of Kossuth and Humboldt Counties*, p. 798.

33. *Woman's Journal* 4 (1872), p. 10.

34. Gordon, *The Second Chapter*, p. 4; Collson, "My Search," p. 10.

35. A list of the ten novels Gordon considered the "noblest available to English readers" was recommended to Unity clubs when it appeared in *Unity* 13 (1884), p. 229. Leach shows how this "affection for George Eliot . . . attested to the strength" of positivistic influence on feminists' thinking. *True Love*, p. 156.

36. Mary Collson to Jane Addams, June 17, 1932, SCPC.

37. Collson, "My Search," p. 22.

38. Gordon, *The Second Chapter*, p. 2.

39. *Unity*, 13 (1884), p. 134.

40. Gordon, *The Second Chapter*, p. 7.

41. *Old and New* 8 (Feb. 1900), p. 5.

42. *Old and New* 3 (March 1893), n.p.

43. *Old and New* 1 (Feb. 1892), n.p.

44. *Unity* 13 (1884), p. 134; Helvie, passim.

45. *Unity* 13 (1884), p. 134.

46. Gordon, *The Second Chapter*, p. 6.
47. Eleanor E. Gordon to Jenkins Lloyd Jones, March 3, 1897, MTSL.
48. Theodore Parker had so revered womanhood that he made it a necessary element of divinity, and prayed publicly to a Father and Mother God. Emerson credited women with a spirituality unattained by men, while Hawthorne expected the coming revelation to be heralded by a woman.
49. Hitchings, *Women Ministers*, pp. 3–4.
50. Safford denounced the plan in a letter written to *The Christian Register* and published in *Old and New* 15 (March 1907), p. 6.
51. Gordon, *The Second Chapter*, p. 6.
52. Collson, "My Search," pp. 21–22.
53. In an unpublished reminiscence entitled "Rainbows I Have Seen," MVC, p. 4, Collson explains that her parents, who moved to Iowa from New York State and apparently honeymooned at the Falls, had a picture of Niagara hanging in their home.
54. Eleanor Gordon to Jenkins Lloyd Jones, Aug. 30, 1900, MTSL.
55. Wing, "Clayton County," pp. 273–274, 281–282.
56. Eleanor E. Gordon, *A Little Bit of a Long Story for the Children* (Humboldt, Iowa, 1934), pp. 10–12.
57. Allen F. Davis, *American Heroine: The Life and Legend of Jane Addams* (New York, 1973), p. 29.
58. Quoted by Mari Jo Buhle in *Women and American Socialism, 1870–1920* (Urbana, Ill., 1981), p. 65.
59. *Old and New* 9 (Sept. 1900), p. 8.
60. Eleanor Gordon to Jenkins Lloyd Jones, March 3, 1897, MTSL.
61. Gordon, *The Second Chapter*, p. 6.
62. *Old and New* 1 (Dec. 1891), p. 6.
63. The quotation is from one of Safford's sermons, reprinted in *Old and New* 4 (May 1895), p. 6.
64. From an article in *The Outlook*, reprinted in *Old and New* 4 (May 1895), p. 5.
65. *Old and New* 10 (Nov. 1901), p. 7.
66. *Unity* 19 (1887), p. 283.

CHAPTER II
1. *Suggestions Respecting Improvements in Education* (Hartford, 1829), p. 46.

2. Mary Collson, "My Search for an All Right World," p. 23.

3. See William Leach on feminism and coeducation, in *True Love and Perfect Union: The Feminist Reform of Sex and Society* (New York, 1980), pp. 78–80.

4. Robert E. Belding, "Iowa's Brave Model for Women's Education," *Annals of Iowa* 43 (1976): 347–348; *The Spectator*, University of Iowa Alumni Association pub., Oct. 1978, p. 8.

5. University of Iowa *1895–96 Bulletin*, p. 84.

6. Collson, "My Search," p. 24.

7. Records of the Iowa City Unitarian Church, SHSI; Collson file, UUA.

8. Records of the Iowa Zeta chapter of Pi Beta Phi, Iowa City.

9. Collson, "My Search," p. 24.

10. Ibid., p. 31.

11. Eleanor E. Gordon, *The Second Chapter of A Long Story* (Humboldt, Iowa, 1935), p. 2.

12. University of Iowa, *1895–96 Bulletin*, pp. 36–38; *1896–97 Bulletin*, pp. 42–43.

13. Collson, "My Search," pp. 30–31.

14. Lester Frank Ward, *Dynamic Sociology* (New York, 1883), 2: 159; Lester Frank Ward, "Sociology and Economics," *Annals of the American Academy of Political and Social Science* 13 (March 1899), p. 233.

15. See Leach on social science as women's work, pp. 316–318.

16. Collson, "My Search," p. 30. Italics are mine.

17. Ibid., pp. 122, 131. Collson's remarks, from a paper on the value of the church's Young People's Religious Union, appeared in *Old and New* 5 (Dec. 1896), p. 5.

18. See Francis A. Christie, *The Makings of the Meadville Theological School, 1844–1894* (Boston, 1927).

19. Rev. Marian Murdock, "Women at Meadville," an address at the Semi-Centennial of the Meadville Theological School, June 1894, MTSL.

20. Meadville Theological School *Bulletin, 1897–1889*, MTSL.

21. Collson, "My Search," p. 24.

22. G. S. Garfield, "What I Like to Hear from the Pulpit," delivered at Ida Grove in Nov. 1897 and reprinted in *Unity* 41 (1898), pp. 42–43.

23. *Unity* 41 (1898), pp. 156–157.

24. In a letter "from the field," published in *Unity* 42 (1898), p.

216, Collson wrote that she had heard many similar reports recently at the Omaha Congress on Liberal Religions and had come back from the meetings with a better appreciation of Kipling's words, "The cub he is small. Let him think and be still."

25. Mary Collson to Rev. Samuel A. Eliot, secretary, American Unitarian Association, Nov. 7, 1898, AUA; Collson, "My Search," p. 25.

26. *Old and New*, 6 (Dec. 1897), p. 346.

27. Collson, "My Search," p. 25.

28. Ibid., p. 35.

29. See Barbara Welter's discussion of "The Cult of True Womanhood, 1820–1860," in *American Quarterly* 18 (1966): 151–174.

30. As Joan Jacob Brumberg points out, missionary work offered many evangelical women the opportunity to show their competence, use their skills, and enlarge the perimeters of their lives. Yet by learning of female mistreatment in non-Christian cultures and seeing themselves in relation to their heathen sisters abroad, America's orthodox churchwomen came to minimize the inequities they suffered in their own culture and more cheerfully accepted the subjugation that marked their True Womanhood. See Brumberg's chapter on "The Apostolate of Women," in *Mission for Life* (New York, 1980), pp. 79–105.

31. Collson, "My Search," p. 25.

32. *Unity* 42 (1898), pp. 39–40.

33. Mary Collson to Jenkin Lloyd Jones, Jan. 24, 1898, MTSL.

34. Mary Collson to Edward Meeman, n.d. (circa Sept. 1934), MVC; Mary Collson to Edward Meeman, Oct. 11, 1934, MVC.

35. See Carroll Smith-Rosenberg, "The Hysterical Woman: Sex Roles and Role Conflict in Nineteenth Century America," *Social Research* 39 (1972), pp. 652–678.

36. *Unity* 41 (1898), p. 192.

37. Clara C. Helvie, "Unitarian Women Ministers" (Boston, 1929), UHS, *passim*.

38. See Donald Meyer, *The Positive Thinkers* (New York, 1965), pp. 28–41.

39. Collson, "My Search," p. 26.

40. Eleanor E. Gordon to Dr. Frederick May Eliot, president, American Unitarian Association, March 25, 1899, AUA.

41. Caroline Dall, *College, Market, and Court*, Memorial ed. (New York, 1914), pp. 233–236.

42. Helvie, "Unitarian Women Ministers," p. 100.

43. *Unity* 44 (1899), p. 447.

44. Addams was one of more than sixty "eminent educators" who were currently lecturing throughout the "North Central West" under the auspices of the University of Chicago's Extension Division.

45. Allen F. Davis, *American Heroine: The Life and Legend of Jane Addams* (New York, 1973), p. 103; *Unity* 42 (1898), pp. 39–40.

46. *Unity* 45 (1900), pp. 262–264.

47. *Unity* 45 (1900), p. 302.

CHAPTER III

1. On the roster were Jane Addams, Ellen Starr, Julia Lathrop, Florence Kelley, Enella Benedict, Rose Gyles, Miss Brockway, Maud Gernon, Eleanor Smith, Alice Hamilton, Mrs. Cronk, Sarah Hill, Gertrude Howe, Edith de Nancrede, Amelia Hannig, Clara Landsberg, Mr. and Mrs. Allessandro Mastro-Valerio, George Hooker, Frederick Deknatel, Robert Hunter, and George Twose. HHP.

2. Mary Collson, "My Search for an All Right World," p. 35.

3. For a profile of the settlement workers as a group, see Allen F. Davis, *Spearheads for Reform: The Social Settlements and the Progressive Movement, 1890–1914* (New York, 1967), pp. 26–39.

4. Collson, "My Search," p. 27.

5. Vivid accounts of the early development and activities of the Juvenile Court can be found in Sara L. Hart's *The Pleasure is Mine* (Chicago, 1947), pp. 95–105; Julia C. Lathrop's "The Background of the Juvenile Court in Illinois"; and Mrs. Joseph T. Bowen's "The Early Days of the Juvenile Court" in *The Child, the Clinic and the Court* (New York, 1925), pp. 290–297, 298–309. The entire Feb. 1901 number of *The Commons* was also devoted to reports on juvenile delinquency, dependency, and rehabilitation in Chicago.

6. Annals of the Chicago Woman's Club, p. 189, CHS.

7. "Report of a Committee, 1912: The Juvenile Court of Cook County, Ill.," p. 31, CHS; Hart, *The Pleasure is Mine*, p. 133.

8. Bowen, "Juvenile Court," p. 300.

9. Edith J. Clarke, "Juvenile Delinquency and Dependency: Report of Inquiry at Chicago," *The Commons* 6 (1901) pp. 3–4.

10. Richard S. Tuthill, "The Chicago Juvenile Court," *Proceedings of the Annual Congress of the National Prison Association* (Philadelphia, 1902), p. 121. Quoted by Anthony Platt in *The Child Savers:*

The Invention of Delinquency, 2nd ed. (Chicago and London, 1977), p. 144.

11. *Hull-House Bulletin* 4 (Jan.-May 1901), p. 12.

12. Collson, "My Search," p. 37.

13. Case Studies—Supplement I, folder 9 (Nov. 1899–Aug. 1901), JPA. As required by law, last names have been omitted. Hereafter, numbers in parentheses refer to casebook pages.

14. *The Chicago Tribune*, Nov. 13, 1900, p. 7.

15. Chicago Woman's Club, *Club Meetings 1900–1901*, pp. 222–223, CHS. In *The Child Savers*, Platt indicts the juvenile court movement for this Romantic overlay.

16. Collson, "My Search," p. 31.

17. Ibid., pp. 28–29.

18. Ibid., p. 29.

19. The episode is recounted by Robert L. Reed in "The Professionalism of Public School Teachers: *The Chicago Experience, 1895–1920*," Ph.D. diss., Northwestern University, 1968.

20. Collson, "My Search," pp. 29–30.

21. Ibid., p. 31.

22. Alice Hamilton, *Exploring the Dangerous Trades* (Boston, 1943), p. 80.

23. Ibid.

24. Mary Collson, "The Damaged Picnic," MVC.

25. Mary Collson to Edward Meeman, undated (c. Sept. 1934), MVC.

26. Collson, "My Search," p. 30.

27. *Hull House Bulletin* 4 (Spring 1901).

28. Collson, "My Search," p. 33.

29. Mary Collson to Edward Meeman, May 5, 1936, MVC.

30. Collson, "My Search," p. 33.

31. For a good account of the socialists' campaign strategy, ideological disputes, and efforts towards unification during the period of Collson's involvement, see Ira Kipnis, *The American Socialist Movement, 1897–1912* (New York, 1952), pp. 93–106.

32. H. Augusta Howard, "Woman Considered as a Human Being," *Social Democratic Herald*, Dec. 29, 1900, p. 3.

33. Kipnis discusses the attitude towards women in the movement at the turn of the century, pp. 261–265. Also see James Weinstein, *The*

Decline of Socialism in America, 1912–1925 (New York, 1969), pp. 53–62.

34. Mary Collson to Edward Meeman, May 5, 1936, MVC.

35. See Mary A. Hill's account of Gilman's association with Hull House in *Charlotte Perkins Gilman: The Making of a Radical Feminist, 1860–1896* (Philadelphia, 1980), pp. 272–281.

36. Mari Jo Buhle's study of *Women and Socialism, 1870–1920* (Urbana, Ill., 1981), discusses the divergent responses of the immigrant women and native-born, middle-class feminists to the socialist programs.

37. Here Collson was taking her text from May Walden Kerr's *Socialism and the Home* (Chicago, n.d.), pp. 30–31.

38. Collson, "My Search," p. 35.

39. Ibid., p. 36.

40. Mary Collson to Edward Meeman, n.d. (c. Sept. 1934), MVC. Collson's frequent impatience with the gentle *mater familias* haunted the former resident in later years. She repeatedly expressed remorse for her lack of gratitude at the time and told Addams how much her love and appreciation had grown. See Mary Collson to Jane Addams, Jan. 12, 1911; June 2, 1932; Jan. 20, 1934; DG1 Series, Box 13, SCPC.

41. Collson, "My Search," pp. 37–38.

42. *The Workers' Call* April 20, 1901, p. 4.

43. Collson, "My Search," pp. 38–39.

44. Ibid., n.p. (fragment for Chapter 2).

45. Eleanor Gordon to Jenkin Lloyd Jones, Aug. 30, 1900, MTSL.

46. Eleanor Gordon to Jenkin Lloyd Jones, Sept. 26, 1900, MTSL.

47. Collson, "My Search," p. 46.

CHAPTER IV

1. Allen F. Davis, *Spearheads for Reform: the Social Settlements and the Progressive Movement* (New York, 1907), pp. 29–33.

2. Charlotte Perkins Gilman to George Houghton Gilman, May 15, 1900, AESL. See Mary Hill, *Charlotte Perkins Gilman: The Making of a Radical Feminist, 1860–1896* (Philadelphia, 1980), pp. 280–281.

3. In the first sixteen months of the court's operation, Richard S. Tuthill, Judge of the Court, found it "impossible to secure persistent service [of probation officers] without the payment of a reasonable compensation for the services rendered." "As matters now stand," he

reported— in *The Commons* 55 (Feb. 1901), p. 8—"the number of probation officers is totally inadequate for carrying on the work."

4. Mary Collson, "My Search for an All Right World," pp. 30, 40.

5. Thomas N. Bonner, *Medicine in Chicago, 1850–1950* (Madison, Wisc., 1957), p. 205.

6. Bradford Sherman's *Historical Sketch of the Introduction of Christian Science in Chicago and the West* (Chicago, 1912) is worth looking at, but not readily available. The Library of Congress has a copy in its rare book room. Robert Peel describes the activity among the Scientists in Chicago in *Mary Baker Eddy: The Years of Authority* (New York, 1977), *passim*.

7. Warren Felt Evans' *The Mental Cure* (Boston, 1869) was followed by *Mental Medicine* (Boston, 1872), *Soul and Body; or The Spiritual Science of Health and Disease* (Boston, 1876), *The Divine Law of Cure* (Boston, 1881), *Healing by Faith; or Primitive Mind Cure* (London, 1885), and *Esoteric Christianity and Transcendental Medicine* (Boston, 1886). The mind cure movement is traced by Donald Meyer in *The Positive Thinkers* (New York, 1965) and by Gail Parker in *Mind Cure in New England* (Hanover, N.H., 1973).

8. Dr. H. Neill, who came to practice in Iowa in 1875, made this observation based on his own training at the University of Michigan Medical School, "which was above average in its requirements." "Taken as a whole," he conceded, "we pioneer doctors were a rotten lot." Quoted by William J. Petersen in "Diseases and Doctors in Pioneer Iowa," *IJH* 49 (April 1951), p. 115.

9. Collson, "My Search," p. 8; see Richard H. Shryock's chapter on "The Popular Health Movement" in *Medicine in America* (Baltimore, 1966); and Joseph Kett's discussion of lay healers in nineteenth-century America in *The Formation of the American Medical Profession* (New Haven, 1968). Glenda Riley, in *Frontierswomen: The Iowa Experience* (Cedar Rapids, Iowa, 1981), p. 77, discusses the frontierswoman's role as a medical paraprofessional.

10. In *The Religion of New England* (Boston, 1926), pp. 171–176, the Unitarian cleric Thomas Van Ness makes this point to explain the appealing facets of Christian Science that prompted him to investigate the movement in the late 1880s. See Donald Meyer's discussion of mind cure's indebtedness to Emerson in *The Positive Thinkers* (New York, 1965), pp. 79–81, and Parker, *Mind Cure*, pp. 5–6.

11. Major biographies of Mary Baker Eddy include the church's

"authorized" study by Sybil Wilbur, *The Life of Mary Baker Eddy* (New York, n.d.); *Mary Baker Eddy*, 3 vols. (New York, 1966 [*The Years of Discovery*], 1971 [*The Years of Trial*], 1977 [*The Years of Authority*]) by The Mother Church archivist, Robert Peel; Georgine Milmine's revealing and uncomplimentary *The Life of Mary Baker Eddy and the History of Christian Science* (New York, 1909); and Edwin Dakin's bitter, but thoroughly researched *Mrs. Eddy: The Biography of a Virginal Mind* (New York, 1929).

12. Mary Baker Eddy, *Retrospection and Introspection*, 1st ed. (Boston, 1891), p. 45.

13. Mary Baker Eddy, *Science and Health with Key to the Scriptures* (Boston, 1910), p. 468.

14. Collson, "My Search," p. 10.

15. See Raymond J. Cunningham, "The Impact of Christian Science on the American Churches, 1880–1910," *American Historical Review* 72 (1967), pp. 887–895.

16. *Christian Science Journal* 5 (March 1888), p. 388.

17. *Unity*, 44 (1899), p. 499.

18. *Old and New* 6 (1897), pp. 293–294.

19. Collson, "My Search," p. 41.

20. Ibid., pp. 102–103.

21. Eddy, *Science and Health*, p. 448.

22. Letter from C. Lewis Lawrence, *Christian Science Journal* 22 (1904), pp. 312–313.

23. Collson, "My Search," pp. 33, 142, 20.

24. Ibid., p. 33.

25. Ibid., pp. 45–46.

26. Safford's report as state missionary appeared in *Old and New* 10 (Sept. 1901), p. 1.

27. *Old and New* 10 (Dec. 1901), passim.

28. Gordon's paper on "The Ethical Implications of the Organic Theory of Society" was printed in *Old and New* 10 (Nov. 1901), p. 2.

29. *Old and New* 8 (Nov. 1899), pp. 5–6. More recently, Iowa Unitarian ministers had addressed the problem of Christian Science and "other outbursts of enthusiasm" trying to recruit their liberal members and were advised to encourage more study of such pillars of the faith as Martineau, Emerson, Channing, and Parker. *Old and New* 9 (April 1901), p. 3.

30. Collson, "My Search," p. 49.

31. Ibid., pp. 53–54.
32. Ibid., pp. 54–55.
33. Ibid., p. 27.
34. The response of the Hull House Woman's Club to a talk by a Christian Scientist—as recounted by Ray Ginger in *Altgeld's America* (Chicago, 1965), p. 129—was probably typical. As Ginger tells the story, the speaker concluded her presentation by suggesting that the next time the group smelled the stench from the river nearby they "declare the truth that it really smelled sweet. To this a German matron replied, "Vell . . . dere must be something de matter with dot woman's nose," and the club members "roared with approval."
35. Rev. Amzi Dixon, *Is Christian Science a Humbug?* (Boston, 1901), pp. 21, 25.
36. Collson, "My Search," p. 55.
37, Ibid., pp. 55–56.

CHAPTER V
1. Donald Meyer, *The Positive Thinkers*, (New York, 1965), p. 72. Also see Carroll Smith-Rosenberg's "The Hysterical Woman: "Sex Roles and Role Conflict in 19th Century America," *Signs* 1 (Autumn 1975): 1–29, and J. S. Haller and Robin M. Haller's *The Physician and Sexuality in Victorian America* (Urban, Ill., 1974).
2. See William Leach, *True and Perfect Union: The Feminist Reform of Sex and Society* (New York, 1980), pp. 171–172; and Regina Morantz, "The 'Connecting Link:' The Case for the Woman Doctor in Nineteenth Century America," in *Sickness and Health in America*, eds. Judith Leavitt and Ronald Numbers (Madison, Wisc. 1978), pp. 117–128.
3. Penny Hansen describes this pattern in "Woman's Hour: Feminist Implications of Mary Baker Eddy's Christian Science Movement, 1885–1910" (Ph.D. diss., University of California, Irvine, 1981), pp. 310–321.
4. Horatio Dresser, ed., *The Quimby Manuscripts* (New York, 1921), pp. 393ff.
5. Robert Peel, *Mary Baker Eddy: The Years of Authority* (New York, 1977), p. 168.
6. Harold W. Pfautz, in "Christian Science: The Sociology of a Social Movement and a Religious Group" (Ph.D. diss., University of Chicago, 1954), pp. 292ff., shows that despite the abnormally high

percentage of women in the movement, the men were "taking over the leadership," even at the local church level, in urban areas and all regions except the West.

7. Mary Baker Eddy, "Miscellaneous Writings," in *Prose Works* (Boston, 1925), p. 245; *Science and Health with Key to the Scriptures* (Boston, 1910), p. 63.

8. Anthony never met the cult's founder personally, but she had heard Eddy speak in Chicago in 1888. Ready to proselytize for her own cause, she sent the religionist the first part of her history of woman's suffrage and had her organization follow up with offers to sell her the subsequent volumes at a reduced price. Harriet H. Robinson (for Miss Anthony) to Mrs. Mary Glover Eddy, Jan. 14, 1887, AMC; Susan B. Anthony to Mrs. Mary Glover Eddy, June 19, 1903, AMC.

9. Mary Baker Eddy to Clara Choate, cited by Robert Peel, *Mary Baker Eddy: The Years of Trial* (New York, 1971), p. 109.

10. Eddy, *Science and Health*, p. 63. "A feasible as well as rational means of improvement at present," Eddy added, "is the elevation of society in general and the achievement of a nobler race . . . having higher aims and motives."

11. Ida H. Harper, *The Life and Work of Susan B. Anthony*, 2 vols. (Indianapolis, 1898), 2:918.

12. Eddy, *Science and Health*, p. 340.

13. George B. Day, "Sheep, Shepherd and Shepherdess," *Christian Science Journal* 5 (1887), p. 232; Carol Norton, *Woman's Cause* (Boston, 1895), p. 15.

14. Mary Collson, "My Search for an All Right World," pp. 55–57.

15. Ibid., p. 55.

16. See Annie M. Knott, "Reminiscences," *Christian Science Journal* 18 (1901), pp. 679–683; "Reminiscences," *Christian Science Journal* 41 (1924), pp. 593–599; "Mrs. Annie M. Knott," *New York Times*, Dec. 21, 1941, p. 40.

17. Knott, "Reminiscences," in *We Knew Mary Baker Eddy*, 3rd series (Boston, 1953), p. 83.

18. Collson, "My Search," p. 56.

19. Alfred Farlow to Mary Baker Eddy, June 11, 1893, cited by Peel, *Years of Authority*, p. 157.

20. Collson, "My Search," p. 94. Peel cites—in *Years of Trial*, pp. 219–220—a letter Farlow wrote to Eddy in 1887 giving essentially the same account.

21. Collson, "My Search," p. 94.

22. In *Science and Health*, p. 560, Eddy also stated that a student could not advance in spiritual understanding if he or she entertained "a false estimate of anyone whom God . . . appointed to voice His Word;" no student could grasp the Scientific Principle without a "correct sense of its highest visible idea."

23. Back in 1901, for instance, she had written one of her deputies whom she was thinking of putting in Farlow's place: "I told [Mr. Farlow] but yesterday the situation has outgrown the incumbent. I like his sturdiness but his education has been not in a literary line which the place demands." And later: "Mr. Farlow is a smart business man and a lovely character but he has not the education and literary taste requisite for his responsible office. . . . I want an officer of the Mother Church *wise* and educated sufficiently to fill his place without having to look after him in anywise." Peel, *Years of Authority*, p. 196.

24. Collson, "My Search," pp. 56–57.

25. See Alice Henry, *The Trade Union Woman* (New York and London, 1915), p. 60.

26. Henry, *Trade Union Woman*, p. 63; also see Allen Davis, "The Women's Trade Union League: Origins and Organization," *Labor History* 5 (Winter 1964), pp. 3–17.

27. See: "A Labor Conflict Without Violence: The Fall River Lockout," *Outlook* 78 (Dec. 17, 1904), pp. 972–977; "The End of the Fall River Lockout," *Outlook* 79 (Jan. 28, 1905), p. 213; "Relief Work in the Fall River Strike," *Charities* 13 (Jan. 21, 1905), pp. 391–392; Philip T. Silvia, "The Spindle City: Labor, Politics, and Religion in Fall River, Massachusetts, 1870–1905" (Ph.D. diss., Fordham University, 1974).

28. Collson, "My Search," p. 60.

29. James J. Kenneally, in *Women and American Trade Unions*, (St. Albans, Vermont and Montreal, 1978), p. 56, gives 130 as the number of workers the Boston League managed to place.

30. Collson, "My Search," p. 60.

31. Henry, *Trade Union Woman*, pp. 68–69.

32. Ibid.

33. Eddy, *Science and Health*, p. 459.

34. Eddy, "Miscellaneous Writings," p. 31.

35. Some of the best accounts of the night watches are provided in

Memoirs of Mary Baker Eddy (Boston, 1927) by Eddy's longtime metaphysical worker, Adam H. Dickey.

36. Similarly, Eddy made Dickey promise that if she "should ever leave here" he would write a history of his experience in her home and say that she "was mentally murdered." Dickey, *Memoirs of Mary Baker Eddy*, p. xv.

37. Collson, "My Search," p. 61.

38. Peel, *Years of Authority*, p. 58.

39. Edward A. Kimball, *Normal Class Notes* (Boston, 1935). Quoted by Charles S. Braden in *Christian Science Today* (Dallas, 1958), p. 345.

40. Collson, "My Search," p. 62.

41. Ibid., p. 63.

42. Ibid., p. 75.

43. Adhering to a practice that has since become obligatory, class members generally treated the specific content of the teacher's syllabus as confidential, guarding it from outsiders in an atmosphere of secrecy that enhanced the curriculum's aura of spirituality. However, the burden of what Collson and her classmates heard can be surmised from an interview Farlow gave *Human Life* two years later, in which he sought to correct the public's misunderstanding of M.A.M.:

> It is magnetism because it refers to a supposed power independent of God; malicious, in keeping with the Scriptural declaration, "The Carnal mind is enmity against God." Mrs. Eddy refers to it as the human antipode of Divine Science. It is a term which is broad enough to include all that is opposed to God. It includes every phase of evil, every phase of human antagonism to truth.

Quoted by Sybil Wilbur, *The Life of Mary Baker Eddy* (Boston, n.d.), p. 240.

44. Eddy, "The First Church of Christ Scientist and Miscellany," in *Prose Works*, p. 210.

45. Collson, "My Search," p. 76.

46. Ibid., p. 63.

47. See Ann Douglas Wood, "'The Fashionable Diseases': Women's Complaints and Their Treatment in Nineteenth Century America," *The Journal of Interdisciplinary History* 4 (1973), p. 25–52; and Regina Morantz, "The Lady and Her Physician," in *Clio's Consciousness Raised*, eds. Mary S. Hartman and Lois Banner (New

York, 1974), pp. 38–53. Pfautz, "Christian Science," pp. 252–253, notes that in a study by Ronald Freedman and P. K. Welpton, in *Milbank Memorial Fund Quarterly* 28 (July 1950), pp. 294–355, Christian Science was one of three denominational groups (out of thirteen) showing the lowest fertility rates, while at the same time occupying only an intermediate position with respect to strict family planning. As Pfautz points out, Scientists' low fertility would appear to be a function of their doctrine's negative value on sex, which discourages sexual activity.

48. Eddy, "Miscellaneous Writings," pp. 288–289.

49. Ibid., p. 286; *Science and Health*, pp. 61, 64.

50. Eddy, "Miscellany," in *Prose Works*, pp. 268–269.

51. *Manual of The Mother Church* (Boston, 1895), p. 83.

CHAPTER VI

1. Clifton J. Phillips, *Indiana in Transition* (Indianapolis, 1968), p. 460. There were roughly 90,000 members of The Mother Church in 1905, and about 7,000 practitioners. Harold W. Pfautz—in "A Case Study of An Urban Religious Movement: Christian Science," in *Contributions to Urban Sociology*, eds. Ernest W. Burgess and Donald J. Bogue (Chicago, 1964), p. 301—charts the movement's rates of growth in the United States from 1880 to 1950.

2. William P. McCorkle, "A New Mariolatry," *Presbyterian Quarterly* 12 (Oct. 1898), p. 513. Cited by Raymond J. Cunningham, "The Impact of Christian Science on the American Churches, 1880–1910," *American Historical Review* 72 (1967), p. 499.

3. Clifford P. Smith, *Christian Science: Its Legal Status* (Boston, 1914).

4. John B. Huber, M.D., "Christian Science from a Physician's Point of View," *Popular Science* 55 (1899), p. 766.

5. Mary Baker Eddy, *Science and Health with Key to the Scriptures* (Boston, 1910), pp. 175, 389.

6. Ibid., p. 370.

7. Albert Stump, "Regulation of the Practice of Medicine in Indiana since 1897," *Journal of the Indiana State Medical Association* 42 Supp. (July, 1949), pp. 53–54.

8. *The New York Times*, Nov. 8, 1904, p. 1.

9. *Evansville Journal-News*, March 19, 1905, p. 20.

10. *The New York Times*, Feb. 19, 1904, pp. 1–5; May 9, 1905, p. 6.

11. *Evansville Journal-News*, April 3, 1905, p. 5.

12. *Evansville Journal-News*, April 4, 1905, p. 5.

13. Mary Collson, "My Search for an All Right World," p. 66.

14. Eddy, *Science and Health*, p. 195.

15. The organization's censorship, which was notorious, was exercised to prevent the circulation of more "dangerous" material (e.g., copies of Eddy's letters, transcripts of class notes or of lecturers' informal talks, and "false" interpretations of Science or "distorted" portrayals of its Founder. It was to suppress this "perverted and unsafe" literature, not the novels, that Eddy had handed down her "obnoxious books" bylaw forbidding the circulation of any material that was "not correct" and the patronizing of any publishing houses or bookstores that sold "obnoxious books." *Manual of The Mother Church*, p. 43.

16. Eddy referred to Catherine M. Yates' *On the Way There* as "a little gem," and she complimented Clara Louise Burnham, the author of *The Right Princess*, for dissecting her character "with the skill of a metaphysician surgeon" (*Christian Science Sentinel* 6 [Aug. 1904], p. 828; 5 [Oct. 1902], p. 72). Articles on the integrity of Christian Science literature appeared frequently in response to readers' requests for "Scientific" guidance. See the *Christian Science Sentinel* 5 (Aug. 1903), p. 791; 6 (Sept. 1903), p. 40; 6 (July 1904), p. 764; 7 (Dec. 1904), p. 216.

17. Collson, "My Search," p. 17.

18. Ibid., p. 81.

19. Kinter described his lobbying with Farlow in the *Christian Science Journal* 16 (1898), p. 96. Because one of Mrs. Eddy's bylaws prohibited wives of teachers from teaching, Mrs. Kinter's professional opportunities were limited to her practice.

20. E.g., *Evansville Journal-News*, Dec. 18, 1905, p. 4. Relatives claimed that at 86 Eddy was no longer physically or mentally competent and sought, unsuccessfully, to take over the management of her affairs. *Evansville Press*, Oct. 11, 1907, p. 4.

21. *Evansville Journal-News*, May 21, 1906, p. 5.

22. *Evansville Journal-News*, Sept. 8, 1906, p. 8.

23. *Manual of The Mother Church*, p. 45; also see the *Christian Science Journal* 20 (1904), p. 184.

24. Edward J. Meeman, *The Editorial We*, ed. Edwin Howard (Memphis, TN, 1976), p. 23.

25. Collson, "My Search," pp. 76–77.

26. Ibid., p. 69.

27. Ibid. p. 70.

28. *Unity* 42 (1898), p. 52.

29. Mary Collson to Edward Meeman, July 19, 1948, MVC.

30. Collson, "My Search," p. 69.

31. Mary Collson to Edward Meeman, July 19, 1948, MVC.

32. Collson, "My Search," pp. 68–69.

33. Letter from Jane Steber, clerk, First Church of Christ, Scientist, Evansville, Indiana, to Cynthia Tucker, Aug. 7, 1978; "A Short History of the Christian Science Movement in Evansville, Indiana" and "History of First Church of Christ, Scientist, 212 Mulberry Street, Evansville, Indiana," mimeographed reports, First Church of Christ, Scientist, Evansville, Indiana.

34. Collson, "My Search," p. 79.

35. *Evansville Journal-News*, Jan. 15, 1909, p. 11.

36. *Evansville Journal-News*, Jan. 19, 1909, p. 5.

37. Collson, "My Search," p. 80.

38. Ibid., p. 81.

39. Ibid., pp. 79–80.

40. Ibid., p. 81.

41. Ibid., pp. 84–85, 94–95.

42. Robert Peel, *Mary Baker Eddy: The Years of Authority* (New York, 1971), p. 202.

43. Similar action was planned when *McClure's* first announced a series of articles on Mrs. Eddy's life; however, when the installments continued despite the threats of a boycott—and the articles' detailed evidence proved unanswerable—Farlow decided to take another tack. He began assembling documentation for a book of his own, and had Mrs. Sybil Wilbur O'Brian, a friendly journalist, write the official Eddy biography to offset the devastation wrought by *McClure's*. As for Michael Meehan's documentary history of the "Next friends suit," which was published in 1908, Farlow had the entire edition bought up and stored away in The Mother Church Publishing House. The following year, when the Milmine biography came out in book form, Farlow arranged for a wealthy friend of the church to purchase the plates and subsequently had them destroyed. For a fuller account, see Henry R. Mussey, *The Christian Science Censor* (New York, 1930), pp. 14–19.

44. Collson, "My Search," pp. 86–87.

45. Ibid., p. 87.

46. Eddy, *Science and Health*, p. 102.
47. Collson, "My Search," p. 88.
48. Ibid., p. 89.
49. Ibid., p. 87.
50. Ibid., pp. 89–90.
51. Ibid., p. 123.
52. Mary Collson to Jane Addams, Jan. 12, 1911, SCPC.
53. Collson, "My Search," p. 91.
54. Ibid., pp. 92–93.
55. Ibid., p. 96.
56. Ibid., p. 97.
57. Ibid., p. 98.
58. Collson file, ATMC.

CHAPTER VII

1. Gertrude Foster Brown's description, quoted by Mildred Adams in *The Right To Be People* (Philadelphia and New York, 1967), p. 117.
2. Mary Collson, "My Search for an All Right World," p. 99.
3. James Weinstein, *The Decline of Socialism in America, 1912–1925* (New York, 1969), pp. 61–62.
4. "Letter to the Editor," *New York Times*, July 28, 1914, p. 11.
5. *New York Times*, July 30, 1914, sec. II, p. 3.
6. Collson, "My Search," p. 99.
7. Ibid.
8. Ibid., p. 102.
9. Ibid., pp. 103–104.
10. Ibid., pp. 105–105.
11. Mary Collson to Rev. Charles T. Billings, Feb. 17, 1917; application for Unitarian ministry, Collson file, UUA.
12. Jane Addams to Rev. Harry Lutz, Committee on Supply of Pulpits, April 28, 1917, UUA.
13. Florence Buck to Rev. Harry Lutz, April 28, 1917, UUA.
14. *Christian Register* 97 (Aug. 1918), p. 775.
15. *Unity* 79 (1917), pp. 133–134, 260; *Christian Century* 34 (1917), pp. 13–14. Also see Ray H. Abrams, *Preachers Present Arms* (Scottsdale, Pa., 1969).
16. *Unity* 81 (1918), p. 160.

17. Thomas Van Ness, *The Religion of New England* (Boston, 1926), pp. 166–171.

18. Ibid., pp. 172, 176.

19. Mary Collson to Edward Meeman, Aug. 13, 1934, MVC.

20. Collson, "My Search," p. 105.

21. Ibid., p. 106.

22. The records of The Mother Church show that her reinstatement followed the usual course of reentry. She was first admitted to probationary status on May 31, 1918, and to full membership a year later.

23. Collson, "My Search," p. 94.

24. Ibid., p. 110.

25. This effect has been widely observed. Bryan R. Wilson—in *Sects and Society: A Sociological Study of the Elim Tabernacle, Christian Science, and Christadelphians* (Berkeley, 1961), pp. 168–169—notes that Christian Science practices and teachings inhibit the development of strong social bonds, emotional ties, and personal acts of charity. Walter I. Wardwell—in "Christian Science and Spiritual Healing," in *Religious Systems and Psychotherapy*, ed. Richard H. Cox (Springfield, Ill., 1973), p. 83—discusses the "alienation of the individual [Christian Scientist] from the world of men" as a function of denying the reality of matter, sin, and suffering. This denial "separates the individual from his own bodily senses and thus from others," Wardwell says. Further, "there is little religious basis for concern with other people. Not only is matter not real, but other people don't really matter."

26. Collson, "My Search," p. 116.

27. Ibid., p. 119.

28. Ibid., pp. 110–111.

29. As Abrams makes clear, the Eddyites held no monopoly on hawkishness during the war.

30. Collson, "My Search," p. 113.

31. Mary Baker Eddy, *Science and Health with Key to the Scriptures* (Boston, 1910), p. 147.

32. Collson, "My Search," p. 113.

33. For reports of this kind, see *Christian Science War Time Activities* (Boston, 1922).

34. Collson, "My Search," p. 115.

35. For Dr. Alice Hamilton's account, see *Exploring the Dangerous*

Trades (Boston, 1943), pp. 265–267. Collson described her own in-volvement in a letter to Edward Meeman, Sept. 16, 1934, MVC.

36. Theodore Draper describes the organization's background and development in *American Communism and Soviet Russia* (London, 1960), pp. 174–177.

37. Mary Collson to Edward Meeman, Sept. 16, 1934, MVC.

38. Mary Collson to Edward Meeman, June 18, 1934, MVC.

39. As Stephen Gottschalk points out in *The Emergence of Christian Science in American Religious Life* (Berkeley, Los Angeles, and London, 1973), p. 269, the Scientists' periodicals always carried numerous testimonials of personal victories over alcholism, but the Eddyites differed with most advocates of temperance in their view that far more had been accomplished in promoting it through Scientific thinking than through "legally coercive measures."

40. Collson, "My Search," pp. 140–141.

41. Ibid., pp. 32–33, plus unnumbered fragment pages.

42. Ibid., p. 132.

43. Ibid., p. 121.

44. Ibid.

45. For an excellent summary of this aspect of Scientific orthodoxy see Charles S. Braden, *Christian Science Today* (Dallas, 1958), pp. 347–349.

46. Collson, "My Search," pp. 16–17.

47. Ibid.

48. Eddy, *Science and Health*, p. 401.

49. *Manual of The Mother Church*, (Boston, 1895) p. 47.

50. Mary Collson to Edward Meeman, Aug. 9, 1934.

51. Collson, "My Search," pp. 127–128

52. Ibid., p. 128.

53. Ibid., pp. 129–130.

54. Mary Collson to Edward Meeman, 14, Dec. 1931; Collson, "My Search," p. 128.

55. Collson, "My Search," p. 131.

56. Ibid., p. 132.

57. Collson file, AMC.

CHAPTER VIII

1. "My Search for an All Right World" was the title she had in mind for a book about her Christian Science experiences.

2. Mary Collson, "My Search for an All Right World," p. 145.

3. Ibid., p. 136.

4. Mary Collson to Jane Addams, June 2, 1932, SCPC.

5. Edward J. Meeman, *The Editorial We* (Memphis, TN., 1976), p. 35.

6. Edward Meeman to Mary Collson, Jan. 12, 1934, MVC.

7. Ibid.

8. Mary Collson to Edward Meeman, July 4, 1933; Nov. 24, 1933, MVC.

9. Mary Collson to Edward Meeman, Nov. 24, 1933, MVC.

10. Edward Meeman to Mary Collson, Jan. 12, 1934, MVC.

11. Mary Collson to Edward Meeman, Nov. 24, 1933, MVC.

12. Mary Collson to Edward Meeman, Jan. 13, 1934, MVC.

13. Mary Collson to Jane Addams, Jan. 20, 1934, SCPC.

14. Mary Collson to Jane Addams, June 2, 1932, SCPC. After Addams was hospitalized in 1931, Collson wrote to let her know she loved and valued her spirit. Newspaper photographs of the reformer's return to Hull House, Collson said, filled her with "the same humility" she felt when she contemplated the picture of Christ carrying the cross to Calvary. This reaction was widespread, as Allen F. Davis points out in *American Heroine* (New York), p. 284.

15. To avoid reviving the stigma of Bolshevism that wartime sentiment had attached to Hull House, Collson portrayed her political life in Chicago as completely detached from her settlement life, even though this meant bending the truth.

16. Mary Collson to Edward Meeman, Feb. 11, 1934, MVC.

17. Collson papers, MVC.

18. Mary Collson to Edward Meeman, March 10, 1934, MVC.

19. Edward Meeman to Mary Collson, March 14, 1934, MVC.

20. Mary Collson to Edward Meeman, March 17, 1934, MVC.

21. Mary Collson to Edward Meeman, Aug. 13, 1934, MVC.

22. Mary Collson to Edward Meeman, April 18, 1934, MVC. Scribner's published Edwin Dakin's brutal presentation of Mrs. Eddy— *Mrs. Eddy: The Biography of a Virginal Mind* (New York, 1929)—but gave way to the pressure of threatened boycotts and recalled it from four-fifths of its distributors. See Henry R. Mussey, *The Christian Science Censor* (New York, 1930), pp. 37–44. Horatio Dresser's sup-

pressed first edition of *The Quimby Manuscripts* (New York, 1921) contained correspondence between Mrs. Eddy and Quimby that cast doubt on the origins of her "divinely inspired" work, *Science and Health.*

23. Edward Meeman to Florence Bowers, Aug. 5, 1934, MVC.

24. Mary Collson to Edward Meeman, June 18, 1934, MVC.

25. Charles H. Trout describes the competition for jobs in *Boston, the Great Depression, and the New Deal* (New York, 1977), p. 178.

26. Mary Collson to Edward Meeman, Aug. 9, 1934, MVC.

27. Mary Collson to Edward Meeman, June 1, 1934, MVC. Walter I. Wardwell—in "Christian Science and Spiritual Healing," in *Religious Systems and Psychotherapy*, ed. Richard H. Cox (Springfield, Ill., 1973), p. 83—discusses this "alienation of the individual from the world of men" as an effect of Christian Science belief.

28. Collson, "My Search," p. 133.

29. Mary Collson to Edward Meeman, June 1, 1934, MVC.

30. Mary Collson to Edward Meeman, July 9, 1934, MVC.

31. Ibid.

32. Mary Collson to Edward Meeman, May 5, 1936, MVC.

33. Mary Collson to Edward Meeman, Dec. 30, 1932; May 5, 1936, MVC.

34. Mary Collson to Edward Meeman, Aug. 13, 1934, MVC.

35. Mary Collson to Jane Addams, June 2, 1932, SCPC.

36. Collson, "My Search," p. 112.

37. Mary Collson to Edward Meeman, July 4, 1933; Collson, "My Search," p. 112

38. Mary Collson to Edward Meeman, Nov. 24, 1933, MVC.

39. Mary Collson to Edward Meeman, Sept. 1934, MVC.

40. Mary Collson to Edward Meeman, Dec. 14, 1931, MVC.

41. See Arthur M. Schlesinger, Jr., *The Crisis of the Old Order* (Boston, 1957), pp. 204–223.

42. John Strachey, *The Coming Struggle for Power* (New York, 1935), pp. 358–360.

43. Schlesinger, *Crisis*, p. 210.

44. Mary Collson to Edward Meeman, Dec. 14, 1931, MVC.

45. Ibid.

46. Albert Parry, writing in *Outlook*, July 15, 1931, reported that

Amtorg, the Soviet trading corporation in New York, was receiving about 350 applications a day from Americans wanting jobs in the Soviet Union.

47. *The World Tomorrow*, Sept. 30, 1930. Cited by Arthur Schlesinger, Jr., p. 212.
48. Rev. Lyman P. Powell, "A Clergyman Looks in on Russia," *Review of Reviews*, October 1934.
49. Mary Collson to Edward Meeman, Sept. 16, 1934, MVC.
50. Mary Collson to Edward Meeman, Sept. 1934, MVC.
51. Mary Collson to Edward Meeman, Sept. 16, 1934, MVC.
52. Ibid.
53. Meeman, *The Editorial We*, p. 35.
54. Edward Meeman to Mary Collson, Sept. 23, 1934, MVC.
55. Mary Collson to Edward Meeman, Oct. 11, 1934, MVC.
56. Ibid.
57. Mary Collson to Edward Meeman, Nov. 4, 1934, MVC.
58. Mary Collson to Edward Meeman, Dec. 30, 1932, MVC.
59. Mary Collson to Edward Meeman, May 5, 1936, MVC.
60. Ibid.
61. Mary Collson to Edward Meeman, July 4, 1947, MVC.
62. Mary Collson to Edward Meeman, June 25, 1952, MVC.
63. Ibid.

Bibliography

UNPUBLISHED WRITINGS

"A Short History of the Christian Science Movement in Evansville, Indiana." Mimeographed report, First Church of Christ, Scientist, Evansville, Ind., n.d.

Collson, Mary E. "My Search for an All Right World" (tentative title). Typescript in the Mississippi Valley Collection, Memphis State University.

Collson, Mary E. "Rainbows I Have Seen." Typescript in the Mississippi Valley Collection, Memphis State University.

Collson, Mary E. "The Damaged Picnic." Typescript in the Mississippi Valley Collection, Memphis State University.

Cunningham, Raymond J. "Ministry of Healing: The Origins of the Psychotherapeutic Role of American Churches." Ph.D. diss., Johns Hopkins University, 1965.

Fox, Margery Q. "Power and Piety: Women in Christian Science." Ph.D. diss., New York University, 1973.

Hansen, Penny. "Woman's Hour: Feminist Implications of Mary Baker Eddy's Christian Science Movement, 1885–1910." Ph.D. diss., University of California, Irvine, 1981.

Helvie, Clara C. "Unitarian Women Ministers." Typescript in the Universalist Historical Society, 1929.

"History of First Church of Christ, Scientist, 212 Mulberry Street, Evansville, Indiana." Mimeographed report, First Church of Christ, Scientist, Evansville, Ind., 1969.

Johnson, Joseph K. "Christian Science: A Case Study of A Religion as A Form of Adjustment Behavior." Ph.D. diss., Washington University, 1938.

Kain, Edward. "The Never Married in the United States, 1890–1980." Ph.D. diss., University of North Carolina, Chapel Hill, 1980.

Kamau, Lucy Jayne. "Systems of Belief and Ritual in Christian Science." Ph.D. diss., University of Chicago, 1971.

Murdock, Rev. Marian. "Women at Meadville." Handwritten paper delivered at the Semi-Centennial of the Meadville Theological School, June 1894. Meadville-Lombard Theological School Library.

Pfautz, Harold W. "Christian Science: The Sociology of a Social Movement and a Religious Group." Ph.D. diss., University of Chicago, 1954.

Reed, Robert L. "The Professionalism of Public School Teachers: The Chicago Experience, 1895–1920." Ph.D. diss., Northwestern, 1968.

"Report of a Committee, 1912: The Juvenile Court of Cook County, Ill." MS in Chicago Historical Society.

Silvia, Philip T. "The Spindle City: Labor, Politics, and Religion in Fall River, Massachusetts, 1870–1905." 2 vols., Ph.D. diss., Fordham University, 1974.

Thorner, Isidor. "Christian Science and Ascetic Protestantism: A Study in the Sociology of Religion, Personality Type and Social Structure." Ph.D. diss., Harvard University, 1951.

MANUSCRIPT COLLECTIONS

Addams, Jane. Papers. Swarthmore College Peace Collection, Swarthmore, Pa.

American Unitarian Association. Letter Books. Andover Library, Harvard Divinity School, Cambridge, Mass.

Annals of the Chicago Woman's Club. Chicago Historical Society, Chicago, Ill.

Collson, Mary Edith. Papers. Mississippi Valley Collection, Memphis State University, Memphis, Tenn.

Hull-House Association Papers. University of Illinois at Chicago Circle, Chicago, Ill.

Jones, Jenkin Lloyd. Papers. Meadville-Lombard Theological School Library, Chicago, Ill.

Juvenile Protective Association Papers, Case Studies, Nov. 1899–Aug. 1901. University of Illinois at Chicago Circle, Chicago, Ill.

Meeman, Edward J., Papers. Mississippi Valley Collection, Memphis State University, Memphis, Tenn.

Records of the Chicago Woman's Club Meetings, 1900–1901. Chicago Historical Society, Chicago, Ill.

Records of Iowa Zeta Chapter of Pi Beta Phi. University of Iowa, Iowa City, Iowa.
Records of the Unitarian Church, Iowa City, Iowa. Archives of State Historical Society of Iowa, Iowa City, Iowa.
Western Unitarian Conference Papers. Meadville-Lombard Theological School, Chicago, Ill.

BOOKS

Abrams, Ray H. *Preachers Present Arms*. New York: Round Table Press, 1933. Rev. ed. Scottdale, Pa.: Herald Press, 1969.
Adams, Mildred. *The Right To Be People*. Philadelphia and New York: Lippincott, 1967.
Awake and Inherit: Supply as Spiritual Reflection. Work. Sufficiency. Faithfulness. Boston: Christian Science Pub. Soc., 1937.
Bannister, Robert C. *Social Darwinism: Science and Myth in Anglo-American Social Thought*. Philadelphia: Temple University Press, 1979.
Beecher, Catherine. *Suggestions Respecting Improvements in Education*. Hartford: Packard and Butler, 1828.
Bonner, Thomas N. *Medicine in Chicago, 1850–1950*. Madison: The American History Research Center, Inc., 1957.
Braden, Charles S. *Christian Science Today*. Dallas: Southern Methodist University Press, 1958.
Brumberg, Joan Jacob. *Mission for Life*. New York: The Free Press, 1980.
Buhle, Mari Jo. *Women and American Socialism, 1870–1920*. Urbana: University of Illinois Press, 1981.
Burnham, Clara Louise. *The Right Princess*. Boston: Houghton, Mifflin and Company, 1903.
Chodorow, Nancy. *The Reproduction of Mothering: Psychoanalysis and the Psychology of Gender*. Berkeley: University of California Press, 1978.
Christian Science War Time Activities. Boston: Christian Science Pub. Soc., 1922.
Christie, Francis A. *The Makings of the Meadville Theological School, 1844–1894*. Boston: Beacon Press, 1927.
Cooke, George Willis. *Unitarianism in America*. Boston: American Unitarian Association, 1902.

Cott, Nancy. *The Bonds of Womanhood: "Woman's Sphere" in New England, 1780–1835.* New Haven: Yale University Press, 1977.

Crunden, Robert M. *Ministers of Reform: The Progressives' Achievement in American Civilization, 1889–1920.* New York: Basic Books, 1982.

Dakin, Edwin. *Mrs. Eddy: The Biography of a Virginal Mind.* New York: Charles Scribner's Sons, 1929.

Dall, Caroline. *College, Market, and Court.* Memorial ed. Boston: The Rumford Press, 1914.

Davis, Allen F. *American Heroine: The Life and Legend of Jane Addams.* New York: Oxford University Press, 1973.

Davis, Allen F. *Eighty Years at Hull House.* Chicago: Quadrangle Books, 1969.

Davis, Allen F. *Spearheads for Reform: The Social Settlements and the Progressive Movement, 1890–1914.* New York: Oxford University Press, 1967.

Dickey, Adam H. *Memoirs of Mary Baker Eddy.* Boston: Merrymount Press, 1927.

Dixon, Rev. Amzi. *Is Christian Science a Humbug?* Boston: J. H. Earle, 1901.

Draper, Theodore. *American Communism and Soviet Russia.* London: Macmillan Co., 1960.

Dresser, Horatio W. *The Quimby Manuscripts.* New York: Thomas Y. Crowell Co., 1921.

Eddy, Mary Baker. *Prose Works.* Boston: Christian Science Pub. Soc., 1925.

Eddy, Mary Baker. *Retrospection and Introspection.* Boston: Christian Science Pub. Soc., 1892.

Eddy, Mary Baker. *Science and Health with Key to the Scriptures.* Boston: Christian Science Pub. Soc., 1910.

Emerson, Ralph Waldo. *Miscellanies.* Boston, New York, and Cambridge: Harvard University Press, 1893.

Evans, Warren Felt. *The Mental Cure.* Boston: H. H. & T. W. Carter, 1869.

Farlow, Alfred. *Christian Science: Historical Facts.* Boston: Puritan Press, 1902.

Fine, Sidney. *Laissez Faire and the General Welfare State: A Study of Conflict in American Thought, 1865–1901.* Ann Arbor: University of Michigan Press, 1964.

Frankfort, Roberta. *Collegiate Women: Domesticity and Career in Turn-of-the-Century America.* New York: New York University Press, 1977.

Ginger, Ray. *Altgeld's America.* Chicago: Quadrangle Books, 1965.

Goddard, Harold Clarke. *Studies in New England Transcendentalism.* New York: Columbia University Press, 1908. Reprint. New York: Hillary House Publ., Ltd., 1960.

Good, Harry G., and James D. Teller. *A History of American Education.* 3rd ed. New York: Macmillan, 1973.

Gordon, Eleanor E. *A Little Bit of a Long Story for the Children.* Humboldt, Iowa, 1934.

Gordon, Eleanor E. *The Second Chapter of a Long Story.* Humboldt, Iowa, 1934.

Gottschalk, Stephen. *The Emergence of Christian Science in American Religious Life.* Berkeley, Los Angeles, and London: University of Calif. Press, 1973.

Grant, Madeleine Parker. *Alice Hamilton.* London: Abelard-Schuman, 1967.

Haller, J. S., and Robin M. Haller. *The Physician and Sexuality in Victorian America.* Urbana: University of Illinois Press, 1974.

Hamilton, Alice. *Exploring the Dangerous Trades.* Boston: Little, Brown & Co., 1943.

Harper, Ida H. *The Life and Work of Susan B. Anthony.* 2 vols. Indianapolis: The Hollenbeck Press, 1898.

Hart, Sara L. *The Pleasure is Mine.* Chicago: Vallentine-Newman, 1947.

Hartman, Mary S. and Lois Banner. *Clio's Consciousness Raised.* New York: Harper & Row, 1974.

Henry, Alice. *The Trade Union Woman.* New York and London: D. Appleton & Co., 1915.

Henry, Alice. *Women and the Labor Movement.* New York: George H. Doran Co., 1923.

Hill, Mary. *Charlotte Perkins Gilman: The Making of a Radical Feminist, 1860–1896.* Philadelphia: Temple University Press, 1980.

History of Humboldt County. Chicago and Cedar Rapids, Iowa: Historical Publishing Co., 1901.

History of Kossuth & Humboldt Counties, Iowa. Springfield, Ill.: Union Publishing Co., 1884.

Hitchings, Catherine F. *Universalist and Unitarian Women Ministers*. Boston: Universalist Historical Society, 1975.

Jeffrey, Julie Ray. *Frontier Women: The Trans-Mississippi West, 1840–1880*. New York: Hill & Wang, 1979.

Kenneally, James J. *Women and American Trade Unions*. St. Albans, Vt. and Montreal: Eden Press, 1978.

Kerr, Howard. *Mediums, and Spirit Rappers, and Roaring Radicals: Spiritualism in American Literature, 1850–1900*. Urbana: University of Illinois Press, 1972.

Kerr, May Walden. *Socialism and the Home*. Chicago: C.H. Kerr & Co., n.d.

Kett, Joseph. *The Formation of the American Medical Profession*. New Haven: Yale University Press, 1968.

Kimball, Edward A. *Normal Class Notes*. Boston: J. Raymond Cornell, 1935.

Kipnis, Ira. *The American Socialist Movement, 1897–1912*. New York: Columbia University Press, 1952. Reprint. New York: Greenwood Press, 1968.

Lasch, Christopher. *The New Radicalism in America, 1889–1963*. New York: Alfred A. Knopf, 1965.

Leach, William. *True Love and Perfect Union: The Feminist Reform of Sex and Society*. New York: Basic Books, 1980.

Levine, Daniel. *Jane Addams and the Liberal Tradition*. Madison: State Historical Society of Wisconsin, 1971.

Lubove, Roy. *The Professional Altruist: The Emergence of Social Work as a Career, 1880–1930*. Cambridge: Harvard University Press, 1965.

Lyttle, Charles H. *Freedom Moves West: A History of the Western Unitarian Conference, 1852–1952*. Boston: Beacon Press, 1952.

Manual of The Mother Church. Boston: Christian Science Pub. Soc., 1895.

Meadville Theological School Catalogue, 1895–1896. Meadville, Pa., 1896.

Meyer, Donald. *The Positive Thinkers*. New York: Doubleday & Co., 1965.

Meeman, Edward J. *The Editorial We*. Edited by Edwin Howard. Memphis, TN.: The Edward J. Meeman Foundation, 1976.

Milmine, Georgine. *The Life of Mary Baker G. Eddy and the History of Christian Science*. New York: Doubleday, Page & Co., 1909.

Mussey, Henry R. *The Christian Science Censor.* New York: The Nation, 1930.

Norton, Carol. *Woman's Cause.* Boston: Dana Estes & Co., 1895.

Noun, Louise. *Strong-Minded Women.* Ames, Iowa: Iowa State University Press, 1969.

O'Neill, William L. *Everyone Was Brave: The Rise and Fall of Feminism in America.* Chicago: Quadrangle Books, 1969.

Ossoli, Sarah Margaret Fuller. *Life Without and Life Within.* Edited by A. B. Fuller. Boston: Brown, Taggard and Chase, 1859.

Ossoli, Sarah Margaret Fuller. *Woman in the Nineteenth Century.* New York: Greeley & McElrath, 1845.

Parker, Gail. *Mind Cure in New England.* Hanover, N. H.: University Press of New England, 1973.

Peel, Robert. *Mary Baker Eddy: The Years of Authority.* New York: Holt, Rinehart, & Winston, 1977.

Peel, Robert. *Mary Baker Eddy: The Years of Trial.* New York: Holt, Rinehart, & Winston, 1971.

Peel, Robert. *Mary Baker Eddy: The Years of Discovery.* New York: Holt, Rinehart, & Winston, 1966.

Persons, Stan. *Free Religion: An American Faith.* Boston: Beacon Press, 1963.

Philips, Clifton J. *Indiana in Transition.* Indianapolis: Indiana Historical Soc., 1968.

Platt, Anthony M. *The Child Savers: The Invention of Delinquency.* 2nd ed. Chicago and London: The University of Chicago Press, 1977.

Putnam, Ruth, ed. *The Life and Letters of Mary Putnam Jacobi.* New York: G.P. Putnam's Sons, 1925.

Riley, Glenda. *Frontierswomen: The Iowa Experience.* Cedar Rapids: Iowa State University Press, 1981.

Scharf, Lois. *To Work and to Wed: Female Employment, Feminism, and the Great Depression.* Westport, Conn.: Greenwood Press, 1980.

Schlesinger, Arthur M. Jr. *The Crisis of the Old Order.* Boston: Houghton Mifflin, 1957.

Sherman, Bradford. *Historical Sketch of the Introduction of Christian Science in Chicago and the West.* Chicago: Privately printed, 1912.

Shryock, Richard H. *Medicine in America.* Baltimore: Johns Hopkins University Press, 1966.

Sinclair, Andrew. *The Better Half: The Emancipation of the American Woman*. New York: Harper & Row, 1965.

Sklar, Katherine Kish. *Catherine Beecher: A Study in American Domesticity*. New Haven: Yale University Press, 1973.

Smith, Clifford P. *Christian Science: Its Legal Status*. Boston: Christian Science Pub. Soc., 1914.

Smith, Henry Nash. *Virgin Land: The American West as Symbol and Myth*. Cambridge: Harvard University Press, 1950.

Smith, Page. *Daughters of the Promised Land*. Boston and Toronto: Little, Brown and Co., 1970.

Stage, Sarah. *Female Complaints: Lydia Pinkham and the Business of Women's Medicine*. New York: Norton, 1979.

State University of Iowa. *1895–96 Bulletin*. Iowa City, Iowa: State University of Iowa, 1895.

State University of Iowa. *1896–97 Bulletin*. Iowa City, Iowa: State University of Iowa, 1896.

Strachey, John. *The Coming Struggle for Power*. New York: Covici, Friede, 1935.

Suggestions Respecting Improvements in Education. Hartford: Packard & Butler, 1829.

Taft, Rev. Stephen H. *The History of Humboldt, Iowa. A Semi-Centennial Address Given . . . on the 11th day of September, 1913*. Humboldt, Iowa: The Jaqua Printing Co., 1934.

Tims, Margaret. *Jane Addams of Hull House, 1860–1935*. New York: Macmillan, 1961.

Trout, Charles H. *Boston, The Great Depression, and The New Deal*. New York: Oxford University Press, 1977.

Van Ness, Thomas. *The Religion of New England*. Boston: Beacon Press, 1926.

Ward, Lester Frank. *Dynamic Sociology*. New York: D. Appleton and Co., 1883.

Weistein, James. *The Decline of Socialism in America, 1912–1925*. New York: Alfred A Knopf, 1969.

We Knew Mary Baker Eddy. 3rd series. Boston: Christian Science Pub. Soc., 1953.

Wilbur, Earl Morse. *A History of Unitarianism*. 2 vols. Boston: Beacon Press, 1945.

Wilbur, Sybil. *The Life of Mary Baker Eddy*. New York: Concord

Publishing Co., n.d. Now pub. by Christian Science Pub. Co., Boston.

Wilson, Bryan R. *Sects and Society: A Sociological Study of the Elim Tabernacle, Christian Science, and Christadelphians.* Berkeley: University of California Press, 1961.

Wood-Simons, May. *Woman and the Social Question.* Chicago: C.H. Kerr & Co., 1899.

Yates, Katherine M. *On the Way There.* Chicago: K.M. Yates & Co., 1904.

ARTICLES

Belding, Robert E. "Iowa's Brave Model for Women's Education." *Annals of Iowa* 43 (1976): 342–348.

Bicknell, A. D. "S. H. Taft: A Sketch." *Old and New* 14 (1906): 33, 35.

Bowen, Mrs. Joseph T. "The Early Days of the Juvenile Court." In *The Child, the Clinic and the Court*, pp. 298–309. New York: The New Republic, 1925.

Cashdollar, Charles D. "European Positivism and the American Unitarians." *Church History* 45 (1976): 490–506.

Clarke, Edith J. "Juvenile Delinquency and Dependency: Report of Inquiry at Chicago." *The Commons* 6 (1901): 3–4.

Cunningham, Raymond J. "The Impact of Christian Science on the American Churches, 1880–1910." *American Historical Review* 72 (1967): 887–895.

Davis, Allen. "The Women's Trade Union League: Origins and Organization." *Labor History* 5 (1964): 3–17.

Day, George B. "Sheep, Shepherd and Shepherdess." *Christian Science Journal* 5 (1887): 227–234.

Farlow, Alfred. "Mary Baker Eddy and Her Work." *New England Magazine* n.s. 41 (1909): 420–429.

Gardiner, Judith Kegan. "The New Motherhood." *North American Review* 263 (Fall 1978): 72–76.

Garfield, G. S. "What I Like to Hear from the Pulpit." *Unity* 41 (1898): 42–43.

Harkness, Georgia. "Pioneer Women in the Ministry." *Religion and Life* 39 (1970): 261–271.

Howard, H. Augusta. "Woman Considered as a Human Being." *Social Democratic Herald*, Dec. 29, 1900, p. 3.

Huber, John B. "Christian Science from a Physician's Point of View." *Popular Science* 55 (1899): 755–766.

Lathrop, Julia C. "The Background of the Juvenile Court in Illinois." In *The Child, the Clinic and the Court*, pp. 290–297. New York: The New Republic, 1925.

Lee, John A. "Social Change and Marginal Therapeutic Systems." In *Marginal Medicine*, eds. Roy Wallis and Peter Morley, pp. 23–41. New York: The Free Press, 1976.

McCorkle, William P. "A New Mariolatry." *Presbyterian Quarterly* 12 (October 1898).

Malkiel, Theresa. "Where Do We Stand on the Woman Question?" *International Socialist Review* 10 (1909): 159.

Morantz, Regina. "The Connecting Link: The Case for the Woman Doctor in 19th Century America." In *Sickness and Health in America*, eds. Judith W. Leavitt and Ronald L. Numbers, pp. 117–128. Madison: University of Wisconsin Press, 1978.

Morantz, Regina. "The Lady and Her Physician." In *Clio's Consciousness Raised*, eds. Mary S. Hartman and Lois Banner, pp. 38–53. New York: Harper & Row, 1974.

Morantz, Regina Markell, and Sue Zschoche. "Professionalism, Feminism, and Gender Roles: A Comparative Study of Nineteenth Century Medical Therapeutics." *Journal of American History* 67 (1980): 568–588.

Nudelman, Arthur E. "The Maintenance of Christian Science in Scientific Society." In *Marginal Medicine*, eds. Roy Wallis and Peter Morley, pp. 42–60. New York: The Free Press, 1976.

Olmstead, Agnes Briggs. "Recollections of a Pioneer Teacher of Hamilton County." *The Annals of Iowa* 3rd ser. 18 (1946): 93–115.

Petersen, William J. "Disease and Doctors in Pioneer Iowa." *Iowa Journal of History* 49 (1951): 97–116.

Pfautz, Harold W. "A Case Study of an Urban Religious Movement: Christian Science." In *Contributions to Urban Sociology*, eds. Earnest W. Burgess and Donald J. Bogue, pp. 284–303. Chicago: University of Chicago Press, 1964.

Porritt, Edward. "A Labor Conflict Without Violence: The Fall River Lockout." *Outlook* 78 (1904): 972–977.

Powell, Rev. Lyman P. "A Clergyman Looks in on Russia." *Review of Reviews* (October 1934).

"Relief Work in the Fall River Strike." *Charities* 13 (1905): 301–392.

Smith-Rosenberg, Carroll. "The Female World of Love and Ritual: The Relations Between Women in Nineteenth Century America." *Signs* 1 (Autumn 1975): 1–29.

Smith-Rosenberg, Carroll. "The Hysterical Woman: Sex Roles and Role Conflict in 19th Century America." *Social Research* 39 (1972): 652–678.

Stump, Albert. "Regulation of the Practice of Medicine in Indiana." In *Journal of the Indiana State Medical Association* 42, Supp. (July 1949): 53–59. Indianapolis: Indiana State Medical Association, 1949.

"The End of the Fall River Lockout." *Outlook* 79 (1905): 213.

Tuthill, Richard S. "The Chicago Juvenile Court." *Proceedings of the Annual Congress of the National Prison Association* (Philadelphia, 1902), pp. 115–124.

Ward, Lester Frank. "Sociology and Economics." *Annals of the American Academy of Political and Social Science* 13 (1899): 230–234.

Wardwell, Walter I. "Christian Science and Spiritual Healing." In *Religious Systems and Psychotherapy*, ed. Richard H. Cox, pp. 72–88. Springfield, Ill.: Charles C. Thomas, 1973.

Walter, Barbara. "The Cult of True Womanhood, 1820–1860." *American Quarterly* 18 (1966): 151–174.

Wing, Amelia Murdock. "Early Days in Clayton County." *The Annals of Iowa*, 3rd ser. 27 (1946): 257–296.

Wood, Ann Douglas. "'The Fashionable Diseases': Women's Complaints and their Treatment in 19th Century America." *The Journal of Interdisciplinary History* 4 (1973): 25–52.

Index

Child welfare, 21, 24, 33–34,
40–44, 51–52, 54, 56
Chodorow, Nancy, xiii
Christian Register and militant
propaganda, 134, 140
Christian Science doctrine: on
celibacy, 98; and common
sense, 65; on demonstrations
as "humanly possible," 141;
and denial of death, 102; as
derived from Quimby, 62;
and elevation of "woman-
hood," 81–82; as escape for
Collson, 67; and fear, 93–94,
112, 113, 114, 116, 120,
125–128; and feminism, 81,
82–85; and insensitivity to
human suffering, 60, 138–
140, 152; on "Malicious
Animal Magnetism," 92–93,
115, 118, 185 n.43; and
New Thought, 68; as "phi-
losophy of getting," 122; and
physical examinations, 101;
and Plato, 132, 168;
psychological effect of, 126–
128, 155; and reason, 96; on
"reflecting divine Love," 78;
and Roman Catholicism, 94,
155; and "scientific statement of being" 62; and
social gospel, 77; transcendentalist overtones of, 66; as
unscientific, 140, 142
Christian Science Hall (Evansville), 111
Christian Science Journal, practitioners' listing in, 75, 123–
125

Christian Science Monitor,
141–142, 144–145, 160
Christian Science movement:
and authorized literature, 64;
Board of Directors, 83, 123–
124, 150; and censorship,
116, 158–159, 187 n.15,
192–193 n.33; in Chicago,
59; as Christian, 168; and
class consciousness, 110;
ecclesiastical hierarchy of,
87, 114; in Europe, 120–
121; First Readers in, 83–84,
102, 103, 104, 105–106,
121; in Indiana, 100; lecturers, 84–85, 105–106, 118;
and legislation, 101, 105,
144–146; male domination
in, 82; and material prosperity, 108–111; Normal Class,
116–117; practitioners of,
80–82, 146, 147–148, 160;
and press, 101–102, 106;
Primary Class, 75, 77, 88;
and Prohibition, 144–145;
public hostility toward, 100–
102, 105–106; and racial discrimination, 110; Reading
Rooms, 92, 111, 120; and reliance on printed word, 103;
and social aloofness, 106,
108, 113; and social reform,
68; teachers in, 82, 85, 88,
99; and war, 140–142; and
women, 80–85
Christian Science novels, 102–
103, 187 n.16
Christian Science therapy: "absent" treatments, 126, 131,

Marx, Karl, 45–47
Matter and Memory, 133
Meadville Theological School,
 24–25, 32
Medical profession: and Christian Science, 100–101, 148–
 149; on frontier, 60; and
 psychiatry, 166; and psychosomatic disorders, 59; and
 women, 80, 97–98
Meeman, Edward J.: and Collson, 107–108, 155–169; and
 communists, 164; and
 Socialist Party, 107–108, 164
Memphis, Tenn., 155
Mental healing: dynamics of,
 65, 70–71, 76, 133; independent of method, 148; as not
 unique to Christian Science,
 73; and primacy of patient's
 belief, 147–148; as profession for women, 98, 123;
 right to practice, 101; and
 Unitarians, 60–62, 133, 135–
 136; unreliable, 161. *See also*
 Christian Science therapy
Mill, John Stuart, 22
Moral Rearmament, 150
Mother Church (First Church
 of Christ, Scientist), The:
 Collson withdraws from,
 128, 153; welcomes Collson
 back, 137–138
Mothering: effect of, xiii, 5; and
 mental healing, 98
Murdock, Rev. Marian, 10, 15–
 16, 18, 24, 120

Nationalist Clubs, 46

National Women's Trade Union
 League, 89–92
New Thought, 68–72
New York City, Collson moves
 practice to, 124–127
New York Suffrage Association,
 129

Okoboji Summer School, 34
Old Age Assistance, 167
Old and New, 13; on Christian
 Science, 65; as voice of Iowa
 Sisterhood, 10
Oxford movement, 150
Oxford University, 120–121

Palmer, Attorney General
 Mitchell, 142
Peabody, Rev. Andrew Preston,
 64
Peace movement, 130–131, 150
Perkins, Charlotte. *See* Gilman,
 Charlotte Perkins
Physical education for women,
 20
Pi Beta Phi (Iowa Zeta chap-
 ter), 21
Plato, 168; and Christian Sci-
 ence, 132; Collson's respect
 for, 67
Positivism, xii, 7, 14
Progress and Poverty, 23
Prohibition and Christian Scien-
 tists, 144–145
Psychology, Collson's interest
 in, 23, 72, 161–162, 166

Quimby, Phineas P.: as basis

tion among New York practitioners, 124–125
Stevens, Alzina P., and Chicago Juvenile Court, 34, 37–38
Strachey, John, 162–163
Suffrage: and Iowa Sisterhood, 14; and New York campaign, 129–130
Swedenborg, Emanuel, 72

Theology: concepts of divinity, 83; Liberal, 6–7; revelations, 132–133, 168; Unitarians' diminishing interest in, 26. *See also* Christian Science doctrine; Unitarianism
Tower Hill, Wis., 34
Transcendentalism, 6–7, 168–169
Trine, Ralph Waldo, 72
"True Womanhood" mystique, 28
Tuthill, Judge Richard S., and Chicago Juvenile Court, 39
Twain, Mark. *See* Clemens, Samuel

Unitarianism: and Bergson, 133; and Calvinist thought, 6; and Christian Science, 64–65, 73; and Comte, 7; discrimination against, 28; and egalitarianism, 87; and positivists, 7; and science, 11, 72; and Transcendentalists, 6–7; and shift of interest from theology to sociology, 26; on social display, 109–110; and women

ministers, 7–9; and war sentiment, 134–135
Unitarian Ministerial Union, 133
United Textile Workers of America, 89
Unity, 8; on Christian Science, 65; on Collson's move to Hull House, 34–35; on war, 134

Vallade, Louis, 104–105, 111
Van Ness, Rev. Thomas; and Christian Science, 135–136

Walker, F. A., 22
Walton, George A., 150
War: and Christian Scientists, 140–142; Collson's stand on, 134–135; and Unitarians, 134–135; and women, 130–131
Ward, Lester Frank, 23
Washta, Iowa, 32–33
"Ways That Are Vain," 97
Whittier, John Greenleaf, 169
Wiggen, Rev. James Henry, 65
Williard, Frances, 17
Wilson, J. Stitt, 47, 49
Wing, Amelia Murdock, 10
Women: bonding among, xiv, xv, 9–10, 160; as campaigners, 129–130; and Christian Science, 80–85; and church-work, 28; and medical profession, 97–98; as mental healers, 80, 81, 84, 98, 123; as ministers, 8, 28–29, 150; as physicians, 80; and social-

AMERICAN CIVILIZATION
A series edited by Allen F. Davis

*Gospel Hymns and Social Religion: The Rhetoric of
    Nineteenth-Century Revivalism*
    by Sandra S. Sizer
*Social Darwinism: Science and Myth in Anglo-American Social
    Thought*
    by Robert C. Bannister
*Twentieth Century Limited: Industrial Design in America,
    1925–1939*
    by Jeffrey L. Meikle
*Charlotte Perkins Gilman: The Making of a Radical Feminist,
    1860–1896*
    by Mary A. Hill
Inventing the American Way of Death, 1830–1920
    by James J. Farrell
Anarchist Women, 1870–1920
    by Margaret S. Marsh
*Women and Temperance: The Quest for Power and Liberty,
    1873–1900*
    by Ruth Bordin
Hearth and Home: Preserving a People's Culture
    by George W. McDaniel
The Education of Mrs. Henry Adams
    by Eugenia Kaledin
*Class, Culture, and the Classroom: The Student Peace Movement
    in the 1930s*
    by Eileen Eagan
*Fathers and Sons: The Bingham Family and
    the American Mission*
    by Char Miller
An American Odyssey: Elia Kazan and American Culture
    by Thomas H. Pauly
*Silver Cities: The Photography of American Urbanization,
    1839–1915*
    by Peter B. Hales
Actors and American Culture, 1880–1920
    by Benjamin McArthur

Saving the Waifs: Reformers and Dependent Children, 1890–1917
  by LeRoy Ashby
*A Woman's Ministry: Mary Collson's Search for Reform as a
Unitarian Minister, a Hull House Social Worker, and a
Christian Science Practitioner*
  by Cynthia Grant Tucker